SCEPTICISM AND P[OETRY]

AN ESSAY ON THE POETIC IMAGINATION

by

D. G. JAMES

> *For every man who thinks and lives by thought must have his own scepticism, that which stops at the question, that which ends in denial, or that which leads to faith and which is somehow integrated into the faith which transcends it.*
>
> T. S. ELIOT

BARNES & NOBLE, INC. NEW YORK

Publishers · Booksellers · Since 1873

PRINTED IN GREAT BRITAIN
BY BRADFORD AND DICKENS
DRAYTON HOUSE, LONDON, W.C.I

TO THE MEMORY OF

MY FATHER AND MY MOTHER

THIS BOOK IS DEDICATED

PREFACE

In the following essay I have tried to set out a view of poetry which is by no means new, but of which I believe there is need of reiteration. This view is that a theory of poetry is primarily a theory of the imagination; that the imagination which is present in the making of poetry is present also in all our knowledge of the world; and that its operation in poetry cannot therefore be understood if considered apart from the activity of the imagination in knowledge. In order to express this view I have started from the writings of the critic who, for such a view, is the obvious point of departure—Coleridge; and in order to emphasize Coleridge's famous statement of the nature of the imagination, I have very briefly stated the essentials of Kant's theory of the imagination in perception. To go far and at any length into philosophical issues in an essay of this kind, which is primarily concerned with poetry, is hardly desirable or possible; but it is equally certain that philosophical matters cannot be wholly avoided if we are to frame an adequate theory of poetry. At the same time I have at every point written for the literary rather than the philosophical reader.

It is difficult in these days to reiterate a doctrine of the imagination as creative without coming into polemic with the associationist psychology which has become so fashionable, the psychology from which Coleridge emancipated himself before his famous passage on the imagination was written. I have therefore criticized the literary aesthetic of Mr. I. A. Richards, an aesthetic which, despite the wide popularity it has enjoyed, will not, I think, bear more than the most cursory inspection. Under the influence of such a psychology, Mr. Richards has sought to transfer interest from the theory of the imagination to a theory of the emotional and volitional response to poetry; and with the greatest respect to Mr. Richards, whose writings have done so much to renew the vitality of philosophical criticism in our time, it is difficult not to believe that he has thereby done a signal disservice to the advance of the theory of poetry. By a curious irony, Mr. Richards has chosen Coleridge as his patron saint in criticism, a striking situation when one considers the utterly different psychologies which Coleridge employed and for which Mr. Richards shows such regard; and I have tried, in a brief discussion of Mr. Richards' book on Coleridge, to show how impossible is his effort to eat his Coleridge and have him too.

As I have said, the detailed discussion of philosophical and psychological issues is not possible in an essay of this size; and to anyone who feels that I skip lightly over a hundred problems of both kinds, I can only say that I do not do so in entire ignorance of those problems. But philosophical criticism is a kind of frontier territory between philosophy and psychology on the one hand and criticism proper on the other. In my essay I have tried, within the limits of what I set out to do, to keep an eye on the neighbouring terrains when detailed exploration was forbidden. I have in some cases indicated where the reader will find detailed informative discussion of matters which I have been compelled to hurry quickly over.

To try to discuss the activity of the imagination in poetry is necessarily to consider, at least in some degree, the relation of poetry to the other major forms of experience—morality, science, religion. But though I have tried to indicate what seem to me to be those relationships properly conceived, my chief purpose has been to try to indicate the limits of poetry and the final breakdown which I suggest must attend upon it. That is to say, that as, in Kant's view, metaphysics is an 'instinct' which we cannot deny but which is yet denied successful achievement, so poetry is finally driven to attempt the impossible and thereby to experience an ultimate failure. The movement of the poetic mind, I have suggested, is towards a powerful sense of the world's limits; but it is compelled by an inward necessity to try to penetrate beyond those limits, and therefore to involve itself in inevitable defeat. And I have tried, by writing of three great English poets, to show that this is so. In the work of Keats, Wordsworth, and Shakespeare there is, I think, a final failure. In the life and work of Wordsworth the situation is indeed different from that which obtains in the case of Keats and Shakespeare, and by writing of Wordsworth I placed myself under an obligation to discuss, however briefly, the relation of poetry to religion. While setting out this view of poetry, I have however sought to emphasize that the imagination can never hope to free itself of scepticism; and that to claim that the imagination can give us what can be known for truth is an extravagance which cannot be upheld. It is for this reason that I have called the book *Scepticism and Poetry*.

In writing of the three poets I have mentioned, I have striven to write from the texts themselves; but it is impossible to be without obligations of many kinds. It is Mr. Middleton Murry who has written most extensively on Keats in our time, and no student of Keats can fail to be profoundly in Mr. Murry's debt. But I cannot help feeling, so far as I understand Mr. Murry's work, that Mr. Murry has misrepresented the direction of Keats' imaginative life. This may be, and very likely is, due to my inability to be clear about Mr. Murry's interpretation. But in my essay on Keats I have simply striven to set out what, from study of his poems and letters, I have been able to grasp of Keats' imaginative life. In writing of Shakespeare I have to acknowledge indebtedness to Mr. Wilson Knight; although I had formed some such view of Shakespeare's last plays as I have here expressed before reading Mr. Wilson Knight's essay, I learnt a great deal from it. The reader will notice that in what I have said of Wordsworth I have made considerable use of the 1805 text of *The Prelude*, thereby seeking to avoid becoming involved in discussion of changes in Wordsworth's attitude and opinions. I trust that my other obligations, which are both numerous and profound, will be clear from my quotations and references.

Finally, I am aware that 'interpretation' of poetry such as I have attempted in the latter part of this essay is likely to be distasteful to many. I can only say that, though I feel that distaste myself, I do not see how, in our approach to great poetry, it can be avoided. And if, in what 'interpretation' we attempt, we remain conscious that poetry is very far from being an affair of opinion and doctrine, we cannot, perhaps, do a great deal of harm. Also, I hope that I have shown myself aware of the many dangers which attach to wide generalization on the subject of poetry.

I wish to thank the delegates of the Clarendon Press for permission to quote five stanzas of a poem by Robert Bridges; and Mr. Walter de la Mare for permission to make some quotations from his writings. Also, I am greatly in the debt of my sister, Mrs. Frank Blackmore, who typed nearly the whole of my MS.; and of Mr. F. Goulden, of Worcester, who gave me kindly and skilful assistance.

CONTENTS

PART ONE

If it were not for the Poetic or Prophetic character the Philosophical and Experimental would soon be at the ratio of all things, and stand still, unable to do other than repeat the same dull round over again.

BLAKE—*There is no natural religion*

As all men are alike in outward form, So (and with the same infinite variety) all are alike in the Poetic Genius.

As none by travelling over known lands can find out the unknown, So from already acquired knowledge Man could not acquire more: therefore an universal Poetic Genius exists.

BLAKE—*All religions are one*

CHAPTER I

THE 'PRIME AGENT'

> The primary Imagination I hold to be the living power
> and prime agent of all human perception. . . .
>
> COLERIDGE—*Biographia Literaria*

I

WORDSWORTH and Coleridge based their view of
the creative imagination on a doctrine according to which
imagination is a primary factor in all knowledge whatsoever.
The activity of the artist, they held, is not something unique,
cut off from the ordinary apprehension of the world, a miraculous gift made to certain extraordinary people who are different
in kind from the ordinary mass of men. They held that the
imagination of the artist and the poet, when rightly seen, is
recognized as essentially of a piece with the most prosaic
knowledge of the world, and has therefore as much claim to be
taken seriously as the everyday perception of objects. The
imaginative life is not a whimsical or fanciful indulgence which
embroiders and decorates, but a development from processes
which are involved in the simplest act of apprehension. Our
ordinary knowledge of the world and the artistic prehension
of reality are not two things, worlds apart, but, so they held,
one thing enjoying in the artist a conscious extension of activity
which is denied it in the ordinary business of life. Poetry and
life therefore are one, and can never be divorced. Whatever
of knowledge the poet may achieve is as fit to be called knowledge as our everyday awareness of objects in perception. It
has the same source, the same sanctions, the same criteria;
and can no more be denied than the processes which condition
the most hard-headed and utilitarian apprehension of our
environment. Hence their defence of imagination in art and
poetry is an assertion of the omnipresence of imagination in

all conscious response to a world. In defending poetry they do not envisage themselves as defending a world removed from the life of the market-place. They turn their defence into attack by asserting the necessity of imagination in the whole of life, and by showing poetry as a growth from processes which are present in all knowledge. To deny poetry the right to be taken seriously is also and equally to deny to everyday perception the right to be taken seriously; for in both the imagination is creative. To impugn poetry is to impugn perception, in so far as both are awareness of imaginative objects and open therefore to the same attack.

This was the belief upon which Wordsworth and Coleridge built. Wordsworth set it out in poetry; Coleridge in prose. Here is Coleridge's statement of it in *Biographia Literaria* (ch. 13): "The Imagination I consider either as primary, or secondary. The primary Imagination I hold to be the living power and prime agent of all human perception, and as a repetition in the finite mind of the eternal act of creation in the infinite I AM. The secondary Imagination I consider as an echo of the former, coexisting with the conscious will, yet still as identical with the primary in the *kind* of its agency, and differing only in *degree*, and in the *mode* of its operation. It dissolves, diffuses, dissipates, in order to create; or where this process is rendered impossible, yet still at all events, it struggles to idealize and to unify. It is essentially *vital* even as all objects (*as* objects) are essentially fixed and dead." The imagination is the "prime agent of all perception"; and the artistic imagination is identical with the imagination operative in perception "in the kind of its agency". The difference is "in degree". Coleridge does indeed say that there is also a difference "in the mode of its operation", and at first sight this appears as a contradiction of the former statement of identity in the "kind of its agency"; for if there is a difference in the mode of its operation, is not this equivalent to asserting a difference in the kind of its agency? But it is likely that in saying that there is a difference in the mode of operation, Coleridge is saying no more than (what he says in the next sentence) that the conscious imaginative activity of the artist has a necessarily *destructive* side which the primary imagination has not. "It dissolves, diffuses, dissipates, in order to recreate." "Coexisting with the conscious will", being that is to say, consciously and deliberately directed by the poetic mind, it is in contrast to the primary imagination present in perception, which is purely constructive. The artistic imagination, unlike the primary, has not only to build up; it has also to break down. It has indeed to break down the world of 'everyday' perception. And in this destructive element, necessarily present in the poetic imagination, consists this difference in the mode of operation. In respect of its destructiveness it is different from the primary imagination; in respect of its constructiveness it is identical with it 'in the kind of its agency'. And Coleridge was right to stress the identity rather than the difference, for its destructiveness is but an aspect of its life, incidental to its passion to create, and inspired by it.

Coleridge goes on (ch. 14) to illustrate the working of the secondary imagination in this way: "Mr. Wordsworth was to propose to himself as his object, to give the charm of novelty to things of everyday, and to excite a feeling analogous to the supernatural, by awakening the mind's attention from the lethargy of custom, and directing it to the wonders and loveliness of the world before us; an inexhaustible treasure, but for which, in consequence of the film of familiarity and selfish solicitude, we have eyes, yet see not, ears that hear not, and hearts that neither feel nor understand." Here then is the creativeness of the "secondary imagination" producing a "charm of novelty", a new world which formerly we have failed to create "in consequence of the film of familiarity and selfish solicitude"; and there is not only created a new world which formerly we had not the energy to create, but we ourselves are changed in senses and mental power alike. The world of familiarity and selfish solicitude is the world of the primary imagination; *that* world is dissolved and dissipated; and, out of the same materials, operated on however by a revivified imagination a new world is made. The first is adequate to the demands of "practical" life; but the creative re-ordering of the secondary imagination results in a world adequate to the demands of the "contemplative" life which, if sufficiently developed, issues in artistic creation.

Yet the burden of Coleridge's argument is that the world as it is for familiarity and selfish solicitude is none the less imaginative, a product of imagination; that the secondary imagination is to the world disclosed to "familiarity and selfish solicitude" what the primary imagination is to the vast plurality of sensation. It is true that the poetic mind breaks down and builds anew; but it is nevertheless also true that the practical world has been constructed, and constructed necessarily by the imagination. It is because the imagination in its primary function has made the world of ordinary life that a rebirth of that power at a higher level is able to destroy it and recreate it. Hence the root of all Coleridge's thinking on this matter lies in the nature of what he calls the "primary imagination", which he holds is a condition and the "prime" condition of all knowledge whatsoever. Unfortunately Coleridge himself never treated his argument in detail. And we must therefore go back to the source of his thought on the imagination, the philosopher Kant, who first propounded the necessity of imagination for all knowledge of the world.

2

Kant's writings are notoriously obscure, and it cannot be said that in the *Critique of Pure Reason* he expressed a clear view of the nature and function of the imagination and of its relation to the other factors involved in human knowledge. But one thing at least is certain, that Kant presented a view of the human mind in knowledge which was radically different from those of his predecessors; and in general this radical difference consists in his regarding the mind, not as essentially passive in the face of a world communicating itself to mind, but as essentially active in exercising certain powers which, he held, are a necessary condition of knowledge, and of knowledge of a world of objects. This activity of the mind is synthetic of what is given, and is creative in the sense that the world is not given as an ordered unity to the mind, and that the mind is not a mirror in which a world is reflected or a blank sheet upon which the world imprints itself. Instead, the mind actively grasps and operates upon what is presented in sensation. Formerly, philosophers had thought that the world came to be known only by association of isolated elements given to the mind in sensation; the world, they said, puts itself together in our minds like a jig-saw puzzle, and somehow the jig-saw puzzle arranges itself into a whole for our convenience; the original bits get fitted together not through active operation of the mind, but mechanically, by a process of association and compounding of elements. It was this view of the occurrence of knowledge which Kant laboured to destroy. The mind, he said, is presented with a "manifold", a plurality of sensation, and works creatively upon this bare, insignificant given, transforming it, by its power, into a system of ordered and interacting objects. There is all the difference in the world, he said, between a mass of barely given elements, unrelated colours, sounds, etc., and a world of enduring objects of which these sense qualities are known as qualities. And to account for the difference between the two, in the genesis and growth of human knowledge, it is necessary, Kant held, to assume that the mind is active in synthesis and in transcending what is merely presented to the mind in sensation. This is the creativeness of the mind in knowledge; and the presence of objects existing in an ordered world is to be explained primarily not by the possible reality of such objects in an ordered world, but by the activity of the mind which operates on the limited material presented to it, synthesizes it in doing so, goes beyond it and represents to itself a world of objects. This is the essence of Kant's doctrine of the mind in its knowledge of the world.

The question then arises as to the nature of the activities

which effect this creative work. And it is at this point that Kant's doctrine of the imagination emerges. His analysis, it should be remembered, is an analysis of human knowledge, and is concerned to give no account of animal perception. And of human perception he says that three elements are involved, which he calls sensibility, imagination, and understanding. What Kant had to say of these mental activities and of their interconnection is by no means clear or consistent; and there is good reason to believe that his views changed a good deal. But the essence of the matter would appear to be as follows: the mental factors involved in transforming what is merely given in sensation into a world of objects are sensibility, imagination, and thought. Through sensibility we become aware of temporal and spatial order, so that colours, sounds, etc., are apprehended as related in space and time. To assert such an activity, he held, was inevitable, in so far as space is not a sensation. Associationist psychology has laboured in vain to show how awareness of spatial order could possibly result from the association and compounding of sensory elements; and Kant cut across any such efforts by asserting the existence of what he called sensibility, an agency whereby the mind apprehends, and creatively apprehends, a spatial and temporal order. This work is accompanied by the activity of the imagination and of the understanding (by which is meant what is generally now called the discursive intelligence). He ascribed to both what he calls a transcendental function, by which he meant a creative function, in the sense that their activity is a necessary condition of the awareness of objects. He had not in mind the function of the imagination which enables us to image known objects, nor the function of the intelligence which contrasts and compares known objects. The higher functions of the imagination and of the intelligence are productive of objects and creative; they are the absolutely necessary condition of a world of objects being known by the mind. Together they supplement the work of sensibility. Of this higher exercise of the imagination and the understanding we are not conscious, Kant held; the mind is creative in this respect without being aware of it; such creativity is not, as Coleridge, following Kant, says, "coexistent with the conscious will".

Admitting so much, the question arises: What is the nature of these activities and the relation between them? As between the imagination and the understanding, Kant gave, in many ways, a primary place to the understanding rather than to the imagination. The understanding, he held, is equipped with a number of fundamental concepts,[1] such as cause and effect, substance and attribute, which are at once creative and interpretative of the world. The understanding, by its very nature, and for no reason which discloses itself, thinks in that way, and synthesizes the vast plurality of sensation in terms of them. Without these concepts he thought there could not conceivably be any world for mind; the creative intelligence grasps and reduces what is given into these forms. But it is clear that in and by itself the conceptual understanding cannot account for perception, our knowledge of a world of particular objects. Kant seems to speak sometimes as if it can. But it may be seen that no amount of abstract rules and concepts can give us the variety of individual objects with which in fact we are acquainted. From a number of empty forms only we cannot arrive at the particularity of the perceived world. On the one hand there is the given mass of sensation, on the other the understanding with its rules and concepts. But the reality which we know is neither merely sensation nor a collection of abstract rules. It is a world of individual things which have sense qualities and about which we make abstract and general statements; and it is precisely the occurrence to the mind of such a world which Kant is concerned to account for.

It is possible that Kant came to see that this is so. At any rate it is certain that he came to give an increasingly important

[1] This is perhaps too crude a statement of Kant's view. It would be a more accurate account of Kant's doctrine to say that these concepts arise as the result of 'schematism' of more fundamental concepts which, in another use, are the basis of the logical relations of subject and predicate, ground and consequence, etc.

place to the imagination, and spoke of it as the common root from which sensibility and understanding spring.[1] And clearly this is more satisfactory; for it indicates 'sensibility' as a form of activity without which we could not be aware of spatial and temporal order; and the understanding as conditional upon the imagination for its operation. Before stating, in this way, the fundamental character of the imagination, he seems to have thought of the imagination as only an aspect of intelligence. The imagination, he seems at one time to have held, is merely the understanding at work, *is* the understanding as, according to its concepts, it is creative of a world. But this was hardly possible, as we have already suggested. For if such a view be true, objects are only grasped and created through concepts which include within their scope a host of other individual objects; in which case the synthesis which is effected is of a logical kind, a classification of objects merely. And while this logical classification is certainly the supreme mark of what we call the discursive intelligence, it does not, in itself, account for the apprehension of the individual object itself which is classed by the intelligence within the concept. For the individual object, though in our human consciousness it is always classified, is not merely an occasion for the discursive intelligence, but is known as a unique individual. Now if Kant's view be true, the individual is known not as an individual but as an exemplification of certain concepts and principles from the beginning of experience. Yet if the individual is to be recognized as an exemplification it follows that there must be a sense in which the individual is known as an individual prior to the reflective analysis which operates upon it. If indeed the imagination is to be thought of as intellectual in its make-up, we are cast upon the horns of a dilemma; either the object is something merely thought, in which case the particularity of perception falls away, or it is known as an individual, in which case it is a synthesis which does not primarily consist in being conceived.

[1] *Critique* (tr. Kemp Smith), p. 146. See also *Commentary* on Kant's *Critique* (Kemp Smith), p. 225.

Clearly we must accept the second alternative, and therefore ascribe the primary labour of synthesis not to reflective analysis but to a logically prior and immediate grasp of the individual; and it is this labour of synthesis which we may call the activity of the imagination in knowledge. In our adult experience at least, such apprehension is never unaccompanied by intellectual processes; we cannot reduce ourselves to a condition of thoughtlessness. But to insist on conceptual analysis as the key to perception is to ignore the central fact of perception, namely that it is perception of individuals. The imagination, conceived of as other than an activity of the understanding, must therefore, if we are to accept Kant's threefold distinction, make the primordial synthesis from the confusion of sense. The discursive operation of the intelligence effects its analysis of what is originally brought together by the imagination. And all our knowledge shows these two sides, the direct and imaginative, prehending individual wholes; the reflective or discursive, analysing and classifying. They necessarily occur together in all adult experience; but they cannot be identified, as Kant at one time thought.

We may believe therefore that in coming to the recognition of the productive imagination as a unique and "fundamental faculty of the human soul", Kant had recognized the necessary infertility of the understanding, and so introduced the notion of a creative imagination operative in "sensibility"; it is this activity which makes possible both the apprehension of sensory wholes, such as patches of colour, and apprehension of objects of which sensory qualities are grasped as aspects or qualities. It became therefore, in his view, the primary creative activity in perception, taking precedence in that respect over the understanding. Kant indeed continued to insist that no knowledge is possible to human being without the activity of the understanding; certainly all our knowledge is discursive. Thought is the mark of our self-consciousness whereby we distinguish ourselves from the known world, the objects of which are known as objects. But the very discursive character of thought shows that it depends upon an activity more fundamental than itself. And Kant's work when it is purely critical is an effort to show the limitation under which the intelligence, he held, must necessarily labour.

Such we may believe was the essence of Kant's doctrine in the *Critique of Pure Reason*, and we may resonably regard it as the source of Coleridge's reflections on the imagination. Following Kant, he believed that the imagination is creative in ordinary perception; for it is primarily due to its activity that what is given as sensation is synthesized together into wholes, so that we become aware of objects interacting and thereby themselves unified into larger wholes. And it is because the imagination in its prehension of the world dissolves the comparative confusion of sense impressions and effects a synthesis, that it may be called, at this "primary" level, creative. Kant in certain parts of his work, and probably Coleridge too, believed that the imagination literally created nature, that is to say, that but for the mind there would be no ordered world in existence. But this doctrine is not necessary in order to see that the imagination as it operates in perception is creative. Nor was it essential to the most important thesis in Kant's book. When it is said that the primary imagination is creative, all that need be implied is that the world as we know it is not given to passive and merely receptive mind, but implies construction from, and interpretation of, given data.[1] As such the imagination is common to everybody; it operates in everyone however unaware of it. It operates unconsciously to bring to our knowledge a world of things and persons in which we may carry on the practical business of life. All our perception of people and things and their reactions one on the other is imaginative in this fundamental sense. For every thing, creature, and person we know, we know as a whole, as an individual thing, and as such in relation to others, and to larger wholes.

[1] On this point, however, see later, p. 60 and footnote.

3

Associationist psychology, the psychology which Coleridge originally held and which he gave up under the influence of Kant, holds, as we have said, that the world forms itself for our minds by the association and compounding of 'sensory atoms', a process which implies no creative operation of the mind. Now such a psychology is at an enormous disadvantage in explaining our awareness of space. For spatial order and spatial wholes, however rudimentary, are not as such given; nor can the given sensational elements conceivably be represented, through a process of association, as supplying such order and wholeness. Whether or not Kant's view of the 'subjective' character of space is true, it is necessary from the point of view of psychology, in its effort to explain the growth of perception, to hold that the mind 'starts with some germinal apprehension of the unity of the world, sufficient to enable it, when occasion arises, to expect and seek for connections not yet disclosed'.[1] There seems to be no possible explanation of our perception of spatial order which does not imply a capacity, natural to our mental constitution, for apprehension of spatial qualities and relations, apprehension for which the sensory elements are the stimuli and occasion. We must assume such a capacity for construction and interpretation; however reluctant we may be to fall back upon elements in our natural constitution as an explanation, it seems unquestionable that spatial apprehension, so far as it can be explained at all, can be explained only in that way.[2] In so far as this is so, we must view the mind as 'interpreting' or 'constructing', into a three-dimensional order, elements which as such could never afford such apprehension.

Similarly, our awareness of objects of which, as experience

[1] Stout, *Manual of Psychology*, pp. 437–8.
[2] See Stout, *Manual of Psychology*, pp. 436–41; and for an informative discussion, McDougall, *Outline of Psychology*, pp. 236–46. In general, modern *gestalt* psychology has presented a mass of evidence against associationism.

develops, we represent sensory elements or "sense-data" as aspects or qualities, illustrates the necessity of assuming creative activity on the part of the mind. That this is so can easily be seen by considering the views of such sceptical philosophers as Hume or Russell, who maintain that the world in reality is nothing more than what is given in sense, "sensations" or, as they are called in recent philosophy, "sense-data". Their argument is, that while the existence of sense-data, patches of colour, sounds, etc., is indisputable, it is altogether questionable whether the world consists of anything more than these. They point out that when we refer to a physical object it is impossible to demonstrate that we are referring to anything beyond a number of actual and possible "sense-data"; and certainly while there can be no difficulty in showing the existence of sense-data we cannot demonstrate the existence of anything else, what ordinarily we call the "thing", a substance which underlies the elements given in sense. Such philosophers therefore proceed to a denial of the existence of a thing at all, except in the sense of being a system of sense-data merely. Similarly with regard to causal connection, they deny the reality of anything but sequences of 'sense-data', and challenge us to show the existence of anything other than these. In other words, their argument is an attempt to reduce the world to the 'given' elements.

Now with the question as to whether or not this doctrine is true we are not here concerned. All we have to point out is that whether or not the world consists of anything in addition to sense-data, it is certain that the world as we represent it to ourselves is not merely a matter of 'sensations'. It is beyond dispute that the world as we represent it to ourselves in perception is a world of objects, of unities, or things, of which the sense-data are apprehended as aspects or appearances. It is no doubt the case that we can speak of what we call 'thinghood' only with the greatest vagueness and uncertainty. But however vaguely we may speak of it, it is the substantial unity into which all sense-data are synthesized. When we look in the direction of what we call a table it is certain that we represent it to ourselves not as a number of sense-data, but as a substantial existence of which certain aspects are given in sense. It is not relevant to our present purpose to try to prove that such a substantial existence is a part of the real world. All we are concerned to observe is that in our perception of the world, what is given to sense is unified in the imagination, however vague and obscure, of such a unity. That unity or thinghood may be only a fiction of the imagination, and we may be helpless to prove that it is otherwise. But it seems clear that in perception the imagination, transcending sense, represents the world in that way. The doctrine of Hume in denying that the world consists in anything but 'sensations' may be true; but that issue does not affect the position that in perception the imagination does synthesize the sense-data in something which is not given to sense.

It is the same with causal connection. Sceptics assert that, when we observe what we call a causal sequence, all that is occurring is a movement and a succession of sense-data, and that there is no inner causal connection. Again, it is possible that this is true. But again, our perception of the event is of the impact of two things between which exists an inner and necessary causal unity. It may be that our imaginative representation of that causal unity is exceedingly vague and mysterious; there can be no doubt that it is. But such a connection is certainly a factor in our representation of the world. Again, such causal connection may be only a fiction of our imagination; yet we certainly represent the world as a scene of such connections between substances. The fact that we cannot speak about that causal connection with clearness has to be admitted. But however helpless we may feel in trying to discuss it, we know that in perceiving what we call the impact of two objects we are aware of a great deal more than a succession of sense-data. We find the greatest difficulty in speaking with anything approximating to reasonable clearness about that 'something more'; but that it is present in our perception of the world is undeniable. Mr. Bertrand Russell, in *An Outline of Philosophy* (p. 121), says "that to say that A is necessarily followed by B is to say no more than that there is a general rule, exemplified in a large number of instances and falsified in none, according to which events such as A are followed by events such as B", and it may be that this is all that actually happens. But when at a later stage Mr. Russell tells us to "purge our imaginations of causality" all we can reply is that we can no more do so than we can fail to see if we open our eyes.

Thus a sceptical philosophy, by insisting that the only demonstrable elements in the world as we are aware of it are those which are given to the senses, compels us to observe how much more than what is given is present in our representation of the world. And the main feature of Kant's work was to emphasize this situation and thereby to indicate the importance of mental creativeness in perception. Kant indeed, as we observed, threw the labour of construction on to the understanding, the conceptual element in human awareness of the world. But there is some reason to think that Kant realized the unsatisfactoriness of doing so, and felt the necessity of regarding the imagination as the 'prime agent', prehending individual wholes in perception, and thereby making possible the work of the understanding—classification and abstraction. Part of the value which attaches to scepticism of the kind of which we have spoken consists in its laying bare the enormous part played by the imagination in our awareness of the world, both in our awareness of what we call 'things', and of the connections which we represent them as having with one another. So that, as we said earlier, and as Wordsworth and Coleridge repeatedly said, the life of the imagination is not a peculiarity of the artist and the poet, but is present, though not in the same conscious way, throughout all perceptual activity. And for our purpose, the primary question is not the validity of the imagination or otherwise, but the undoubted reality of the imagination in its awareness of a world of objects.

4

It follows, from what has been said above, that if science is to place itself beyond the attacks of sceptical philosophers, its statements can necessarily be taken to refer only to elements which are undeniably 'discoverable', to use Mr. Russell's word; that is, to sense-data. Mr. Russell points out (*Mysticism and Logic*, p. 145) that all that can be learnt by observation and experiment is about "certain patches of colour, sounds, tastes, smells, etc., with certain spatio-temporal relations". Hence, as one who is anxious to give a philosophical foundation to physics, he has formulated a philosophy according to which objects are exhibited as systems of actual and possible sense-data, and nothing more. But whether or not this philosophical doctrine be true, Mr. Russell insists that scientific knowledge is, in all strictness, knowledge of sense-data, and must consist in the statement of general rules relating to the succession of sense-elements. He says (*Outline of Philosophy*, p. 154) that "we now realize that we know nothing of the intrinsic quality of physical phenomena except when they happen to be sensations". And, speaking of the possibility of the 'thing' being anything more than sense-data, he points out (p. 126) that "it can be no part of legitimate science to assert or deny the persistent entity; if it does either, it goes beyond the warrant of experience".

Hence, to use a word which Mr. I. A. Richards has adopted, strictly scientific statements have 'reference' only to objects viewed as systems of actual and possible sense-data. Mr. Richards, however, has been content to speak of scientific 'reference' without pointing out this fundamental aspect of the situation. And he goes on, it will be recalled,[1] to distinguish between language used 'for reference' (the scientific use of language) and language used 'emotively' (the poetic use of language). But we must realize what is implied in the notion

[1] *Principles of Literary Criticism*, p. 267. This matter is further discussed below, Ch. III, Section I.

of scientific reference, in the way, following Mr. Russell, we
have indicated. And having realized this, we see that Mr.
Richards' distinction between language used for reference
and language used 'emotively' is fundamentally misleading.
The true distinction is between language having reference
in the last resort only to sense-data, and used therefore for
purposes of barest indication, and language used *imaginatively*.
For in poetry the poet endeavours to convey his sense of the
inner unity and quality of the object as embracing and transcending what is given in sense.[1] And we may say here, what we
shall emphasize at a later stage, that the aim of poetry is *never*
to create emotion; its aim is to convey an imaginative idea or
object. It may be that that conveyance is accompanied by the
occurrence of emotion; but such emotion is incidental to the
main end of poetry, which is the expression and communication
of an object or objects as they are present to the imagination of
the poet. Indeed, we may go so far as to say that, so far as its
intention goes, poetic language is no more 'emotive' than
scientific language.

5

Now although we must view scientific knowledge in
the way Mr. Russell shows, it is equally certain that the scientist
cannot 'purge' himself of his imagination, an imagination like
that of the rest of us which transcends sense and unifies sense-
elements in imagined wholes acting upon each other. However
scientific he may be he cannot reduce himself to representing
the world to himself as only a succession of sense-elements,

[1] But we have, in strictness, to bear in mind that what is called
a 'sense-datum' such as a patch of colour is not, as such, given at all.
That we should be aware of it as a 'whole' shows that this is so. Actually, however much we may speak of the 'given' as over against what
is added by way of interpretation and construction, it seems impossible
to say where the 'given' ends, and the 'interpretation' begins. Sensation, or the merely given, is in the last resort only an ideal limit. See
below, Ch. II, Section 2.

colours, scents, etc. Like everyone else he apprehends the world concretely, as a system of things causally connected. For, although we may use the word science to indicate a body of general rules relating to observed sequences of sense-data or of objects expressible as functions of sense-data, it is nevertheless true that the working scientist does not represent objects to himself in that way. His atoms and electrons are for him not functions of sense-data but the imagined entities of which sense-data are the functions. "If physics," Russell writes (*Mysticism and Logic*, p. 146), "is to be verifiable, we are faced with the following problem: Physics exhibits sense-data as functions of physical objects, but verification is only possible if physical objects can be exhibited as functions of sense-data." But it is none the less the case that the physicist represents scientific objects to himself as 'things', as in everyday life we represent tables and chairs as 'things', of which sense-data are aspects or qualities. The scientist may think, rightly or wrongly, that he is envisaging an actual situation in the real world when he talks of atoms, electrons, and so on. But whether or not he thinks so (and it is certain that all scientists do not), it remains true that he has gone beyond what "sensations" have been given him by his experiments, and has grasped them imaginatively within an imagined whole. And this procedure is analogous to what happens in perception; it is, as it were, an extension of perception, and the scientist can no more avoid imaginative synthesis in science than in his ordinary perception of the world.

Moreover, such imaginative apprehension of the world in science is not an idle addition to the work of formulating generalizations and formulae expressing what is actually observed of successive sense-elements in experiment. It is a very important aspect of scientific method and of the greatest usefulness. For the scientist will approach his experimental work with an imagined state of affairs before his mind which he entertains as possibly representing the actual state of affairs. His hypothesis issues from an imagined concrete situation which inspires and controls his experiment; and either the fresh data which accrue from the experiment fit in with his imaginings or they do not. The important point is that the scientific imagination, suggesting and controlling experiment, is of the greatest value for the discovery of fresh facts which as such are verifiable; and if the new facts may not be synthesized into the previous imaginative scheme a new imaginative scheme is forthcoming and takes its place. As Kant saw, all the generalizations of science which go beyond sense are hypothetical, or, as he called them, regulative. William James was content to call them useful. And these generalizations are the abstract expression of what are in the first place concretely imagined situations which the scientist has in mind, and which determine the method in which he will seek to acquire new and relevant facts. Thus the imagination is indeed, in science, subordinated to the discovery of fact, but it is none the less of the greatest value. Now it may be that the scientist, so long as his facts accord with his imaginative synthesis, may think that his synthesis is a true picture of reality. But, as Russell says, if, having gathered his fresh facts, the scientist wishes to restrict himself to scientific knowledge, he will be content to make generalizations and formulae which express the bare factual result of the experiment, and be indifferent to any claim to describe or picture the physical world except in so far as the physical world is expressible in terms of sense-data. Yet the importance of the imagination in the creation of hypothesis remains. The atomic doctrine, as a picture of the physical world, springs from the imagination of the scientist, controlled by the data observed, just as 'things' of everyday life are the objects of the imagination at once transcending and unifying what is given in sense. And this activity of the imagination is as inevitable and necessary in science as in the perception of the everyday world of objects.

In this sense science may be said to be a triumph of the imagination; within the limited sphere to which the scientist bends his attention, his activity must involve an imaginative element, an imaginative construction from the limited given.

It is easy perhaps to overlook this, for it is true, if we regard science as concerned ultimately only with the strictly verifiable, that the scientific imagination is only instrumental to the work of science in discovering fresh data and sequences. In science there is no resting, so to speak, in the imagination. The scientist presses on to the discovery of demonstrable fact. It is not his business, as Wordsworth said it ought to be the business of the poet, 'to carry sensation into the midst of the objects of science itself, and to contemplate these objects as an enjoying and suffering being'. It is not in the enjoyment but in the use of the imagination that the scientist is absorbed. But, though the function of the imagination in science is subordinated to the discovery of fact, it is none the less vital and important.

The imagination, then, is an integral part of all our experience. It is the necessary condition of all perception, and is present in the simplest apprehension of the world; for it is that which in all experience, of whatever kind, gathers the limited and fragmentary data which are given to the senses into unity.[1] It gives order to the data by transcending and unifying them into imagined wholes, which as such have no place in scientific knowledge; for scientific knowledge, proceeding by observation and experiment, has to do, as Russell rightly insists, only with sense-data.

We observed that Kant, in introducing the notion of imagination as necessary to all apprehension of the world, looked upon it as merely the understanding in action, as an aspect merely of the understanding. Later, indeed, he seems to have ceased to view it in that way, and to have come to regard it as a distinct faculty, conditioning the activity of the understanding. This later view which he took of the imagination is more satisfactory, for the difference between the two activities is striking. For whereas the life of the imagination consists in the apprehension of individual wholes, the life of intelligence

---

[1] See, on this matter, Prof. Kemp Smith's discussion in his *Commentary* on Kant's *Critique*, pp. xxxix–xlv.

consists in classification and abstraction. It is the case, indeed, that these two elements are always present together in our knowledge of the world and supplement each other. Yet the object must be imaginatively apprehended as an individual as well as be classified. It is known as unique as well as being identified, in judgment, with a number of other objects. And these two aspects of our experience cannot be set apart, and are indispensable to each other. They may, indeed they must, vary in the degree of predominance which each gains at the expense of the other, according to the interests of the mind. In everyday life and in science the imagination is subservient to the intelligence. In everyday life it is subordinated to the life of practical purpose; in science to the quest of general rules. In poetry, on the other hand, the imagination suffers a release from the life of purpose and the formulation of general principles; yet it cannot dispense with the intelligence any more than everyday life and science could survive without the exercise of the imagination. The imagination and the intelligence cannot be free of each other; so that just as a poem or play is never wholly divested of meaning, or of implicit meaning, so science can arrive at the most abstract generalizations only by means of a labour of imaginative synthesis. As art is the showing forth in the form of particularity what is general and universal, so that, as Kant said, it appears to have meaning without stating what it is, so the abstract rules of science issue from the scientific imagination of the concrete.

6

The major and inclusive imaginative scheme within which scientific knowledge progresses is the mechanical representation of natural process. As we observed, a philosopher of science such as Russell, in order to give a firm philosophical basis to physics, effects a reduction of objects to systems of sense-data, actual and possible. Yet, though scientific knowledge must in strictness be expressed in such terms, the scientist

does not, in his investigations, throw off his concrete imagination
—representation of the world as composed of 'things' having
causal relation with each other. And guiding his investigation
is a representation of the world as a mechanical system, a
representation within which all his lesser syntheses take their
place; he thinks concretely of objects as part of an inclusive
mechanism. If indeed the scientist undertook to assert that the
structure of the world is mechanical in character, he would no
doubt be saying something for which his investigation, proceeding by observation and experiment, gives him no warrant.
If we accept Russell's judgment, and there seems no way of
avoiding it, we must necessarily confine scientific knowledge
to sense-data and decline to allow that science can tell us the
'intrinsic quality of physical phenomena'. But it is none the
less the case that science naturally tends to represent mechanism
as the 'intrinsic character of physical phenomena', and to
envisage or imagine the physical world as a gigantic mechanism.
Whether the world is or is not of this nature is not now the
issue, but that science finds it convenient thus to represent
the world is certain. It is the case also that science is not in a
position to tell us whether or not the world is a mechanism;
there seem no grounds for believing that it can. The position
seems to be that it is natural to science to have, as the natural
imaginative background to its work, the representation of the
world as mechanical in nature.

That this should be so is at once natural and inevitable.
The condition of the formulation of general and universal
rules is a uniformity of nature which, when imaginatively
presented, becomes a mechanical scheme. The generalizations
of science derive their possibility from the respects in which
objects resemble other objects, so that a mass of instances
may be brought together under a single assertion. The process
of generalization is necessarily one which ignores individuality,
or reduces the individual to an instance of a general rule; it is
the classification of many into an abstract unity, unlike the
concrete unities present to the imagination. And because this

is so, and because in science the imagination is subservient to the main end of discovering universal rules, the imagination of the scientist represents the world in a way in which the individual is as nearly as possible represented as merely instancing the generalization. That is to say, it is stripped of its individuality so far as the essentially concrete character of the imagination will allow; the world is represented as composed of a number of ultimate units entirely similar to each other, so that the variety of objects in the world is explicable in terms of the different ways in which such ultimate units are conjoined with each other. The world therefore becomes a composition of individuals which are as nearly as possible imagined as resembling every other unit. This is natural and inevitable when we realize the final purpose of science, which is abstraction and generalization. And it is futile to complain that it should be so. The surprising thing would be if it were otherwise. And it is to be noted that the exercise of the intelligence, concerned with the formulation of generalizations, does not extrude the imagination or reduce its activity; it merely restricts it, so far as it can, to a representation of the world which is consonant with the abstract process of classification in which science is absorbed, and which aids and stimulates that process.

We say that the scientific imagination strips the object of its individuality 'so far as the essentially concrete nature of the imagination will allow', because in reality the effort of the scientific imagination to hold before itself a representation of the world as a pure mechanism is only partially successful. For the imagination is such that it cannot envisage a perfect mechanism, and will not lose complete hold of concrete individuality. Our perception of the world is penetrated, to a degree which we hardly realize, with an anthropomorphic interpretation, a representation of the world as the scene of the operation of 'forces' and 'energy' which we represent after the analogy of our own motor experience.[1] That is why we cannot give

[1] This matter is further discussed in Chapter III. For an authoritative discussion see Prof. G. F. Stout, *Mind and Matter*, Chapter II.

any description of the world which we may think we imagine
is a mechanism without the use of metaphor which surrepti-
tiously, as it were, defeats our purpose. We describe matter
as 'blind' or 'passive'; Mr. Russell, describing his material
universe in *A Free Man's Worship*, speaks of the 'march of
matter'; Professor Whitehead, describing the scientific philosophy of the seventeenth century, speaks of it as representing
nature as the 'hurrying of material, endlessly, meaninglessly';
Professor Alexander speaks of the 'restlessness of space-time'.
These metaphors are not rhetorical ornaments; they are a
necessity to the imagination. Hence, while it is true that the
scientific imagination strives, in its work of classification of
abstract elements, towards a mechanical representation of the
world, it does not in fact succeed. The truth is that we simply
cannot imagine a perfect mechanism; for the imagination is by
its nature concerned to contemplate only concrete unities and
cannot encompass bare abstractions. Though science may
strive to envisage the world as being one of objects which are
'essentially fixed and dead' the imagination, which is 'essentially
vital', defeats its purpose. All that the scientific imagination
can do is to envisage the world drained of as much individuality
as the imagination, which can live only in the contemplation
of individuality, will allow. And reflection shows that the
mechanical representation of nature is far from being dis-
infected of metaphor; it bears the marks of the concrete
imagination. And this is as true of scientific determinism
to-day as of the representation of the physical world in the
work of Lucretius.

But it is not only that the scientific imagination is one which
strives to prehend the world as a mechanism. It is equally
necessary to the scientist to imagine the world as material.
This, of course, goes inevitably with the mechanistic representation of nature. Science cannot, for obvious reasons, contemplate the material mechanism of the world as broken into,
or rendered incomplete. Materialism is a necessity to the
scientific imagination because a uniform material substance is

the only guarantee of the possibility of universal generalizations; the envisagement of the world as made up of one
uniform substance underlying all the variety of individuality
is the way in which the imagination, in science, seeks to turn
away from individuality to identity and uniformity. Once
again, materialism, like mechanism, is the inevitable imaginative
accompaniment of an effort to achieve completeness of generalization; and in it the variety and individuality of the world is
seen as lost in the uniformity of matter and motion. And the
position is not affected by the fact that matter is differently
represented at different times in the history of science. In
earlier centuries matter was imagined as composed of solid
'pushy' bits, which together made up a gigantic mechanism;
it is now imagined as made up of events or occurrences, and
is called space-time. But though differently represented from
formerly, it serves the same purpose; it is that in which sensations (as Russell calls them) inhere, and is the stuff out of which
the mechanism of the physical universe is made. That matter is
less 'material' than it was is in this connection of no importance.
And it is to be noted that here too the scientific imagination is
defeated; for to view the world as merely material, 'fixed and
dead', is an ideal to which the scientific imagination strives,
but which it necessarily fails to reach. Here too we must
say that the imagination seeks 'as nearly as possible' to
envisage the world as material; for in reality our imagination of the material world, as we call it, fails, and must
necessarily fail, to divest itself of what is concrete and
individual.

Such is the all-inclusive imaginative scheme, so far as it
can possibly be successful, within which science proceeds to its
work. What is important is to see the necessity of this imaginative
scheme on the part of science in its pursuit of rules. Nor can
it ever be rejected by science; it is the indispensable background to its inquiries. To abandon it would be the death
of science, for it is the condition of hopeful research. And
it will not do for science to relax from the rigour of this

scheme.[1] The rapid advance of scientific knowledge in the last three centuries has been attended by and has depended upon the entrenchment of the scientific imagination in the mechanistic representation of the world.

7

In his book *Science and the Modern World*, Whitehead quotes the following passage from Bacon. "It is certain that all bodies whatsoever, though they have no sense, yet they have perception; for when one body is applied to another, there is a kind of election to embrace that which is agreeable and to exclude or expel that which is ingrate; and whether the body be alterant or altered, evermore a perception precedeth operation; for else all bodies would be alike one to another. And sometimes this perception, in some kind of bodies, is far more subtile than sense; so that sense is but a dull thing in comparison of it: we see a weatherglass will find the least difference of the weather in cold or heat, when we find it not. And this perception is sometimes at a distance, as well as upon touch; as when the loadstone draweth iron; or flame Naphtha of Babylon, a great distance off. It is therefore a subject of very noble enquiry, to enquire of the more subtile perceptions; for it is another key to open nature, as well as the sense; and sometimes better." And we might add similar quotations from Vaughan, who claimed to be something of a scientist along the lines indicated by Bacon, and to have made discoveries in this way:

> I summon'd nature; pierc'd through all her store;
> Broke up some seals which none had touched before;

for Vaughan's poetry is full of such a representation of nature as Bacon describes, and his 'discoveries' would make an interesting footnote in the history of science.

[1] This is particularly to be remembered in these days when we hear so much of 'contingency' and 'probability' in the physical world. Doctrine of this kind issues from the scientific consciousness only when the latter has become contaminated by philosophical predispositions.

But our immediate concern is with what Whitehead proceeds to say (p. 53) after quoting Bacon: "In this respect Bacon is outside the physical line of thought which finally dominated the century. Later on people thought of passive matter, which was operated on externally by forces. I believe Bacon's thought to have expressed a more fundamental truth than do the materialistic concepts which were then being shaped as adequate for physics." But whatever the 'fundamental truth' may be, no one doubts the enormous success of the 'mechanistic' representation of the world, nor can we conceive that the line advocated by Bacon, and pursued possibly by Vaughan, could offer a foundation for the purposes of science. 'For else', says Bacon, 'all bodies would be alike one to another.' But so to represent objects is not undesirable when one's end is the discovery of general, inclusive formulations. And science therefore laboured to empty its imagination of such a view of nature as Bacon propounds. Actually, as we have noticed, it could not and cannot do so with complete success; the 'essential vitality' of the imagination cannot be destroyed, and the materialistic and mechanical view of nature is in reality never wholly free of the view Bacon is urging. It does not view matter as active, as Bacon wishes it to; it views it as completely passive. But this complete passivity cannot be imagined other than as the complete passivity of what is essentially active and sensitive. In poetry indeed we may expect to find such a view of nature as Bacon expresses; nevertheless such a view would be a fatal hindrance to the abstract investigations of science. In science the imagination is a servant, and must be kept in the strictest subordination to the purposes of science; if it got out of hand it might turn the scientist into a poet, a very undesirable metamorphosis surely. And the success of science has depended on the activity of the imagination trained to the greatest possible degree to represent nature as 'passive' and 'blind'; and its success must continue to depend upon such a disciplined imagination.

It is foolish therefore to complain that when science

approaches the study of the behaviour of what are called organisms, it should refuse to yield up its imaginative scheme. For it is as necessary in biology and psychology as in what are called the physical sciences; and the only hope of a scientific biology and psychology lies in its retention in these spheres. Just so far as human beings and the lower organisms are in any degree a part of the physical world, they must be incorporated into the inclusive scheme which science has developed in its inquiries into the physical world. The reasons which make a materialistic and mechanistic scheme necessary for the investigation of the physical world make it equally necessary in investigating the behaviour of organisms; and organisms must come therefore to be regarded, as far as is possible, as only differentiations in the uniform self-identical matter of the world; if biology and psychology are to consist in anything but comparatively vague observations, it cannot be otherwise. There is no point at which the mechanistic imagination of science can stop; for to make it do so is to abandon the hope of arriving at rules of universal application. And it is therefore mistaken to resent the incursion of the scientific imagination into biology and psychology. The scientific study of human behaviour is necessarily the study of the nervous system, imagined as a mechanism; and all observations about human behaviour which are not propositions about the body and the nervous system are not, whatever else they may be and whatever value we may ascribe to them, scientific. So far from its being the case that, as Whitehead suggests, the mechanical and materialistic imagination should be sacrificed even in the investigation of the physical world, it is rather the case that it is necessary and inevitable even in the investigation of the most complex organisms. Entities such as life and mind, because in them 'sensations' do not inhere, must be extruded, so far as is possible, from the scientist's imagination of the world.

8

At the same time we must remember that we are speaking of the scientific *imagination*. And the imagination, as we have already said, is that which goes beyond the order of fact. Hence though in science the imagination is disciplined, for scientific purposes, to contemplate a world as nearly mechanical as possible, it would be a great error to think that science is able to say that such is indeed 'the intrinsic quality of physical phenomena'.[1] It is convenient for science so to imagine the world. But that is all that can be said. To think that materialism can be asserted as a metaphysical theory of reality, the validity of which is shown by science, would be to fail to distinguish fact from imagination. Science, in all strictness, can give us, as *knowledge*, only verifiable fact; that it should find certain imaginative schemes useful in its work is a matter of interest but no foundation for metaphysical doctrine. Materialism is the unavoidable, all inclusive, imaginative scheme (or, if we give abstract expression to it, hypothesis) of science. But to treat it solemnly as a true picture of reality arises from failure to recognize the nature of imagination. Finally, we may repeat that, in any case, if we watch our imagination carefully, we shall see that in reality we cannot envisage nature as 'merely fixed and dead'. Although we may speak of the imagination of nature as a mechanism, what is meant is the effort of scientific imagination to approximate to such an apprehension of nature. For it can be only an approximation. For materialism is merely the effort of the imagination to overcome itself, to commit suicide, a feat which it cannot encompass. To try to imagine the world stripped of individuality, which is what the scientific imagination endeavours to do, is to try to destroy the imagination in the act of using it. But because the imagination is the primary agent in our apprehension of the world this cannot be done, nor the 'essentially vital' character of the imagination denied.

[1] But it is important to observe that to say this is not to deny that the universe is wholly mechanical.

9

The quotation from Coleridge with which we began embodies the foundation of the romantic aesthetic and is, I would add, the only possible starting-point for any aesthetic, or, if we wish to use a less presumptuous word, any comments upon literary art. But though what Coleridge says in that quotation is fundamental, Coleridge and Wordsworth never, I believe, overcame what they felt to be a deep opposition between poetry and science. In their view of the relation of perception to imaginative art they are essentially right, yet they never succeeded in establishing in their minds a concord of science and poetry. We shall have occasion later on, in speaking of Wordsworth, to see how falsely he represented the relationship between the two. And I have therefore, in addition to trying to expound their view of the place of the imagination in perception, tried to outline the place of the imagination in science in order to see how that falsely imagined opposition may be overcome. For if we once see that science, in so far as it undertakes to represent to us the nature of the world, is imaginative and not operating at the level of fact, the position is vitally changed, and we are in a fairer way to compare and assess the activity of the imagination in scientific and poetic apprehension of the world. Only in this way can we free ourselves from the endless controversy of opposing claims which, if we are to judge by the writings of 'scientific' minds and 'artistic' minds, divide science from poetry.

CHAPTER II

A DENIAL OF THE 'PRIME AGENT'; AND THE CONSEQUENCES

Mr. Bain collects that the mind is a collection. Has he ever thought who collects Mr. Bain?

F. H. BRADLEY—As a footnote to a discussion of Bain's associationism in *Ethical Studies*

I

IN the present chapter I wish further to emphasize the activity of the imagination in perception and poetry; and to do so by commenting upon the aesthetic of Mr. I. A. Richards. In the preceding chapter I have tried to give an interpretation of Coleridge's famous statement on the imagination; and it is one in which the creativeness of science is seen as a development of, or extension from, the creativeness of the imagination in perception. The scientific imagination may, if we choose to retain Coleridge's phraseology, be classed as secondary, as developing from the imaginative labour which goes to the making of the everyday world of perception, but as also recreating that world. For, though it develop from the 'perceptual' imagination, the world as it is present to the scientific imagination is vastly different from the world as it is present to ordinary perception. So much so that philosophers who regard science as capable of describing to us the 'essential nature of phenomena' are puzzled as to how to reconcile, into a single scheme of reality, the world of perceptual objects and the world of scientific objects, as they are sometimes called. But we are not concerned here with this matter; and, in any case, the problem is an unreal one arising from a false view of the situation. Our present purpose is only to observe that the scientific imagination reforms and recreates the world to an extent which amazes the everyday imagination. Yet it is the case that, like the everyday imagination, its attitude is practical and its concern is with facts. This is so because, as we pointed out, although scientific inquiry is concerned with matters which do not come within the ambit of our everyday lives, it yet subordinates the exercise of the imagination to a status of function or of usefulness with a view to the discovery of fresh fact.

This is the most obvious characteristic of the scientific imagination. Yet its reconstruction of a world different from that present to perception places it nearer to art than everyday perception. For in the first place it has one of the marks which Coleridge, although no doubt he was writing only with regard to the artistic imagination, attributed to the secondary imagin-ation—it is consciously exercised or it is "coexistent with the conscious will"; it is deliberately exerted in an effort to gather a mass of fact into a single concrete scheme. Also, in so far as this is so, it shares with the artistic imagination a destructive aspect; it destroys in the interests of further construction. The history of science is a sequence of construction and destruc-tion, of rebuilding an imagined world. On the other hand, it is true that there is always in science a purpose which finds its fruition outside the imaginative, namely, in fact. It is also true that where science 'dissolves, diffuses, dissipates', what is dissolved leaves behind it a legacy of ascertained fact which is carried over. Yet, though the end and aim of science is not imaginative, there is involved in its process a re-creation of the world which makes of the scientific imagination a 'secondary' process.

Coleridge, however, in speaking of a secondary imagination was no doubt writing of the imagination as it is exercised in the processes which issue in the creation of a work of art. And of the secondary imagination in this sense, we may say that it is neither practical, as everyday life is practical, nor subordinated, as it is in science, to an ulterior purpose which has to do with what lies outside the world of imagination. Actually, as we shall see, there are dangers enough in describing the life of the artistic imagination as unpractical, purely disinterested, and so forth. For it is clear that no activity can be merely unpractical or merely disinterested in the sense of being unrelated to the total life of personality; no such activity is conceivable. Yet it is at least true that its chief concern is not with the usefulness of objects, nor with generalities expressive of fact. Having no such purpose, it dissolves the world of familiarity and selfish solicitude, and brings about a magical enhancement of our apprehension of the world by a re-creation of it at a new and almost undreamed of level. The life of the secondary imagination is one of "struggle to unify"; of steady refusal to allow experience to come in a broken-up way, of absorption of unitary experiences into a patterned whole. It is, as it were, a going back to the beginning of experience and a starting all over again, at a new level of interest; a secondary synthesis, no longer devitalized by use, and vivifying, in its creation, sensational response.

As such it takes its rise out of the necessity, felt by the poet, for a coherent ordering of the world of his experience. No one indeed can live a life wholly devoid of what Coleridge is here calling the secondary imagination; and the difference between the poet and the ordinary man lies in the strenuousness with which the former refuses to allow any imaginative experience to occur without seeking to embody it in a wider imaginative pattern. Such an effort makes demands which the poet devotes his life to satisfying. And certainly, for the poet, that effort is not a pleasurable pastime, but a necessity of his experience. Coleridge believed that the imagination, so far from being a pleasurable indulgence, is indispensable to all apprehension of the world whatsoever; and though we can, for a number of reasons, and in a hundred ways, deaden the life of the secondary imagination, yet when it comes into strenuous life, as it does in the poet, it has its springs in a deeply felt need, the satisfaction of which becomes an increasing necessity to him. This need is for a single imaginative grasp or prehension of life, by the achievement of which life may be mastered and fully lived. The scientist is under a compulsion to draw the fragments of sensible data into the unity of an imagined scheme; the poet endeavours to build out of the fragments of his experience a unified prehension of the whole of life. But whereas the scientist is concerned with the exploration of a field of fact, the poet, in his effort to make an imaginative integration, can hold nothing beyond his regard, not even, as Wordsworth said, the objects of science themselves. His activity is therefore concrete and wholly imaginative; the scientist's abstract and only partially imaginative. Hence, though poetry is not practical, as is common sense, nor interested, as science is, it is yet practical and interested in a sense in which neither everyday life nor science is. However much we may stress the disinterestedness and contemplative power of poetry, poetry arises nevertheless from the felt need for an augmentation of life which carries it far beyond common sense and science alike. Detachment and release may be among the marks of poetic experience; but such detachment and release occur as instrumental to vital need; they arise within an experience which issues from a desire to encompass life, and, by encompassing it, to master it. To re-create the world in a perfect unity of imaginative pattern is its end—a labour which springs from the feeling of helplessness and impotence in the face of an initially disordered and confused mass of experience provided by the primary imagination.

2

It may well be that it was to emphasize this essentially purposive character of the imagination that Coleridge came to elaborate his distinction between the imagination and the fancy, thereby bringing into stronger relief his view that the imagination is essentially serious, of momentous importance to the total life of personality, arising from profoundly practical demands and seeking to issue in a richer practice of life. The primary imagination is the condition of our having a world of experience at all; the secondary imagination the condition of our having a world which, grasped in a fuller unity of pattern, may then yield a maximum of harmonized and vital experience. To bring out this quality, he contrasted it with the fancy which, he held, is essentially unserious. The imagination is always a process of organizing and synthesizing experience, whether at the lower and rudimentary level of the primary imagination, or at the higher level of the secondary; and the secondary imagination is only an extension of the former, released indeed from the restraints which operate at the lower level, and labouring, unlike science, for no abstract end. It is an activity whereby the world is prehended, and, in that prehension, at once dissolved and re-made. Its object, that is to say, is what is always present to the imagination as the real world; when the imagination withdraws itself from this conscious labour of creation into the contemplation of a world to the reality of which it is indifferent, and when it exercises its processes for their own sake, it is no longer imagination, but fancy. Some aesthetics set out the imagination as being what, in effect, Coleridge calls the fancy. When, for example, we read that "to imagine an object is not to commit oneself in thought to its unreality; it is to be wholly indifferent to its reality. An imaginary object is, therefore, not an unreal object, but an object about which one does not trouble to ask whether it is real or unreal",[1] we are reading a description not of the imagination, but of the fancy. It may be, of course, that we are indifferent to the reality or unreality of Hamlet, or as to whether Othello ever lived; but although we are indifferent to the reality of the symbols, or 'objective correlatives', which the poet chooses, the imagination grasps through them a world which, for the imaginative experience, is real, and of which that imaginative experience is a creation. It is true, of

[1] R. G. Collingwood, *Outlines of a Philosophy of Art*, p. 13. I would add that, though I have here quoted Mr. Collingwood to criticize him, I owe a great debt to several parts of his remarkable book, *Speculum Mentis*.

course, that we can imagine for the sake of imagining; and no doubt there is a natural pleasure to be found in playful indulgence of the imagination. But such is not the imagination of which Coleridge is speaking; on the contrary, such activity is productive of the artificial and is fancy,[1] which is deliberately trivial, though of course it may be a source of great delight. What the imagination makes is the world to which the deepest and most strenuous life of personality responds, and to which it adapts itself in all its activities. It is only when it relaxes from this task that it becomes indifferent to reality, and enjoys itself in fancy. The works of fancy supply a release from the serious business of living, a playful enjoyment of that to the reality of which we are indifferent; the works of imagination, on the contrary, compel a strong sense of the real world, re-created at a new and unique level, and with a novel integrative and imaginative pattern. This comprehensive imaginative pattern may be but a background to the particular imaginative prehension which is conveyed in the lyric; in the play or novel, it finds a full expression, as a single prehension of the whole of life, within which the poet has sought to "balance or reconcile" all the opposite and discordant qualities which his experience has brought with it.

It is not perhaps true to say that this generalization applies to all poetry whatsoever. It may be that many lyrical poems do not issue from an inclusive imaginative pattern which seeks to manifest itself in a particular selected situation. It is not necessary for our main argument to deny that frequently the imagination is content to body forth a particular situation entirely for its own sake. But more frequently, and certainly in the case of the greater poets, a total imaginative pattern, originally perhaps vaguely felt, clarifies itself in the exploration of a situation or plot which has been felt to be relevant to that pattern. Such a unity, inclusive of the poet's imaginative universe, seeks to crystallize itself, with varying degrees of

---

[1] A good example of fanciful writing is a stanza of Southwell's quoted on p. 105.

completeness, in lyric, narrative, and drama. The situation or
plot may indeed prove itself an inadequate means of such
crystallization and may call for rejection; and such rejected
attempts have enormous interest for criticism. But where
success has occurred, the agitation of the imagination in
manipulating situation or plot is itself a discipline which
clarifies and gives definition to an originally vague apprehension.
Because this is so, the resulting work is inadequately described
as simply an expression of an all-inclusive pattern, or as simply
the bodying forth of a particular situation. It would be truer
to say that the former is created (or perhaps, more fully dis-
covered) through the discipline involved in the latter.

The situation presented in a poem or play then becomes, in
varying degrees, a revelation of the poet's imaginative universe.
And this is in accordance with Coleridge's doctrine. For the
imagination, creative of wholes at all levels of experience,
operates in the great poet with a degree of power which seeks
wider and wider integration, and which cannot rest from
exploration of the entire universe of his experience, continuously
endeavouring to effect more inclusive 'idealization and
unification'. Such unification is an ideal for the imaginative as
it is for the intellectual life. Reason must seek the unification
of the sciences, as Plato envisaged, in certain principles of
universal validity and self-evident necessity. But where reason
seeks wider and more inclusive propositions, the imagination
of the great writer cannot rest until life is apprehended with
whatever of wholeness and concreteness is possible. In this the
imagination may indeed fail, as also reason may fail. But
because its life consists in the apprehension of wholes, it is
impelled to a pursuit of an inclusive unity within which
experience is integrated. And the creation of this pattern is
paradoxically effected through the expression of it in the selected
situation or plot.

Such is the essence of Coleridge's doctrine of the imagination,
according to which the poem is the representation of a created
world, which is held up as the real world. Poetry, that is to

say, discloses to us an imaginative idea or prehension of the world. In perception, tables, chairs, and pens are imaginative objects, at a rudimentary level of interest; they are present to the mind as imaginative wholes which control our behaviour in an enormous variety of ways. It may be that we are mistaken in thus representing the world to ourselves; tables, chairs, and pens may not be, in reality, what we imagine them to be. Nevertheless they are, as we represent them to ourselves, elements in our real world, the world to which in action and behaviour we respond, and factors effective for the life of personality. At the level of the "secondary" imagination, the world as it is grasped by the poet, through a process of dissolution and recreation, is the world to which in behaviour he responds; it is his world. He may have no means whereby he can show that the world as he imagines it is the real world, the world as it really is; nevertheless it is the world in which he lives, and to which, in all his behaviour, he reacts. This world, his real world, he seeks to convey in his poetry; he compels it, by his poetry, upon us. That world is, of course, personal to him, the creature of a unique imagination synthesizing its own experience of life. In this respect it is at the other extreme from the mass of impersonal and scientific knowledge which merely embodies the common and verifiable properties of the world as it is for all of us; which is, so to speak, the bare skeleton which each of us clothes with his own imaginative creativeness. Hence verisimilitude is a quite useless concept; indeed it is that which must be abandoned—for of what can poetry be an imitation, except of a world which is personal to a unique imagination?

3

Poetry then is the conveyance, by the imaginative use of language, of imaginative objects, the compulsion upon the reader by the poet of his own imaginative prehension of the world or of some aspect of or object within it. And it is only with poetry in this sense that criticism is concerned. Now the view of poetry as the expression of imaginative prehension is a sufficiently ordinary one, and is certainly not new. But there are grounds for believing that it is not wholly idle to repeat it. For example, a book in which Mr. I. A. Richards undertook to set out the principles of literary criticism seems to be built up out of disregard for this simple and, one would have thought, obvious truth. So completely does Mr. Richards ignore it that his book is for the most part taken up by an attempt to describe the psychological and physiological conditions which he holds are necessary for the writing of great poetry. Now such an inquiry, could it be accomplished with any considerable degree of scientific precision, would have great interest. But such interest as it might have would be irrelevant to what alone is the concern of the critic, namely, poetry. Such knowledge as might be achieved by such an inquiry would have as much relevance to poetry as an attempt to inquire into the psychological and physiological condition of a scientist would have to what we call science. To know the psychology and physiology of a scientist is of no aid to a critic of his work, though it might have interest for him; it certainly would be unimportant for judgment on the adequacy of the work he is criticizing. And it is equally true that in poetry, which is the conveyance of an imagination of the world, either in whole or part, the details of psychological and physiological description are irrelevant. The primary concern of the critic, which is the only strictly literary interest, is with the degree of adequacy with which the poet has conveyed his imaginative object, and with the means he has adopted for such conveyance. There are indeed a hundred and one other matters connected with poetry, historical and perhaps scientific, with which we may busy ourselves. But we should not delude ourselves into thinking that such interests are literary.[1]

[1] To avoid possible misunderstanding, I may add here that it is no part of my purpose to deny (what would obviously be absurd) that emotional endowment and temperament, coupled with the course of

This may seem so excessively dogmatic that it may be worth while to consider Mr. Richards' book in more detail, where a quotation from *The Defence of Poetry* sets the theme: "The greatest poets have been men of the most spotless virtue, of the most consummate prudence, and, if we look into the interior of their lives, the most fortunate of men." Mr. Richards is concerned with the 'interior of the lives of the poets', that is to say, their mental states, bodies, and nervous systems. And writing of critics, Mr. Richards says: "The qualifications of a good critic are three. He must be an adept at experiencing, without eccentricity, the state of mind relevant to the work of art he is judging. Secondly, he must be able to distinguish experiences from one another as regards their less superficial features. Thirdly, he must be a sound judge of values."[1] (By values here is meant, one supposes, the value or values of the 'experiences'.) It is to be noted that in this statement of the indispensable qualifications of a good critic (although it is granted, though perhaps incidentally, that the business of a critic is to judge a work of art), it is urged that what the critic has to bear in mind are 'experiences'; what he has to judge are 'experiences', and their value. And Mr. Richards goes on (p. 226) to eliminate even explicit reference to the work of art by saying, "The critic is throughout judging of experiences, of states of mind", and it is urged that critics are needlessly ignorant of the detailed psychology of such 'experiences'. It is therefore, if we are to follow Mr. Richards, with states of mind that the critic is concerned—such as are 'relevant' to the work of art in question; and it is these states of mind which the critic is to judge.

There can, I think, be no doubt that this is what Mr. Richards intends. And in another chapter he undertakes to define a poem. This definition is of the greatest interest. It is suggested

the writer's experience, actively determine the nature of his imaginative life. As I have tried to emphasize (p. 46), the imagination is the organ of the total personality.

[1] *Principles of Literary Criticism*, p. 114.

we may define a poem by reference to the poet's 'experience', to a qualified reader's 'experience', to an 'ideal reader's' 'experience', or to our own 'experience'. Mr. Richards, however, refuses to choose any one of them. "We must be more ingenious. We cannot take any single experience as the poem; we must have a class of more or less similar experiences instead. Let us mean by W*estminster Bridge* not the actual experience which led Wordsworth on a certain morning about a century ago to write what he did, but the class composed of all actual experiences, occasioned by the words, which do not suffer within certain limits from that experience" (p.226). This is, incidentally, an astonishing instance of definition-making, for the poet's 'experience', by virtue of which it is to be decided whether or not other 'experiences' are to be included in the class of 'experiences' which is the poem, is unfortunately not known. (Mr. Richards has immediately before refused to define the poem as the poet's experience 'since nobody but the artist has that experience'.) But our concern is with the definition of a poem as an 'experience'. And on this definition we are given further enlightenment.

'The process in the course of which a mental event may occur, a process apparently beginning in a stimulus and ending in an act, is what we have called an impulse' (pp. 86–7). An impulse then is the entire process which includes stimulus, mental state and action; it is, that is to say, the causation of a mental event, along with the quality and consequences of that event. (It is particularly to be noted that Mr. Richards likes the 'causal' statement of the occurrence of mental experiences.) And 'sensation, imagery, feeling, emotion, together with pleasure, unpleasure, and pain are names for the conscious characteristics of impulses'. In any given situation, of course, there is no such thing as a single impulse. Moreover, 'a stimulus must not be conceived as an alien intruder which thrusts itself upon us, and, after worming a devious way through our organism, as through a piece of cheese, emerges at the other end as an act'. The organism is selectively receptive and the resultant action will depend, for its character, upon the organism as well as upon the stimulus, and memory is a constant factor determining such selection and response. In addition, imagery is constantly substituted for sensation and 'incipient activities or tendencies to action' for overt response; the imaginal or incipient action such as occurs in contemplation of works of art is called an "attitude". An attitude is therefore a highly complicated affair, gathering into itself a mass of impulses. Psychology has not as yet achieved any considerable classification of attitudes, on account of their complexity. "Yet it is in terms of attitudes, the resolution, inter-inanimation, and balancing of impulses . . . that all the most valuable effects of poetry must be described" (p. 113). As an illustration of this the effects of tragedy are quoted. Tragedy supplies a poise or balance of two opposed impulses, pity, the emotional accompaniment of an impulse to approach (the word 'impulse' is here used apparently of the result of the mental state caused by the stimulus), and terror, the emotional accompaniment of an impulse to retreat. It is in the 'attitudes' that value resides; and of attitudes and their value the critic must be an expert judge. Yet since impulses deriving from the stimulus which is the poem are received by the mind, which is an 'organized system' of possible impulses, attitudes will vary from reader to reader. It is for this reason that the poem must be defined as a class of 'experiences'; and this must mean, in effect, that the poem is not one but many, as many as there are readers.

Valuable attitudes are those in which stability and poise is achieved. Such stability and poise are general characteristics of the most valuable experiences of the arts. But, it must be observed, "we must resist the temptation to analyse its cause into sets of opposed characters in the object. As a rule no such analysis can be made. The balance is not in the structure of the stimulating object, it is in the response" (p. 248). For this reason there is nothing peculiarly "aesthetic" in this poise of impulses; and apparently a large number of stimuli, very different from works of art, can give rise to them. Poems and plays are only among a number of stimuli which can produce such valuable experiences. States of inner harmony or reconciliation of impulses when enjoyed by poets, issue in the writing of poetry; and such states of inner adjustment tend to be accompanied by 'transcendental descriptions', of which Wordsworth's *Tintern Abbey* is an example.[1] Such a mental state is apt to cause the poet to look for its origin in a divine source. But such beliefs result from an inner condition, and not vice versa.

4

This is, I think, the essence of Mr. Richards' aesthetic. And it is summed up by what he has to say of Coleridge's remark that the "sense of musical delight is a gift of the imagination". This, he thinks, is one of Coleridge's 'most brilliant feats'; and he goes on to say, "It is in such a resolution of a welter of disconnected impulses into a single ordered response that in all the arts imagination is most shown".[2] The imagination is "most shown in this resolution"; but what the imagination is and how it produces this desirable result we are not told, 'for the reason that here its operation is most intricate and most inaccessible to observation'; and the remaining and bigger part of the chapter, which was intended to be a chapter on the imagination, talks of impulses and their resolutions, but not of the imagination. And this is in accordance with Mr. Richards' comparative lack of interest in the act of awareness as contrasted with its volitional and affective accompaniments (the 'attitude'); 'for a theory of knowledge', he goes on to say, 'is needed only at one point, the point at which we wish to decide whether a poem, for example,

---

[1] But to meet all the facts, Mr. Richards should have added that such states may give rise, apparently, to 'materialistic descriptions', as in the case of Lucretius.

[2] Op. cit., p. 245. Whether such 'resolution' always occurs, and if so, n what sense, is discussed in Chapter IV, Sections 6 and 7.

is true, or reveals reality, and if so, in what sense; admittedly a very important question. Whereas a theory of feeling, of emotion, of attitudes and desires, of the affective-volitional aspect of mental activity, is required at all points of our analyses" (p. 91). Mr. Richards' predominant interest in feelings, emotions, attitudes, is at the expense of recognition of the activity of the imagination. He holds the critic to be primarily concerned with the resultant attitudes. "It is the attitudes invoked which are the all-important part of any experiences". What is emphasized is not our awareness of an object or set of objects, but the emotional-volitional results in us of the action of a "stimulus", which acts together with certain subjective conditions. What is important is not what is present to our minds, but what is wrought in our minds in feeling and tendencies to action. The whole regard of this aesthetic is away from the object to its results; his concern is not with the beholdment of an object but with the trains of results set up by the "stimulus". Hence Mr. Richards' love of poetry may be said to be of the cupboard variety; it is a means to an experience which is valuable for life. And his interest in poetry is therefore but an interest in one particular means by which such "experiences" can be produced; for presumably a "balance and reconciliation of impulses", such as great poetry is said to afford, might conceivably be produced by a harmless drug, in which case poetry and drugs are alike stimuli productive of valuable experiences such as it is the business of the critic apparently to judge. Accordingly, what has happened in Mr. Richards' aesthetic is that poetry has simply fallen out of it, and it has become one stimulus among many which can produce desirable results. The qualifications for a poetry-critic and a drug-critic would be, on Mr. Richards' showing, identical; they both would have to be adepts at experiencing states of mind (though for one the states of mind would be "relevant" to a work of art, and for the other those "relevant" to a drug, but such states could conceivably be identical); they would both have to be able to distinguish experiences from one another as regards their less superficial features; and they would both have to be sound judges of value.

Now there is no way in which so impossible a position can be avoided except by giving due recognition to the primacy of the imagination in poetic experience. So long as we fail to do so we necessarily look away from the imaginative object which the poet seeks to make us create, to a number of accompanying effects, emotional and volitional, which, however important, are not the central feature of poetic response. We must, on the contrary, view poetic experience as an awareness of an imaginative object; and the central "experience" is not effects wrought in us, but beholdment by the imagination of an object. It is what is present to our minds which is vital in the experience, and not the emotional-volitional effects. Such effects, of course, there will and must be. But they are attendant upon an act of apprehension which is central. The act of imaginative awareness may indeed be an 'incomprehensible ultimate', but it is a unique 'incomprehensible ultimate' which cannot be reduced to an effect in the nervous system. "To say", says Mr. Richards, "that the mental (neural) event so caused is aware of the black marks [the poem on paper] is to say that it is caused by them" (p. 90). It is to be noted that "mental" is here, for convenience, equated with "neural"; 'for convenience' because Mr. Richards, by his use of the brackets, would have us believe that we can represent mental events as 'caused' by physical stimuli in the same way as neural occurrences may be caused by physical stimuli. But in fact this is not possible. The act of awareness has a uniqueness which cannot be summarily dismissed in that fashion. And the whole purpose of Kant's work, which inspired Coleridge, was to insist that this is so, and that the act of awareness is a creative act which may require for its occurrence the presence of certain physical factors, but which cannot be reduced to them. The act of awareness is a unique and creative act, not susceptible of such a convenient reduction to neural events as Mr. Richards would have us believe.

Hence the primary situation which we have to bear in mind is not our neural susceptibility to stimuli, but the imaginative synthesis of sensations which are presented to the mind on the occurrence of certain physical and neural processes. Similarly in the arts the vital factor is our imaginative activity in its awareness of an object. In perception and in poetry alike an object is present to the imagination, a presence which, of course, is accompanied by affective-volitional factors, but is nevertheless primary to such factors. In the absence of this recognition Mr. Richards is naturally at a loss to explain Coleridge's statement that a 'sense of more than musical delight' is the gift of the imagination. 'The sense of more than musical delight' Mr. Richards at once interprets as a poise of impulses; but how is it a 'gift of the imagination'? We are not told. Whereas there can be little doubt that Coleridge viewed such effective-volitional effects as incidental ('gifts') to the major fact of the imagination's activity. Mr. Richards' aesthetic concentrates on the gifts. It apparently ignores the giver. No doubt these 'gifts' are valuable, and valuable for life; but the critic, if he concentrates on them to the exclusion of the imaginative object, is simply not fulfilling his function. In the 'impulse', which is the inclusive name for the entire process from stimulus to attitude, nothing is indicated to show the creative act which is present and fundamental to the rest. We hear a great deal about sensation, tied and free imagery, references, emotions, and attitudes; but nothing of the primary activity without which sensation, imagery, and references are abstractions, and emotions and attitudes impossible. It is all *Hamlet* without the Prince. If we are to remedy this omission, we must cease to speak of the reception of 'stimuli' which cause certain results which may be valuable, and speak instead of an 'active agency' which creates its object, and in that creation enjoys certain emotional and volitional accompaniments.

5

In a more recently published book, *Coleridge on the Imagination*, Mr. Richards deals at great length with Coleridge's views on the imagination. It is, in the light of what has gone before, of the greatest interest to observe what he has to say, and what validity he is prepared to grant to Coleridge's doctrine. Speaking of Coleridge's desertion of Hartley for Kant, Mr. Richards says that 'the two systems (or sets of assumptions), violently opposed though they seemed to him, may each—to a Coleridge—be ways of surveying our mind' (p. 17). Now 'materialist associationism' is certainly one way of surveying our mind; it is the way which is dictated by a psychology which sets out to be 'scientific'. This we noticed at the end of our first essay, and we shall return to it at the end of this one. Over against 'materialist associationism' Mr. Richards sets 'transcendental idealism'. But transcendental idealism is not that which is opposed to it. What should be opposed to it, as another 'way of surveying the mind', is a psychology which realizes that 'materialist-associationism' is not, when clearly understood, anything more than a form of scientific methodology, and which, while admitting that it itself is not 'scientific', asserts that the mind is creative in knowledge. This it may clearly do without asserting any epistemological idealism. Now Coleridge once and for all threw over all that Hartley stood for, and ceased to hold an associationism, whether as a 'way of surveying the mind' or in any other way; it is true that in so doing he adopted an idealism. But this, for our purpose, can be separated out from his view of the mind as an 'active agency'.[1] And the choice is not between,

[1] Although it is true that Coleridge took Kant to be an idealist in the usual sense of the term, it may be emphasised that by 'transcendental idealism' Kant intended a doctrine indifferent to both 'idealism' and 'realism'—a doctrine which regarded idealism and realism as raising (and trying to answer) questions which go 'beyond experience' and which therefore should not be discussed. Although Kant certainly gives ground for being regarded as a subjectivist,

as is suggested, the materialist and the idealist. The choice is between a materialistic psychology which does not see its materialism merely as a necessity of scientific inquiry, and a psychology which sees materialism as a necessity to scientific method, and, by rejecting it, is content to be open to the charge of being 'unscientific'.

Then, at a later stage, after Coleridge's remarks on the primary and secondary imagination have been quoted, come the following astonishing sentences. "Taken as psychology", writes Mr. Richards, "—not as metaphysics—there is little in such an account of mental *activity* with which a modern psychologist—even though he combines with it a metaphysical materialism, and supposes that the mind is just certain ways of operation in the body—will treat now as other than a commonplace. Data are for him facta; he knows too much about the dependence of every mental event upon former mental events to regard any of their products as simply given to us. For him the activities of the self . . . are results of past activities . . . and this prior experiencing determines how it will experience in the future" (p. 60). What these remarks are apparently intended to convey is that Coleridge, in these sentences, was stating a trivial commonplace and what any associationist could accept. But between all that is implied in Coleridge's view of imagination as the 'prime agent of all human perception' and what Mr. Richards reduces Coleridge's remarks to mean, there is, of course, a whole world of difference. This is not the place in which to enter into the detail of the controversy which centres about associationism. But it is plainly absurd to seek to reduce Coleridge's statement, whether taken as psychology or metaphysics, to meaning nothing more than a modern form of associationism could accept. Certainly Coleridge intended something very different from materialistic

this was certainly not what he intended. It is probably true to say that there are eminent contemporary writers who, while insisting on 'interpretation' and 'construction' by the mind in perception, adhere to an uncompromising epistemological realism. But Kant's own view is the most satisfactory.

and associationist psychology. There is reason to believe that
Mr. Richards occasionally suspects that this is so; and he
then falls back on the suggestion that there is no essential
difference between the two views. "We cannot", he says,
"reasonably satisfy ourselves, or take either party's word for
it, that they are as opposed to each other as they seem to be.
We could only be satisfied if we were able to perform a perfect
analysis exhibiting them in common terms. We need, in other
words, to discover just what each is doing, and a means of
comparing these doings—a common framework in which
the rival speculative machineries can be examined" (p. 70).
Such an analysis and such a technique of comparison are at
present beyond our powers. "But we should not", we are told,
"hold that there is any irreconcilable clash between their
results." This is indeed making the best of two worlds; and
doing so on the strength of the lack of an analysis and technique
of comparison competent to show how the reconciliation
can be made. This kind of argument is, if I may say so, a form
of the self-mystification which in his book Mr. Richards
attributes to Mr. Herbert Read. It is also a form of 'dodging
the chief difficulty' which again, in another part of the book,
is attributed to others.

There is good reason why Mr. Richards should seek to make
the best of the two worlds. For he recognizes, in spite of all his
liking for associationism, that Coleridge's view of the mind as
active and creative has advantages that 'associationism of the
Hartley–Condillac type' had not. "As an instrument for explor-
ing the most intricate and unified modes of mental activity—
those in poetry—its superiority seems overwhelming." There
is indeed little doubt of this; Mr. Richards will hardly allow
himself to be drawn into the view of literary creation which
Mr. Russell sets out in *An Outline of Philosophy* (p. 200) as
resulting from the poets having a store of 'unusual associations'.
Yet, by one of those astonishing reconciliations of opposition
which from time to time occur in Mr. Richards' mind, we
find him saying on the preceding page that 'were Coleridge

alive he would, I hope, be applauding and improving doctrines of the type he, as a metaphysician, thought least promising —the very materialistic-mechanistic doctrines that he was attacking'. Mr. Richards, therefore, will not have the imagination as Coleridge tried to explicate it; or, rather, he accepts it in the act of saying that it will be shown, by the psychology of years hence, to be at one with 'materialist associationism'. If he could show how, in but one slightest respect, this is conceivable, we might perhaps take this seriously.

6

We may now return to the *Principles of Literary Criticism*, in which we are told that the only point at which the theory of knowledge has any relevance for criticism is when we wish to decide whether or not a poem is true or false, or reveals reality. The theory of knowledge has, in Mr. Richards' view, a slighter use in criticism than a theory of feeling, emotion, and attitude, which is required at every point. Now reflection will show that though some theory of apprehension is necessary for criticism, it is not in the least necessary for that purpose which Mr. Richards indicates. In the first place, Mr. Richards apparently believes that *Othello*, *Tintern Abbey*, or any other poem we wish to mention, is either true or false, does or does not reveal reality. And it is implied that there is at hand a theory of knowledge which can tell us whether or not *Tintern Abbey* does or does not reveal reality. It is a matter of great interest to know that there is such a theory; but if it exists it has not yet come to light. Incidentally, one would have thought that to know whether *Othello* is true or false, or *Tintern Abbey* reveals or fails to reveal reality, a conclusive metaphysic, were such a thing possible, and not only a theory of knowledge, would be necessary. But our present point is that the question of the abstract truth or otherwise of a play or poem simply does not occur in imaginative experience; for poetry is not a number of propositions, but the conveyance of imaginative prehension.

The poet sees the world in a certain way; thus has his imagination created it, and thus is it real to him, the world in which he lives and to which in his life he responds. The world as it is represented is the poet's world; and in so far as his poem is successful, he will make it the reader's world by compelling his vision upon him. And this is so whether the poet be a Lucretius or a Wordsworth. In great poetry we at once receive and create an imaginative vision of the world; a new world becomes acutely present to us, or, as Coleridge says, the poet makes us creators, after him, of such a new world. And to ask is *Tintern Abbey* true or false is to put an impossible question from outside the imaginative experience, and, in any case, a question which surely no one can claim to have answered or be able to answer once and for all. Our response to such a world as the poet places compulsion upon us to create may indeed quickly fade after our reading, and that world may soon cease to have a compelling reality for us. But all that is of relevance and importance for criticism is that the poet makes it real for us and compels us to his vision. However Christian a man may be, however much, that is to say, his life may be controlled by the Christian imagination of the world, he may yet enjoy the *De Rerum Natura* as the expression of an amazing vision of the world. It is surely not the business of the critic to make pronouncements upon the "truth" or otherwise of poems and plays; we do not want, say, a Christian critic to point out objections to Lucretius' scheme; we want him to help us enjoy an imaginative synthesis which is not Christian. And if he cannot do that he is no critic; he has to be "chameleon-like", and for the purpose of his work to live in not one world but in a "thousand worlds".[1]

When Mr. Richards undertakes to describe the genesis of

[1] I do not wish to suggest that this is the sole function of the critic; but I do suggest that the critic should avoid the use of the word 'truth'. Incidentally, in view of Mr. Richards' view of what he calls 'revelation theories' of poetry (see later, p. 67), it is surprising that he should think it worth while to discuss whether or not a poem is 'true' or 'reveals reality'.

the writing of poetry he again shows his interest in "experiences" and "attitudes", not in the object present to imaginative activity. When we read a poem, and enjoy an "experience" of poise of impulses, the stimulus is the poem, though of course the stimulus is complicated in its action by 'interior' conditions. What then is the stimulus to the poet which gives him his "experience"? Not, it seems, an imaginative object. Instead, "some system of impulses not ordinarily in adjustment within itself or adjusted to the world finds something which orders it or gives it fit exercise. Then follows the peculiar sense of ease, of free, unimpeded activity and the feeling of acceptance, of something more positive than acquiescence. This feeling is the reason why such states may be called beliefs."[1] Thus we are asked to believe that the labour of imaginative synthesis is a product of a rather mysterious and fortunate adjustment of impulses; and that the literary masterpieces of the world, the *Iliad*, the *Aeneid*, the *Inferno*, *Paradise Lost*, *The Tempest*, were stimulated into existence 'by something'—possibly a good meal, or a comfortable chair.

We are further told that in order to have "experiences" two conditions are necessary, first mental health, and secondly 'frequent occurrence of such experiences in the recent past' (p. 248). These two conditions are interesting. For what, in the first place, is mental health? What can it mean for Mr. Richards but the possession of a mental organization which is likely to result in "experiences"? So that, in order to have "experiences" we must have a mind likely to have "experiences". And secondly, in order to have "experiences" in the present and future, we must have had such "experiences" (and frequently) in the past. This is equivalent to saying that in order to have the experience of digesting a meal well we should have a sound constitution, a constitution of the kind likely to digest a meal well; and, secondly, we should have successfully digested meals previously, indeed in the recent past. But all this, to say the least, is not very enlightening.

[1] *Principles of Literary Criticism*, p. 283.

E

7

Mr. Richards, no doubt, is the more willing to take up this attitude because there can be no doubt that a great deal of the world's best poetry is religious—represents, that is to say, a religious imagination of the world. Mr. Richards, however, disapproves of such apprehension of the world. He does so apparently on the basis of his distinction between the scientific and the emotive uses of language, and religious belief is an 'emotive' affair. Now as we endeavoured to point out in the previous chapter, this distinction is superficial in comparison with the distinction between language used for mere indication and language used for imaginative conveyance. This failure to see the more significant distinction is again due to a persistent emphasis upon emotional and volitional reactions at the expense of the initial imaginative activity. And when, it is argued, language is used emotively, what is occurring is an effort to bring about 'effects in emotion and attitude produced by the reference it occasions'. That is to say, a poise or balance of impulses 'brought about by something' easily results in a reference being occasioned—in Wordsworth's case, for example, it is God, the immortality of the soul, etc. But these 'references' arise out of an emotional-volitional state; they are fictions, and should not therefore be taken seriously —'it is still the attitudes, not the references which are important'. "For strong belief-feelings, as is well known, and as is shown by certain doses of alcohol or hashish, and pre-eminently of nitrous oxide, will readily attach themselves to almost any reference, distorting it to suit their purpose."

Now the matter of the explicit expression of belief in poetry is by no means so important as Mr. Richards would have us believe. For the poet's belief can ultimately be interpreted to be only the presence to his imagination of a world which is the world in which he lives, and which, as he responds to it in his life, is his real world.[1] The poet's belief in other words is not a matter of mere explicit assertion; it consists in his emotional-volitional response to the world of his imagination, which is shown by that response to be his real world. Whether or not the poet makes formal assertion of belief is not important. Mr. Richards, in accordance with his view of the place of belief in poetry, is strongly opposed to what he calls 'revelation' theories—views which hold that poetry can claim to give us truth. For our part, we should agree that the 'revelation' theory is a useless and impossible doctrine; but for reasons other than those which Mr. Richards holds. For against the 'revelation' theory it is necessary to maintain that, as we do not know 'for truth' (as Keats says), the ultimate nature of the universe, we must be content with a situation in which the poet is seen as conveying to us the world as it is for his imagination, which controls his life, and which is thus real to him. Ultimately, whether or not the world is really as it exists for his imagination neither he nor we can in all strictness be said to know.[2]

Yet it is of interest to find that apparently, according to Mr. Richards, poetry does not always use distorted 'references';

[1] A relevant discussion will be found in an essay 'The Nature of Believing', by R. B. Braithwaite, in the *Proceedings of the Aristotelian Society* for 1933, where belief is defined as (1) entertainment of a proposition *p*, and (2) a disposition to act as if *p* were true. I suggest that in poetry, whether or not the poet explicitly states propositions which he can be said personally to believe, we have belief-situations. *King Lear* (see later, p. 69) contains no explicit expression of Shakespeare's belief about human life; but it expresses the kind of world which at the time Shakespeare 'entertained' in his imagination and which, as thus entertained, affected his behaviour. If this is true, *King Lear* and, say, *Tintern Abbey* (which contains explicit statements of belief) both alike express belief, and the question of formal expression of belief loses its importance. This is confirmed by the fact that Mr. A. C. Bradley was able to state in propositional form what Shakespeare at the time of writing the tragedies may be said to have believed about human life. No doubt these beliefs were not present in propositional form to Shakespeare's mind; but they are none the less embodied or implicit in the plays.

[2] See the chapter on Keats later, Section 5.

and it is claimed that there are some poems, not using such references, in which we are 'attuned to existence'. What are these poems? Here is the answer.

For clear and impartial awareness of the nature of the world in which we live and the development of attitudes which will enable us to live in it finely are both necessities, and neither can be subordinated to the other. They are almost independent, such connections as exist in well-organized individuals being adventitious. Those who find this a hard saying may be invited to consider the effect upon them of those works of art which most unmistakably attune them to existence. The central experience of Tragedy . . . is an attitude indispensable for a fully developed life. But in the reading of *King Lear* what facts verifiable by science, or accepted and believed in as we accept and believe in ascertained facts, are relevant? None whatever (p. 282).

Thus *King Lear* 'attunes us to existence'. Then apparently Mr. Richards knows what sort of a thing 'existence' is, since *King Lear* attunes us to 'existence', but *Tintern Abbey* attunes us to a fiction? One gathers from the quotation (though Mr. Richards carefully avoids being too explicit) that *King Lear* gives 'clear and impartial awareness of the nature of the world'. We may presume therefore that Mr. Richards is in possession of a clear and impartial awareness of the nature of the world. Now if *King Lear* has perhaps not given it him, what has? For either he has derived his 'clear and impartial awareness' from *King Lear*, or he has obtained it elsewhere, and can therefore judge as to when an attitude is in tune with 'existence'. But in either case *King Lear* either does or does not reveal the nature of the world. If it does, what becomes of Mr. Richards' antagonism to the revelation theory; if it does not, how does it 'attune us' to existence?—by being a 'drug' which involves no distortion of references? But if it does not distort references, does it not reveal reality?

8

But Mr. Richards seeks to elude us by speaking of belief. There are, he says, no 'beliefs' in *King Lear*; and music

similarly states no 'beliefs'. In the sense of explicit statements
of belief, that is so. Yet to the imagination which is suborned
to *King Lear* the world of Lear is a real world; it was for Shakespeare, if only during the time of its composition, the world
in which he believed. Similarly, the world of *Tintern Abbey*
was for Wordsworth his real world, that to which he responded
in behaviour, and it may become so for the reader. The fact
that Wordsworth, for obvious reasons, had explicitly to express
beliefs to help conveyance of his object, and that Shakespeare,
for equally obvious reasons, had not, does not alter the identity
of the two situations.[1] Two imaginative apprehensions of the
world are being conveyed. That is all that is relevant. Mr.
Richards says, and rightly, that in the reading of *King Lear*,
no facts verifiable by science, or accepted and believed in,
as we accept and believe in ascertained facts, are relevant.
But in *Tintern Abbey*, apparently, there are facts verifiable by
science which are relevant, and which apparently prove that
Tintern Abbey is a case of distorted reference, of reference
to a fiction. If so, we should be glad to know what they are,
and to have mention of a single fact 'verifiable by science,
etc.', which is relevant to *Tintern Abbey*, and shows it to have
fictitious reference. The fact that in one poem there is, and in
the other there is not explicit expression of belief, does not alter
the fact that in each case 'facts verifiable by science' are irrelevant. In each case language is being used to evoke an imaginative
world; and as we have seen, the question of ultimate truth
remains unanswered.

There is, however, little doubt as to the source of Mr.
Richards' 'clear and impartial awareness of the nature of the
world'. He finds that source in science, a source which
apparently, by the information it gives, is able to tell us whether
or not an attitude is valuable and 'attunes us to existence'.

---

[1] Of course, if a poet *can* convey his 'work' without explicit expression of belief, he should most certainly do so. But clearly there is a
large class of poems in which this is impossible. Poetry should *show*
and not *say*; expression of belief in poetry is justified only when it is
unavoidable.

In a little book called *Science and Poetry*, Mr. Richards develops this point for us. There he tells us that what he calls the 'magical view of nature' (by which is apparently intended the religious view of nature whether primitive or Christian) has been dispelled by the 'neutralization of nature', the new 'world-picture of science'. Science has brought about a 'revolution' in these matters, has given us 'genuine knowledge', and the former 'edifices of supposed knowledge' have simply toppled down. Thus science has apparently told us what sort of a thing 'existence' is, and we know now where we stand. Such doctrine, as I have tried to reiterate, is founded on an erroneous view of scientific construction; but in this respect, Mr. Richards not only reveals a failure of comprehension; he adds to such failure self-contradiction of an extreme kind. Having set out such a doctrine as the above, he proceeds to tell us that science 'cannot tell us what we are or what this world is; not because these are in any sense insoluble questions, but because they are not questions at all' (p. 53). And this follows the statement on the preceding page to the effect that science has shown us that the 'magical' view of nature (which after all is a view of what man and the world is) has been exploded by science. It also immediately follows a statement in which we are told that 'science can tell us about man's place in the universe and his chances; that the place is precarious, and the chances problematical'. But one would have thought that to tell us this is to tell us a great deal about what we are and what the world is. For what is meant by 'chances'? Does Mr. Richards include under 'chances' the 'chance', for example, of personal immortality or of a supra-temporal existence? One supposes that he must do, since they are 'chances' about which human beings have always been concerned. Does, then, science tell us *nothing* of what man and the world is?

9

The whole tenor of Mr. Richards' philosophical criticism is due to a very simple failure of discrimination.

Building up his views on the misleading distinction between language used for reference and language used emotively, he has failed to realize the imaginative character of scientific construction.[1] And therefore he has failed to see that the 'world-picture of science' is an imaginative construction, evolved with a view to the formulation of generalizations of strictest fact. He therefore takes it seriously for an account of the nature of existence. In his psychology, materialistic-associationism accordingly becomes inevitable, the mind becomes for him the nervous system, and it is indifferent to him whether or not we call awareness a mental or a neural event. That being so, Mr. Richards believes that criticism instead of being what it necessarily now is, something vague and uncertain, can be made 'scientific' and to consist of precise generalizations and judgments—all that is required is greater knowledge of neurology. When a really adequate knowledge of neurology is obtained, a poem will be susceptible of precise expression; it will be expressible no longer even as an "experience", but as a system of nervous discharges in the mechanical nervous system. No doubt it will be expressible also in mathematical formulae. When poems have thus become reducible to formulae, the critic, who will be an expert neurologist and mathematician, will be able to say, with the utmost precision, which of two poems is the more valuable, which, that is to say, liberates the greatest quantity of nervous energy in the present and for the future. Criticism will thus have become a precise science. It is true that at present neurology is a 'jungle'. But 'it should be borne in mind that the knowledge which the men of A.D. 3000 will possess, if all goes well, may make all our aesthetics, all our psychology, all our modern theory of value, look pitiful'. Certainly, this should be 'borne in mind'. In the meanwhile, it is convenient to regard Coleridge's view of the mind as

[1] It is only fair to Mr. Richards to point out that in Chapter VII of *Coleridge on Imagination* he shows signs of recognizing this. But as this recognition, if he is to be consistent, involves fundamental changes in his entire aesthetic, I have thought it right to criticize his former view.

actively creative as not altogether foolish. But as we saw, in case we should think that Mr. Richards is abandoning his materialistic-associationism, we are assured that an 'analysis and technique of comparison' (of which presumably the men of A.D. 3000 will be in possession) will show that there is no irreconcilable clash between James Mill's view of the mind and Coleridge's. It is, no doubt, an advantage to know what knowledge the men of A.D. 3000 will possess; Mr. Richards blandly gives himself the advantage of Coleridge's way of thinking while sublimely assuring us that in a thousand years it will be shown to be a form of materialistic-associationism. I hesitate to describe this kind of argument as unfair. But Mr. Richards would probaby have a harder word for anyone who, in discussion, asserted that two utterly different things were really the same, on the grounds that, although he could not for the life of him see how they could be, people of a thousand years hence will be able to.

I have written at such length about Mr. Richards' work in order to bring out the character of the conclusions to which we are brought if we ignore the primacy of the imaginative act in artistic creation and enjoyment. Denying such primacy the virtual result of Mr. Richards' work is to ignore poetry and give us formulae instead. Putting the active agency of the imagination on one side, Mr. Richards introduces us to science and scientific psychology; and we are told a great deal about morals and value. These things are no doubt of great importance, but they are not poetry, and the critic, be he ever so philosophical or scientific, who gives them priority over the activity of the imagination is forgetting the main task of criticism. It is not, of course, the case that matters relating to science, psychology, and problems of morals and value do not arise in the discussion of poetry; and it is of great importance that the inter-relation of these things should be discussed and realized. But it is of still greater importance that we should recognize the arts as the expression of the unique activity of the imagination, instead of setting out to reduce the imagination to something other than it is, And when we say that the imagination is 'unique' we do not mean that it is something merely 'aesthetic', but that it is an irreducible factor present in all experience whatsoever, yet operative in the arts with a high degree of power and concreteness.

10

It is surprising how, in critics differing radically from Mr. Richards, there is a curious vagueness on the subject of the imagination, and how frequently the use of the word is avoided. For example, we find Mr. Murry writing in *The Problem of Style* (p. 19): "In adopting the notion that style stands in a direct relation to a core or nucleus of emotional and intellectual experience, we have cut away some of the difficulties that seemed to surround one of the most common meanings of the word style." What is striking in this passage is that Mr. Murry traces back the writing of poetry to "emotional and intellectual" elements. There is no doubt that in the writing of poetry, emotional and intellectual elements are present. But surely there is, more important than either, an imaginative element. It may be, of course, that Mr. Murry is using emotion in a very vague way, to include imaginative creation. But if so, this is surely a reprehensible use of a word which carries for everybody, the plain man and the psychologist alike, an indication of forms of feeling which in themselves are not imaginative. And again, in a passage which Mr. Richards quotes from Mr. Lascelles Abercrombie, we find Mr. Abercrombie speaking of the 'quality and force of the *emotion* symbolized by the imagery'. But is the main use of imagery to symbolize emotion? One would have thought that its main use was the expression of imaginative idea or object; and Mr. Richards, criticizing Mr. Abercrombie, insists that what is important in imagery is not emotion, but meaning. He falls back from the emotional to the intellectual elements involved.[1]

[1] *Coleridge on Imagination*, pp. 35–7.

Certainly, again, emotional and intellectual elements are present; but surely they are part of a total experience central to which is imaginative prehension. Such prehension cannot occur in poetry unaccompanied by emotion and thought. But we cannot agree with Mr. Abercrombie to reduce it to emotion or with Mr. Richards to reduce it to meaning. Or again we find it said in a recent work by Mr. John Sparrow[1] that the aim of the poet is to express and create a 'state of feeling'. It may be that the word 'feeling' is being used loosely. But the loose use of a word can be extremely dangerous, and lead to failures to distinguish the important factors in the situation. For 'emotion' and 'feeling' are in themselves 'blind', states of mind which depend for their occurrence upon an activity of mind which is a prehension of an object and carries us outside ourselves. Such activity is creative, in the sense that the object as it is prehended is not given to the mind, but is the outcome of imaginative synthesis. And this activity is necessary in perception, science, and art alike. In the two former it is subordinate, functional to certain ends; in the latter it is free and suborned to neither utility nor abstraction. And the primary fact about poetry is that in and through it an imaginative object is conveyed. This, as it seems to me, is true of all poetry whatsoever, including, as I hope to show, lyrical poetry. And the dangers which accrue to overlooking this seem overwhelming. The weight of emphasis must always be on the vividness with which we grasp an imaginative object or situation, and not on the quality or value of the other aspects of our mental condition associated with that apprehension—'emotion' and 'attitudes'.

[1] *Sense and Poetry*, p. 27.

CHAPTER III

THE IMAGINATIVE USE OF LANGUAGE

I

IN the last chapter our argument was that the essence of poetry, of its creation and enjoyment alike, consists in creative prehension of an object; and that while such prehension is accompanied by emotion and impulse, emotional-volitional effects, it is an error to give a primary place in poetic experience to emotion and attitudes. They are the accompaniments, however necessary, of a central process which is one of creative imagination. Poetry, that is to say, is the use of language in such a way as to convey awareness of the imaginative wholeness of objects or of their imagined unity. In everyday life all the objects of which we are aware are, as we have seen, present to the imagination; but the imagination of objects is there subordinated to and limited by the demands of practical life. In science also there is necessarily a process of imaginative construction; but here again the scientist does not rest in contemplation of his objects; he is concerned with them for a purpose, and they are instrumental to his real quest, which is one for fact which can be placed beyond dispute. But in the life of what Coleridge calls the 'secondary' imagination, imaginative creation and contemplation are not so subordinated. They are free; and in the writing of poetry that process of creation is for its own sake enjoyed, untrammelled by directly practical considerations, and is communicated to the reader. Objects of which we feel ourselves to be the creators become present to our minds.

As we noted in the first chapter, Mr. I. A. Richards has distinguished between the scientific use of language and the 'emotive' use of language. But we observed also that science, if it is to place itself beyond the range of sceptical attack, must confine itself to speaking of sense-data only; if, as Mr.

Russell says, the scientist chooses to speak of forces, for example, he is speaking of something for the existence of which his investigations give him no warrant. Strictly scientific reference is to sense-data only. This is not, of course, to say that the scientist may not, for convenience, speak of 'forces' and what he represents to himself as 'things'. Mr. Russell's point is that his statements are really scientific in so far as they have relevance only to 'sensations.'

Similarly, in everyday life, we are constantly using language 'for reference' as Mr. Richards would say; indicating what we take to be 'things'. If I say 'There is a chair' I am referring to what I represent as being a 'thing'. Mr. Russell may bring his sceptical guns to bear on my belief; but it is certain that I am referring to what, to me, is more than a bundle of sense-data. This is the everyday use of language for reference—reference to what is, as I represent it to myself, a whole of perception including and transcending sense-elements. But in poetry, language is used chiefly not to indicate objects but to convey the poet's imagination of objects. The poet's imagination rests in the contemplation of objects to a degree far greater than is the case in everyday practical life; and he seeks therefore to use language in such a way as not merely to indicate objects, but to compel us to create in imagination the object as he himself has imagined it.

2

Before we go further there is a matter upon which we may comment. Objects, we have said, are present to the imagination, and are present as wholes to the imagination. We should, therefore, avoid thinking that it is possible to divide, so to speak, the object into two; that part which is given to us in sensation, and that which is not. Although it is the case that for the artificial purpose of making theoretical distinctions we might appear to speak in that way, it is clear that such a division is unreal. For the sense-elements, although we may make 'reference' to them, are nevertheless only known to us as aspects of imaginative unities; and therefore their existence and character is for us conditioned by the nature of the total object as it is present to imaginative prehension. We may illustrate this in the following way, using a favourite instance given in text-books of psychology. It is well-known that a number of lines may be described on paper which to one person may indicate a representation of a staircase, to another an overhanging cornice. That is to say, to the minds of the two people concerned the objects present to their respective imaginations are quite different. But although this is so, there would be no difficulty in securing agreement between the two people as to the correctness of a matter of fact description of what was actually on the paper. They might both be in perfect agreement on the correctness of a matter of fact description; yet, in so far as there were present to their respective imaginations two quite different objects, it is undeniable that what was on the paper looked entirely different to each of them. That is to say, the 'sensations' were caught in two different imaginative syntheses; and if that is so, they must have appeared differently; in each case the character of the sensory elements was conditioned by the nature of the imaginative processes at work. What was given in sensation and agreed upon in that way is really an abstraction from the total object present to the mind.

Nor is this an extreme case. It is perhaps an extreme case at the level of the 'primary' imagination; but when we consider the 'secondary' imagination, it typifies the general situation. We all know how an artist can transfigure an object which we have known, and to which we have given little attention. Two men may be 'seeing' the 'same thing'; yet if one, who has a strong imagination, undertakes to paint it, the other may quickly realize how differently the object appeared to the painter's imagination and to his own. The object present to their respective imaginations was really not one and the same, though no doubt they could, if they took the trouble, agree on an 'objective' description of it. But such an objective description, if it is to be agreed on, must be extremely unimaginative; for here, as in the former case, the strictly 'given' and 'discoverable' elements are an abstraction from a whole present to the imagination, and become transformed when they are re-integrated into the total object which the imagination prehends. It is because this is so that 'verisimilitude' is precisely what is not desirable in art. A photograph, for example, records only those elements upon which agreement of the kind we have spoken of is possible.[1]

We must therefore realize that the total object is an object to the imagination; and that what of the world is 'discoverable' is a world eviscerated of imaginative content, if indeed it can be called a world at all. The sensory elements which we describe as 'given' to the mind are not therefore, in the strictest sense, 'given'; for they are changed by the imagination which creatively integrates them into the unity of the imagined object. And the total object is 'created' by the imagination; for as a totality it certainly is not given but is at once made and contemplated by the imagination. Because this is so, the poet may seek to compel us to imaginative creation either by the use of sensuous description or suggestion (as in onomatopoeia), or on the other hand by more directly suggesting the inner vital quality of an object (as by metaphor). Let us notice the latter method first.

---

[1] The general point made here is applicable to what Professor L. J. Russell calls the 'general form of organization of visual material in a spatial order' 'which is capable of many subtle variations, according to the mode of life, or the training, or the aesthetic experiences of the individual. . . . I would suggest, for instance, that the illustrations in the modern books and newspapers tend to modify the vision of man to-day, so as to produce a common pattern of organization of the visual field very different from that of the man living in medieval England or of the ancient Egyptians.'—In his Presidential Address to the Aristotelian Society, 1932.

3

Both Wordsworth and Coleridge, both of whom liked to write about imaginative processes as well as to indulge them, have each given instances of this creative process. It may be of interest to notice them both. Coleridge's example are the lines from *Venus and Adonis:*

> Look! how a bright star shooteth from the sky;
> So glides he in the night from Venus' eye!

and Coleridge adds: "How many images and feelings are here brought together, without effort and without discord, in the beauty of Adonis, the rapidity of his flight, the yearning, yet hopelessness, of the enamoured gazer, while a shadowy ideal character is thrown over the whole!"[1] And again: "You feel (Shakespeare) to be a poet, inasmuch as for a time he has made you one—an active creative being." All that is relevant in the image and feelings such as occur when we behold a shooting star are emptied into our imagination of Adonis and of Venus, so that our awareness of them is greatly and significantly enlarged. A perception, at once more complex and more clear, is afforded us. And as Coleridge says, we ourselves are made into poets, for the various elements present in our perception—all that is introduced by the simile of the star— have to be freed into our awareness of Venus and Adonis. Shakespeare cannot actually do that for us, but he does all that is possible to ensure the union by our imagination of a number of elements in an enhanced perception of the departure of Adonis from Venus.

And here is Wordsworth's illustration—

> As a huge stone sometimes is seen to lie
> Couched on the bald top of an eminence,
> Wonder to all who do the same espy
> By what means it could thither come, and whence,
> So that it seems a thing endued with sense,

---

[1] *Lectures on Shakespeare,* Section I.

Like a sea-beast crawled forth, which on a shelf
Of rock or sand reposeth, there to sun himself.
Such seemed this Man; not all alive or dead,
Nor all asleep, in his extreme old age.

And he goes on to say: "In these images, the conferring, the abstracting and the modifying powers of the imagination immediately and mediately acting are all brought into conjunction. The stone is endowed with something of the power of life to approximate it to the sea-beast; and the sea-beast stripped of some of its vital qualities to assimilate it to the stone; which intermediate image is thus treated for the purpose of bringing the original image, that of the stone, to a nearer resemblance to the figure and condition of the aged man; who is divested of so much of the indications of life and motion as to bring him to the point where the two objects unite and coalesce in just comparison."[1] The point of these two illustrations is identical. To the powerful imagination of the poet the first situation is not just the desertion of a lover, and the second is not just an old and decrepit man. The poet is aware of more than this in each case; this 'something more' in the imaginative idea Shakespeare brings out by his simile of the star; Wordsworth by his similes of the stone and the sea-beast; and what is present in our imagination of these objects is united with the predominant perception, that of Adonis leaving Venus, and of the old man. Wordsworth's awareness of the old man was a very much more complex and sharp affair than which most people would have on seeing him. The 'same object' is 'given' in each case to the poet and the ordinary person alike; yet as it is prehended by the mind of each it becomes vastly different. In this case the poet, in beholding the old man beheld also a huge stone 'couched on the bald top of an eminence', and a sea-beast 'crawled forth to sun himself'; and the stone, the sea-beast and the old man are one. Such imagination is creative; for it works upon a very limited given, making out of it an object which, when under the compulsion of the poet we

[1] Preface to edition of 1815.

ourselves re-create it, we find amazing; or, had Wordsworth
been a painter we should have been amazed at the face of the
old man on his canvas. And, as Coleridge says, we know a
poet by the fact that he makes us one; we know the activity
of bringing together into a synthesis, and of making an object
which formerly did not exist, and which indeed has existence
only so long as we imagine it. And we know the conscious joy
of creation because what happens is not that the image of stone,
sea-beast, and man are put alongside each other in our minds,
but that our imagination is active in selecting various relevant
elements and fusing them into a unity. So that as Wordsworth
says, 'the conferring, abstracting and the modifying powers of
the imagination immediately and mediately acting are all
brought into conjunction', to produce a single object of contemplation. It is little wonder that there are times when Mr.
Richards rejects his associationism.

The business of poetry then is to make conveyance of
imaginative objects; or better, so to use language as to compel
re-creation by the reader of the objects which were formerly
present to the mind of the poet, objects which owed their
existence to his activity. It is the total object for which he
seeks to obtain our contemplation; and this is in contrast to
that use of language which can convey information of what is
an abstraction from that total object. We may therefore go on
to consider (a) the general character of the objects for which
the poet seeks to win our contemplation, and (b) the methods
whereby he secures this result.

4

It will be remembered that Coleridge, in speaking
of the imagination as 'essentially vital', contrasts it with objects
which 'as objects are essentially fixed and dead'. There is in
this statement an apparent contradiction. By 'essentially
vital' Coleridge appears to mean that power of the imagination
to 'inform and animate other existences' whether human or
not. Yet in the same breath he can say of objects that they can

F

be 'fixed and dead'. Now this is contradictory in so far as all objects are objects only for the imagination; or better, it is only through the imagination that we can be aware of objects at all. If so, and if the imagination is 'essentially vital', how can objects be fixed and dead? We must therefore interpret him as meaning that the 'vital' character of the imagination is only shown forth when the object which is imagined is present to the 'secondary' imagination, and is the conscious creation of the poet. When, as in everyday life, we view objects not primarily as objects of imagination but as useful; or as in science when the imagination is subordinate to an ulterior purpose; or as in the operation of fancy which is predominantly intellectual and not an active imaginative creation—in these cases he describes the objects as 'fixed and dead'. But when they arise from the imagination which is serious and subordinated by no ulterior purpose, they are 'vitalized'. Actually, this is not a wholly true description of the situation, as we saw in discussing the imagination in science; we cannot, however hard we try, devitalize the world as it is present to the imagination. Yet it is no doubt true that to the 'secondary' imagination objects take on an obvious vitality and animation which for the 'primary' imagination they have not, or have to a much lesser degree. There seems to be no doubt that this is so. As Bosanquet said, 'feeling gets into objects'—spring fields are joyous, the rose is proud, the lute is soft and complaining, and so forth. And it is particularly to be noted that this vitality is, so to speak, 'put' into objects by the imagination, and not as at first we might think by the fancy. Again and again Coleridge insists that this is so. Indeed it is the case that all objects, even of the 'primary' imagination, are vitalized; but we are hardly conscious that this is so—our concern is with something ulterior to the object. But by the secondary imagination the world is consistently represented as 'vital'.

There can be little doubt that in everyday life we present the world to ourselves as enjoying activity similar to our own. We may not, indeed we do not, recognize the extent to which this is so. "The tension", writes Professor G. F. Stout, in discussing what he calls the animism of common sense, the attribution of vitality to objects, "of the stretched bow is no more taken to be itself akin to will or striving than the felt tension of the archer's hand as he pulls the string. Both are apprehended as secondary tendencies. So far as active tendency is ascribed to matter, it is always in this way derivative. If we drop all reference to an initiative analogous, however vaguely, remotely and mysteriously, to our own, the word 'tendency' as standing for something actual and positive loses all meaning. There is nothing left but the bare relations of co-existence and sequence which alone are discoverable in the content of sense-experience."[1] And it is certain that when we are aware of a sequence of events, we are certainly aware of something more than the bare relations of co-existence and sequence. There can be no doubt that our representation of causal action is a representation of such an initiative in the object as Mr. Stout speaks of. Hence we can say that Coleridge in holding that any objects can be 'fixed and dead' (that is for the imagination) was mistaken. All objects have a vitality, even for the 'primary' imagination; and we cannot, it seems, help ourselves in thus representing the world. But it is perhaps necessary to emphasize the fact that to hold, as it seems we must do, that we vitalize the world in the act of apprehending it, is not to hold that the world is vital and that the world, as Schopenhauer held, is throughout will. All that we are concerned to point out is that we certainly appear to represent the world to ourselves as informed by will. There is in a later chapter (Chapter 4) in Professor Stout's book the following interesting passage: "Wordsworth in Book IV of *The Excursion* attempts to trace the belief in nature-gods and spirits to aesthetic motives.

> Sunbeams, upon distant hills
> Gliding apace, with shadows in their train,
> Might, with small help from fancy, be transformed
> Into fleet Oreads sporting visibly.

[1] *Mind and Matter*, p. 20.

Wordsworth was wrong. The primitive belief in spirits and gods somehow present and operative in sun, moon, and stars, in mountains, streams, and trees, had not, in the main, an aesthetic origin." Wordsworth was certainly wrong; and Wordsworth, of all people, should have known better. The primitive apprehension of the world was genuinely imaginative; and primitive men were not at play when thus they represented the world. And, in general, it is not that we deliberately and playfully 'put' vitality into objects, but that the imagination cannot, when representing objects to itself, do other than see objects as 'vital'. We have indeed gone far from primitive polytheism; but the 'essentially vital' activity of the imagination is still with us. No doubt a process of 'self-projection' is always involved in imaginative construction; but whatever the subjective processes involved may be, the important matter is that the objects of imagination have vital quality.

As we have said, we do not generally realize (apparently Coleridge himself did not) how 'vital' the imagination is, even in everyday life. Yet Coleridge, we suggested, had some ground for distinguishing between the 'essentially vital' quality of the secondary imagination and the 'fixed and dead' objects of the primary. 'Dead' the latter are not, but they are different from the objects of the secondary imagination in so far as the 'primary' does not dwell, as does the 'secondary', with enjoyment upon the 'vitality' of its objects, and is therefore greatly less aware of that 'vitality'. In the life of the 'secondary' imagination the 'vitality' which is in objects for the 'primary' imagination in a dim and unrecognized way springs into full and unashamed life. There is no need to give instances of this; indeed the two passages from Shakespeare and Wordsworth will serve; in Wordsworth's poem a stone, a sea-beast, and an old man become one.

It may in passing be of some value to notice Ruskin's famous comments on what he called the pathetic fallacy. This fallacy, he held, occurs in the 'false appearances of things to us, when we are under the influence of emotion or contemplative fancy; false appearances which are entirely unconnected with any

real power or character in the object and only imputed to it
by us'.[1] He gives many examples—here are two:

> The spendthrift crocus, bursting through the mould,
> Naked and shivering, with his cup of gold.

and

> They rowed her in across the rolling foam—
> The cruel, crawling foam.

and Ruskin goes on to say: "If we look well into the matter,
we shall find the greatest poets do not often admit this kind of
falseness—that it is only the second order of poets who much
delight in it." Well, if we 'look well' into the matter, we shall
find that Shakespeare indulged the 'pathetic fallacy' not a
few but innumerable times. What are we to say of daffodils
'taking' the wind, of 'envious slivers', of 'marigolds that go
to bed with the sun and with him rise weeping', and a thousand
other instances that could be found in Shakespeare? And if
the greatest poets indulge the pathetic fallacy, so too does the
ordinary person, who talks of water leaping, of the sea dashing
itself against the rocks, and so forth. Neither the poet nor the
most prosaic person in the world can apparently help himself.
Ruskin goes on to tell us that writing of this kind may be beautiful, but is nevertheless untrue; the crocus does not 'burst'
through the mould, the foam is not cruel, marigolds do not
weep, water does not leap, etc; all this he holds is a false
representation. The 'simple' 'plain' natures of things are
distorted apparently for the sake of pretty writing. Nor is
this view of Ruskin's one which fails to make its appearance
today. Speaking of Sappho's lines

> οἶον τὸ γλυκύμαλον ἐρεύθεται ἄκρῳ ἐπ' ὕσδῳ,
> ἄκρον ἐπ' ἀκροτάτῳ· λελάθοντο δὲ μαλοδρόπηες,
> οὐ μὰν ἐκλελάθοντ', ἀλλ' οὐκ ἐδύναντ' ἐπίκεσθαι.[2]

---

[1] *Modern Painters*, Vol. 3, Pt. 4.
[2]
> Like the pippin blushing high
> On the tree-top beneath the sky,
> Where the pickers forgot it—nay,
> Could not reach it so far away.—(Loeb Trans.).

Mr. M. R. Ridley says:[1] "That is all perfectly clear and perfectly straightforward; the apple is an apple." And he goes on to contrast with Sappho's lines the lines of Coleridge—

> The one red leaf, the last of its clan,
> That dances as often as dance it can.

So that apparently Ruskin and Mr. Ridley can tell us just what a plain crocus and a plain apple is; and having told us, be able to show that the poets are writing what is untrue. We are not for a moment concerned to say that crocuses do 'burst through the mould', or leaves 'dance'; but it is curious to find Ruskin and Mr. Ridley assuming that we can, if we wish, stop this anthropomorphic foolishness and represent to ourselves 'just an apple' or 'just a crocus'. The truth is that we cannot help it. Such is the imagination, and in that way do we represent things to ourselves. This representation of things as having, as Mr. Stout says, an existence analogous, however obscure, to our own, may or may not be nonsense; that is not here the point. Schopenhauer, indeed, who was no fool, roundly asserted that will is the essence of what we call inanimate nature;[2] Bacon seems to have said much the same thing, and we find Whitehead today approving of Bacon. But our present concern is not to say that these writers are right, but to express surprise that there are some writers who apparently know that they are wrong, and also think that the imagination can avoid this 'pathetic fallacy' and thus 'truly' represent things to itself. There is no avoiding recognition that the imagination is 'essentially vital' even when, as Ruskin and Mr. Ridley would apparently have us do, we try to represent nature as a mechanism; that effort as we have seen is a failure. This is not to say that a poet must necessarily seek in his writing to repre-

---

[1] *Essays and Studies, English Association*, 1933, p. 115.

[2] "Spinoza says that if a stone which has been projected through the air had consciousness, it would believe that it was moving of its own will. I add to this only that the stone would be right."— Schopenhauer, *The World as Will*, Vol. 1, p. 164 (tr. Haldane and Kemp).

sent all things as, in this way, vital; effects of great beauty can be obtained without his doing so. But it does mean that it is mistaken to condemn such representation as misplaced.[1]

5

So much then for the 'essentially vital' character of the imagination. The 'secondary' imagination, we said, following Coleridge, recreates objects at a level of greater complexity and significance than belongs to the 'primary' imagination of objects; and in poetry there is placed upon us all the compulsion the poet can use to re-create that object for ourselves. Such re-creation of the total object also transforms and changes the sensory elements; such elements are not left untouched, but are taken up and changed by the new object so that we 'see' the object in a new and different way. What then are the essential factors involved in the imaginative use of language, language, that is to say, likely to result in such creation of the object for ourselves? To deal fully with this subject is far beyond the scope of this chapter. We can only indicate the most important elements which are involved. We may deal first with descriptive poetry, poetry, that is to say, which is not primarily marked by the use of metaphor; then we may proceed to consider the various forms of metaphor, employed for various uses, which occur in poetry. Here are the first four stanzas of Bridge's poem *Winter Nightfall*—

> The day begins to droop,—
> Its course is done:
> But nothing tells the place
> Of the setting sun.
>
> The hazy darkness deepens,
> And up the lane
> You may hear, but cannot see,
> The homing wain.

[1] On this subject, see Coleridge *Biographia Literaria*, Chapter xv.

> An engine pants and hums
>   In the farm hard by:
> Its lowering smoke is lost
>   In the lowering sky.
>
> The soaking branches drip,
>   And all night through
> The dropping will not cease
>   In the avenue.[1]

Here is an attempt, and I should say a successful one, to make us aware of the quality of a November nightfall. Bridges attempts to do so by a method of the simplest description. The lines are not indeed free of metaphor; but then there is very little writing, however prosaic even in intention, which is wholly free of metaphor. But it is clear that Bridges in this poem is not relying here on metaphor—everything, as Mr. Ridley would say, is, if not 'perfectly clear and straightforward', at least nearly so. Now it is noticeable in the first place that there is in the lines very little indeed of 'poetic diction'; there is indeed the 'drooping' of the day, which is a metaphor, and therefore smacks of 'poetry' and there is the 'homing wain'. But otherwise there is nothing but the utmost simplicity of statement. Almost every word is directly informative, as much so as in the barest piece of prose. In Shakespeare's lines the simile of the star is not, directly at least, informative; that is not the case in any of Bridges' lines, and 'poetic' words such as 'chorasmian' in 'a wild chorasmian waste', are conspicuously absent. A prosaic person, asked to describe the scene, might conceivably come quite near to using the same words. He might say: the day has come to its end and there is nothing to tell where the sun set. The haze and the darkness are deepening; and in the lane you can hear the wain coming home, but you cannot see it. There is an engine humming near by, and the smoke from it does not rise but sinks. The sky is on top of us. The branches of the trees are dripping, and they will be dripping

---

[1] *Shorter Poems of Robert Bridges*, Clarendon Press, Oxford, 1931.

all night in the avenue. That would be a fairly straightforward description. Of course a prosaic person might not perhaps pick out the same elements, and he might add a lot more. It differs of course, in some of its words, from the poem; but in its bareness of statement it is not beyond the possibility of being written by anyone who had never thought of poetry. The difference of course between the two passages is in respect of their rhythm. Bridges in the poem has used a slow rhythm used in very short lines, which compels a difficult and laboured breathing. We cannot read the lines quickly. The prose version can easily be read in a quick, efficient way; but if we treat the poem in that way, we do so in deliberate rebellion against poetic control. Now in content the poem is identical enough with the prose statement, and in its choice of words it is quite near to it. The difference therefore is to be found in (1) slowness of rhythm and therefore of utterance, (2) control of the pitch of the voice, (3) what we may call 'heaviness', (4) the rhyme, (5) difficult breathing. The first and the second factors are inevitable in the reading; we cannot read it quickly, and our voice is kept low. By that means the poet captures all the suggestiveness of the human voice for his purpose, and thereby adds to his description the emotional suggestiveness which occurs when a voice speaks slowly and in a low tone. Hence a great deal which he cannot say in his poem is conveyed by the reading, the nature of which he carefully determines. He meets his bareness of speech with the rich suggestiveness issuing from the voice. The third factor is not merely as we might think slowness of rhythm. It is possible to have a slow rhythm which is not heavy, as it is possible to have a fast rhythm which is not light.. For example, here are lines which are slow but not heavy:

> Daffodils,
> That come before the swallow dares, and take
> The winds of March with beauty,

and here are lines which are quick but not light:

> I have heard
> That guilty creatures sitting at a play
> Have by the very cunning of the scene
> Been struck so to the soul . . .

But in Bridges' poem we have an impression of weight in addition to slowness, which greatly adds to the effect. The shortness of the lines compels a frequent intake of breath, an effect which really creates for us, in the reading, the experience of almost stifled breathing which we experience on a dank November evening. This latter is a device which resembles onomatopoeia—the creation for our reading experience of a part of the experience described. Finally, there is the use of a sustained rhythm and of rhyme. The importance and effects of rhythm and rhyme have been described by Coleridge, and need not be repeated here at any length. Briefly, it is that rhythm and rhyme together create a pattern into which our mental activities fall; there is thus created a cycle of expectancy which naturally creates opportunity for surprise. The effect of such expectancy occurring with a repeated rhythmic cycle, is to capture interest and attention to such a degree that Coleridge called it a kind of hypnosis. Rhyme should thus be regarded as integral to the rhythm; it takes its place as part of a pattern and contributes therefore to the general effect of the rhythm. Together they make of the words used a unity by, so to speak, arresting the mere onward flow of the words, capturing movement within an embracing pattern.

Taken together these factors make of the language used what we may call imaginative. Of these, it is the power of rhythm, and the control of the pace and pitch of the voice in reading, which are the most powerful. In Bridges' poem the imaginative effect which is obtained by the pace and pitch of the voice is very great, and invests the scene so barely described with a vivid imaginative quality; so much so that when we pass on to the remaining stanzas of the poem we do so only with a surprise which occurs within an established frame of mind; though a surprise it is yet of a piece with what has gone before. The slow extinction of life in the old man is one with the winter scene.[1]

I have taken Bridges' poem for our example because the bareness of its statement called for an unusual and strong technique in the imaginative command of language. Relying on neither metaphor nor on the associative power of words, all the poet's skill and subtle technique was required. It is true of course that, using the effects of the voice, he makes of the scene a sad and melancholy one; and in doing so he uses association— the associations which gather round the various exercises of human speech. On the other hand, a good deal of poetry can be found which, using plain, straightforward statement, has not so great an imaginative effect. For example, Arnold's

> And as afield the reapers cut a swath
> Down through the middle of a rich man's corn,
> And on each side are squares of standing corn,
> And in the midst a stubble, short and bare.

Or, for narrative verse, Wordsworth's

> The cottage door was speedily unbarred,
> And now the soldier touched his hat once more
> With his lean hand, and in a faltering voice
> He thanked me—

consist of plain statements but are little more than prose— the words do little more than indicate the various objects as does the everyday use of language, and come very near to prose. Bridges' poem illustrates therefore to an unusual degree what additions technique can make to what otherwise would come very near to being a prose statement. Bridges' words over and above their 'reference' are so used as to do a great deal more than merely indicate the objects or give us information about them. It is not what he says only, but equally important how he says it which counts, and upon which the creation of a vivid imaginative object depends.

[1] He thinks of his morn of life,
His hale, strong years;
And braves as he may the night
Of darkness and tears.

6

We need not delay long in noticing the operation of the other factors mentioned—they have been greatly studied. All the great poets are masters of the pace of verse and can vary it to suit their purposes with surprising effects. There is an instance of it in Wordsworth's *Ode on the Intimations of Immortality*, where towards the end, after the quick sweep of—

> truths that wake,
> To perish never:
> Which neither listlessness, nor mad endeavour,
> Nor Man, nor Boy,
> Nor all that is at enmity with joy,
> Can utterly abolish or destroy!—

there at once comes the slowing up of

> —Hence in a season of calm weather
> Though inland far we be . . .

This use of pace is an incomparably more important matter than onomatopoeia. In Bridges' poem we noticed an effect comparable to onomatopoeia. In onomatopoeia proper, it is not of course organic effects and sensations which are created, but sensations of a non-organic kind—'the long wash of Australasian shores.' But more frequently poets use not a strict onomatopoeia, but words which by association suggest strongly an element in what is described. For example

> And a bird flew up out of the turret,

is not strictly onomatopoeic, but is nevertheless by its consonants suggestive of the sudden, surprising movement of a frightened bird; or again 'the plunging hoofs were gone' is not strictly onomatopoeic, but is again suggestive of the thump of hoofs against soft turf.

Again, it is often said that one of the primary instruments of the poet is the association which words have—other than those suggestive of sensuous qualities. There is of course no doubt that poets do use this power which words in this sense acquire. Mr. Santayana stresses this factor in his book *The Sense of Beauty* (p. 211)—he writes of "moonlight and castle-moats, minarets and cypresses, camels filing through the desert—such images get their character from the strong but misty atmosphere of sentiment and adventure that clings to them. Such images are concrete symbols of much latent experience, and the deep roots of association give them the same hold upon our attention which might be secured by a fortunate form or splendid material." There is no doubt that this is so, though we should beware of viewing it as indispensable to great verse. There is great poetry in which this associative value of words is deliberately used by the poet; most often when what is set out is of a vague character. Milton, moving in the vastness of Heaven and Hell, was a master of it. Or here are two stanzas by Vaughan which perfectly exemplify its use—

> O tell me whence that joy doth spring
> Whose diet is divine and fair,
> Which wears heaven, like a bridal ring,
> And tramples on doubts and despair?
>
> Whose Eastern traffique deals in bright
> And boundless Empyrean themes,
> Mountains of spice, Day-stars and light,
> Green trees of life, and living streams?

where 'eastern traffique', 'empyrean themes', 'mountains of spice', 'day-star', 'light', 'trees of life', 'living streams' have all an enormous wealth of association. These words thus used are not informative, in contrast to the words in Bridges' poem, but all exemplify what Santayana is saying. But it should be noticed that Vaughan is trying to convey something by its nature vague and unexperienced, and is driven therefore to words of vague significance but wealthy associated experience. Or again Mr. de la Mare, akin indeed to Vaughan, is a master of this use of uncontrolled association, as we may call it—

> They slide their eyes, and nodding, say,
> 'Queen Djenira walks to-day
> The courts of the lord Pthamasar
> Where the sweet birds of Psuthys are.'

On the other hand we should greatly beware of thinking that the poet, except in regard to such vague objects, relies on the associative power of words. On the contrary, the great poet frequently uses the most prosaic words for the most powerful poetic effects. The great poet is never, I think, controlled by words to such an extent as to find any words incapable of becoming vehicles for his imaginative communications. It is rather the case that either, as in the verses from Vaughan and de la Mare, he deliberately uses the vague association of words for his purposes, or if his purposes are not of that kind, he can master the associations which a word may have to the extent of dispelling them, if it should so suit his purpose, from our minds. Consider, for example, two such words as 'catalogue' and 'superfluous'. No two words could be more prosaic in their associations. Yet when we hear

> Ay, in the catalogue ye go for men;

and

> O, reason not the need: our basest beggars
> Are in the poorest thing superfluous:—

these prosaic associations are controlled and expelled, and each becomes charged with the most powerful emotion, the one with contempt, the other with pity. It is not the case therefore that the poet is limited by previous associations; rather he is able to destroy those associations from our minds, and in the act of stripping the words of all but their bare meaning, enriches them with a new context of association.

7

It is easy therefore to exaggerate the place of association in poetry. It is also easy to exaggerate the importance of onomatopoeic device. The associative power of words is something which poets are sometimes compelled to use for their purpose; but it is an error to hold that poets are uniformly dependent on it. And onomatopoeic device is, when all is said, very limited in its scope. The compulsion on the reader to create is brought about far more, as we have said, by the control of the movement and tone of the voice, and all the suggestiveness which attaches to it. But in general, simile and metaphor are the most powerful means of imaginative conveyance; and we may now briefly consider how these forms of speech, as they are sometimes called, exercise such strong effects. The main difference between merely descriptive poetry (such as *Winter Nightfall*) and poetry which relies to any considerable degree upon simile and metaphor, is this. In descriptive poetry the poet speaks of the various objects contemplated, and gives information about them in a way which, up to a point, is that of the outside observer who is recording certain observable elements. In Bridges' poem, for example, we noticed that the poet uses all his words in an informative way, as a prosaic person asked to describe the scene would do; and, for the rest, has to rely upon the suggestiveness of the voice as in our reading of the poem the poet succeeds in controlling it. When, on the other hand, the poet uses metaphor, he abandons the merely informative method; yet, at the same time, he suggests the inner quality of the objects more directly than by reliance on voice. For example, we observe in Bridges' poem a metaphor which a prosaic observer of the scene would not, in all likelihood, use—'The day begins to droop', which we may contrast with 'The soaking branches drip'. The latter line is an entirely straightforward statement; it does not avoid imaginative use of language in the sense in which all our statements, as we have said, are imaginative; but it is the kind of statement which a person would use if he were making a report which was going to be verified in every detail. But in such a report he certainly would not say 'The day begins to droop'. For the word 'droop' derives its significance only from our making of the day a living thing, which, like a flower, or a human being, can 'droop' from weakness; it arises only by a frank attribution of vitality to the 'day'. At the primary level we cannot help ourselves vitalizing things; but our minds, concerned with matters of practical importance, are hardly aware that we do so. If, for example, the observer writing up a report for verification, took the trouble to ask himself how exactly he represented the branches of trees to himself he would see that he represented them as things having a life, however vaguely analogous to his own. But when the poet says 'the day droops' he is frankly enjoying this 'vital' representation of objects. Yet in so doing he would not be using language informatively. 'The soaking branches drip' is a sentence which gives information in a concise way—it conveys observation of a strict kind. You can observe the water falling. But you cannot observe the day drooping, for drooping is an experience of inner weakness which we may have from time to time, but which we cannot, in all seriousness, say we know the 'day' to have. The two statements are different. And although we took *Winter Nightfall* as an example of 'informative' verse, actually the metaphor with which the poem opens, the drooping of day, is the key to the whole poem. The day droops and so does the old man—an inner feebleness has seized them both and is carrying them to their end. Now by the use of the metaphor, of a word which is not straightforwardly descriptive, as when he says 'the day begins to droop', he is able to suggest the inner quality of the scene before him. In a sense of course he may thereby be said to be giving information; but it is information, in so far as it is information at all, about the way in which the poet is imagining the scene, and it is not information of the kind which is conveyed when he says that the trees drip. You may, of course, say that it is sheer nonsense to say that a 'day' can droop. But the fact remains that thus the poet represented to himself the scene; and we may believe that in writing the poem Bridges was not trying to amuse himself, or being fanciful. It is clear, therefore, that by the use of the word 'droop' he conveys what was, for his imagination, the inner quality of the scene more effectively than by long description; and in his poem the 'informative' description which he gives is really additional to an initial and fundamental metaphor. By saying that metaphor suggests quality more directly than description, we mean that in description he has to rely, for imaginative conveyance, upon the effects of his rhythm and pace controlling the voice; but his metaphor is not dependent upon such purely sensuous factors and their suggestiveness.

It would, however, be a mistake to imagine that all metaphor and simile is of this type, a type which is effective through the 'essentially vital' quality of the imagination, and which illumines prehension of natural objects through the representation of them as enjoying a life analogous to our own. We have mentioned it at the outset as the most striking kind of metaphor perhaps, and we shall return to it again. But we may first take notice of many similes which are descriptive of certain sensuous aspects of the object or objects presented. Here are two well-known passages which exemplify this type of simile. Writing of Satan's shield, Milton says

> The broad circumference
> Hung on his shoulders like the moon;

and Browning writes

> These early November hours
> That crimson the creeper's leaf across
> Like a splash of blood, intense, abrupt,
> O'er a shield else gold from rim to boss.

In these two passages the similes are directly informative, the one as to size, the other as to colour. They both involve a distinct 'equivalence' between two images between which comparison is made. In each case the information could have been given by description, description that would be laborious and unwelcome, yet correct and adequate. Instead, it is given by the creation by the mind of a distinct image of the secondary object (the moon, the shield); and without fairly distinct visual imagery of these secondary objects the point of the similes would necessarily be lost. To obtain the information which the poet wishes to convey, we must clearly visualize the moon and the shield, and then proceed to the endowment of the primary objects (the shield, the leaves) with the appropriate qualities. This explicitness and equivalence of two distinct images is the mark of the descriptive figure of speech.

It seems impossible to arrive at a general rule on which a hard distinction of the uses of simile and metaphor respectively can be effected. It is probable that when the figure of speech is descriptive of certain sensuous aspects of the object simile will be used, and not metaphor. Milton could have said 'the broad circumference hung, a moon, upon his shoulders'; or Browning might have called the crimson on the leaves just 'splashes of blood, intense, abrupt'. But in each case there would have been a serious weakening of effect. By the use of the simile in each case the force of 'moon' and 'blood' is increased by the development of the secondary image, a process which simile admits to a much greater degree than does metaphor. And in general such development of the secondary object is desirable when fairly precise conveyance of sensuous aspects of the primary object is sought. On the other hand, elaborate development of the secondary image can easily occur to the detriment of the effect, and to a degree which threatens excessively to transfer attention away from the primary object. But in general, where development is desirable, simile is unavoidable; but in the use of metaphor, the second image is only suggested, and concentration on it in any explicit way is undesirable. Metaphor, as we shall see, seeks what may be called identification rather than equivalence. In metaphor the secondary imagery is caught up and dissolved into the primary, and any explicit equivalence tends to be lost. This occurs (though it must be repeated that emphatic generalization is not possible) when what the poet endeavours directly to convey is the unity of the object as transcending, while yet embracing, the sensuous. For this purpose the metaphor has enormous advantages over the formal and developed simile, for it leaves the mind undivided for concentration upon one primary object.

8

Mr. Herbert Read in his *English Prose Style* writes (p. 25): "The nature and importance of metaphors was clearly stated by Aristotle, in the *Poetics* (xxii, 16, 17):

. . . Much the most important point is to be able to use metaphors, for this is the one thing that cannot be learned from others; and it is also a mark of genius, since a good metaphor implies an intuitive perception of the similarity in dissimilars.

But in this passage Aristotle is writing of poetry. The ability to invent new metaphors is a sign of a poetic mind; and the main use of metaphors is always poetical. To say that a metaphor 'is the result of the search for a precise epithet' is misleading. The precision sought for is one of equivalence, not of analytical description." Mr. Read, it will be noticed, insists, as against Mr. Murry, on the necessity of equivalence, and quotes Aristotle for an authority. Actually, the quotation from Aristotle is not a fortunate one, since there is nothing peculiarly poetical in the activity which Aristotle is describing. The 'perception of the similarity in dissimilars' is as much a mark of the scientist, for example, as of anyone else; and the poet is certainly not concerned merely to observe similarities between dissimilar objects. That is to say, it is not his concern to make such observations of relations, but to convey vivid apprehension of one object, and the awareness of any relationship between two objects must finally be lost in what Mr. Read himself calls, in the previous paragraph, 'one commanding image'. And the test of a good metaphor is the degree to which the poet can at once suggest and destroy an 'equivalence', so that, as Wordsworth says, the 'two objects unite and coalesce' and, as Mr.

Murry says in his admirable discussion of metaphor,[1] metaphor becomes 'a mode of apprehension'. But how is this possible? Mr. Read is doubtless right in saying that equivalence is in some way present; yet the most effective result is reached when the sense of equivalence and comparison is lost, and a single object is grasped in its unity. The danger of developed simile, as has always been recognized, is that this singleness of effect tends to disappear. The art of metaphor is that of reducing the element of equivalence to the minimum, while yet greatly enriching our apprehension of the primary object.

These forms of speech, as conveying something more than information as to sensuous detail, may be viewed as the conveyance of imaginative presentation of objects by means of comparison with other objects drawn from different levels of existence; or, if not from a different level of existence, the objects introduced are drawn from the same level, but are yet markedly different from the object which it is the primary business of the passage to convey. We may distinguish between the natural, the animal, and the human worlds, taking the natural to include both the inanimate and plant life. Now in respect to human life, we must distinguish between its mental and its bodily aspects; and our experience of ourselves as both mental and physical gives rise to a crucial and extensive class of metaphor in which mental activities are expressed in terms of perceptual and motor experience. An obvious example is

> Vaulting ambition, which o'erleaps itself,
> And falls on th' other.

No doubt we may say that here is a comparison between ambition and the act of vaulting. But what happens is that the suggestion of strenuous effort, mental and physical, with its accompanying knowledge of a possible fall which the mention of 'vaulting' gives is caught up into our apprehension of ambitiousness, vivifying and enriching it. Detailed repre-

---

[1] In *The Problem of Style.*

sentation of the act of jumping an obstacle would damage
the desired effect; all that is required is a suggestion, and no
more, of great effort and risk. In

> When to the sessions of sweet silent thought
> I summon up remembrance of things past,—

the process of recollection, is one which involves at most a
very slight degree of accompanying motor action, and is as
merely mental an activity as possible; the poet seeks to give
it body by associating with it the action of calling up an inferior
or a prisoner, an activity more directly associated with definite
bodily action than that of memory. To give metaphorical
expression to an act of memory is by the nature of the case
strikingly difficult; and Shakespeare's metaphor, to be effective,
had necessarily to do no more than suggest in the vaguest
manner an equivalence which, were it emphasized, would
destroy the desired impression of the unique act of recollection.
Shakespeare could not, for his purposes, go outside human
experience; and too boldly to equate the public, authoritative
atmosphere of a court with the private intimacy of recollection
would have been disastrous. The effect of the metaphor
depends on the very slightness of the suggestion of summoning
a prisoner. As the lines stand, they succeed in giving body,
so to speak, to so spiritual an act, but vivid imagery of a court
of sessions would be fatal to the effect. Hence though we must
admit the presence of an implied equivalence, in fact the
secondary imagery is fused into unity with the primary, and
all sense of comparison is lost. In both these metaphors
the poet makes his conveyance of two mental states by the
suggestion of appropriate perceptual and motor experience.
The imagery of leaping and of a court fall away, leaving a
suggestion of physical and mental activity, which is easily
carried over into our apprehension of a total subjective state,
mental and bodily.

9

The most comprehensive class of metaphors is that in which the human is expressed in terms of the natural, and the natural in terms of the human, a type of metaphor in which 'equivalence' is present to a still slighter degree. We may take the following as typical—

> For his bounty,
> There was no winter in 't; an autumn 'twas
> That grew the more by reaping . . .

> As cedars beaten with autumnal storms,
> So great men flourish . . .[1]

> Give me a spirit that on this life's rough sea
> Loves t'have his sails fill'd with a lusty wind,
> Even till his sailyards tremble, his masts crack,
> And his rapt ship run on her side so low,
> That she drinks water, and her keel ploughs air.

On the other hand,

> Leaning on the bosom of the urgent west . . .

> Crossing the stripling Thames at Bablockhithe . . .

> Small is the fane through which the sea-wind sings . . .

> Make their wine peep through their scars . . .

All these metaphors will, I think, bear out Mr. Murry's contention that metaphor may be regarded as the result of a search for a precise epithet rather than as a precise equivalence. Taking the second group first, in 'leaning on the bosom of the urgent west' it is not the case that we enjoy two images from which we extract a similarity or a number of similarities. It is the ship which is leaning; we are aware of the ship as enjoying motor activity and will—the metaphor is, so to speak, the way

[1] It will be observed that this is not a metaphor; but the difference between metaphor and simile is not so great as to make its removal necessary.

in which the poet is aware of the object. Similarly in 'the stripling Thames' we have no visual imagery of a lanky youth; the river is imagined as a young and living thing; and it is the wind which sings and the blood that peeps. The metaphor here, instead of implying a comparison, is the form which the imagining of the object takes, an apprehension however obscure of the natural world as enjoying a life similar to our own.

In the first group, the element of comparison is stronger; yet again these metaphors depend for their power upon the fact that to the secondary imagination the natural and the human are not merely different levels of existence, but are one in their enjoyment of vitality.[1] The 'spirit' becomes a ship; and becomes so in the poet's imagination because the ship is not 'just a ship'. A great man is seen as a cedar because to the poet a cedar is not 'just a cedar'. If this were not so, the metaphors would be impossible; for their justification is that they suggest the extremity of struggle and effort, and unless the ship and the tree 'enjoyed' such extremity of struggle and effort they could not occur in the poet's lines. We may consider what Ruskin says of the simile in Dante, in which lost souls are compared to leaves—"When Dante describes the spirits falling from the bank of Acheron 'as dead leaves flutter from a bough' he gives the most perfect image possible of their utter lightness, feebleness, passiveness, and scattering agony of despair, without, however, for an instant losing his own clear perception that *these* are souls and *those* are leaves." And yet how could this effect be obtained unless fluttering leaves were for us the extreme of helpless, passive things? It

[1] "The metaphors which pass either from nature to man, or from man to nature, are without point and relevance if nature is regarded as mere matter, or man as mere mind. The use of such words as 'spirit' and 'anima' has been rashly taken as evidence that primitive man took a purely materialistic view of that which feels, thinks, and wills. But so to argue is to forget that air and breath are not, for the primitive mind, what they are for the abstract science of the modern chemist."—Professor G. F. Stout, in *Mind and Matter*, pp. 56–7.

is precisely because they are imagined as helpless and passive that they serve the poet's purpose. If they were 'merely leaves' they could serve no purpose in the poet's lines. Antony is bountiful—to the degree that autumn is bountiful; the great man struggles—as in a supreme degree a cedar struggles—against opposition. And the ground of comparison is the vitality in which, to the poetic imagination, all things have their being. By mention of a cedar beaten by strong wind we derive an impression of superlative and unyielding effort; and this impression we carry over into the imaginative idea we form of the great man. We do not, in the enjoyment of the poetic perception, balance one set of imagery over against another; the mention of the tree suggests an extreme degree of strenuousness and self-maintenance, which is carried over and blended into our idea of human greatness. Fundamentally, this great class of metaphors is of the same type as that in which Shakespeare speaks of 'vaulting ambition'; and as the movement of the body in vaulting is not merely a physical affair but is in association with a state of mind, so the secondary objects in metaphors in which the poet endeavours to convey the human in terms of the natural are never grasped as merely physical. The natural is represented as possessed of will and motor experience; in—

> daffodils,
> That come before the swallow dares, and take
> The winds of March with beauty,

the 'taking of the wind with beauty' is the apprehension of the flower as adapting itself to the force of a wind after the fashion of our own experience under such circumstances; in 'the swallow dares' the appeal is primarily to mental experience, to the experience of will.

The type of metaphor in which the natural, the animal, and the human are expressed in terms of each other is no doubt the most frequent. But we observe, in passing, that although it is the case that perhaps the greater number of metaphors are of this type, it is noticeable how easily such metaphors, if carried beyond a certain point, fail in effectiveness. Metaphors of this kind depend on their vague suggestiveness. In the following passage from Southwell it will be seen how the detailed development of the metaphor makes of the lines a passage in fanciful writing, however fine—

> Launch forth, my soul, into a main of tears,
> Full-fraught with grief, the traffic of the mind;
> Torn sails will serve, thoughts rent with guilty fears;
> Give care the stern, use sighs in lieu of wind:
> Remorse thy pilot; thy misdeeds thy card;
> Torment thy haven, shipwreck thy best reward.

We may contrast this with Chapman's 'Give me a spirit——', where there is no such attempt to create equivalences within the metaphor. Or again, where Milton's

> The Windes with wonder whist,
> Smoothly the waters kist,
> Whispering new joyes to the milde Ocean,

is of the finest imaginative writing, he becomes absurd with his

> So when the Sun in bed,
> Curtain'd with cloudy red,
> Pillows his chin upon an Orient wave. . . .

There is another kind of metaphor of which we can perhaps say that it is more an epithet than an equivalence—what may be called the 'associative' type of metaphor in which what we may call 'uncontrolled association' is the major factor. A good example is when Cleopatra exclaims of Antony

> The crown of the earth doth melt.

Here it is obvious that vivid imagery would be extremely harmful of the desired effect and equivalence therefore undesirable. What happens in this case is that there is cast around Antony the vague but rich suggestiveness which hangs about the word 'crown'—associations of wealth, dignity, power, splendour, supremacy, which amplify and vivify our perception of Antony. Two sets of imagery would be fatal in this case, which illustrates how, although we may assert that there is here a formal equivalence, there is in the enjoyment of the lines but one controlling idea.

On the other hand it would be erroneous to deny the importance of 'equivalence' in many cases. Mr. Read, in asserting that there must always be precision of equivalence, may be mistaken; but it is undeniable that in many similes and metaphors equivalence is not merely present but is of the greatest importance for the final effect. There are two examples of this, one a simile, the other a metaphor, in *Antony and Cleopatra*. They are the famous

> The stroke of death is as a lover's pinch
> Which hurts, and is desired—

and

> Dost thou not see my baby at my breast,
> That sucks the nurse asleep?

In these cases the sense of similarity in the midst of dissimilarity is essential for the full ironical effect; equivalence is here necessary, and it is equivalence which hangs upon violent contrast. The effect depends in each case upon this two-fold situation, the torture of the mind by identity and contrast in one.

10

When we come finally to the figurative expression of abstract ideas, we find that again there are two main kinds, the one illustrative and relying on equivalence, the other avoiding it. Chapman provides good illustrations of both—

> there is no truth of any good
> To be discern'd on earth; and, by conversion,
> Naught therefore simply bad: but as the stuff

Prepared for arras pictures, is no picture
Till it be form'd, and man hath cast the beams
Of his imaginous fancy thorough it,
In forming ancient kings and conquerors
As he conceives they look'd and were attired,
Though they were nothing so: so all things here
Have all their price set down from men's conceits,
Which make all terms and actions good or bad,
And are but pliant and well-colour'd threads,
Put into feigned images of truth.

and

—in this one thing, all the discipline
Of manners and of manhood is contain'd;
A man to join himself with th' universe
In his main sway, and make (in all things fit)
One with that all, and go on, round as it;
Not plucking from the whole his wretched part,
And into straights, or into naught revert,
Wishing the complete universe might be
Subject to such a rag of it as he.

In the first passage we have a general statement enunciated in
the first three lines which is continued in the tenth, eleventh,
and twelfth. The rest of the passage is taken up by a simile
by which the imputation of goodness and badness to situations
is likened to the weaving of pictures on tapestry which is in
itself without design. But in the latter no general or abstract
idea is propounded; it is present throughout the passage, and
is conveyed in every aspect through metaphor. In the former
passage the idea is paralleled by the illustration; in the latter
the two are fused and indistinguishable—the general idea is
kept alive by the metaphors of joining, going, plucking;
identifying an attitude to life with the adjustment of our
bodies to a swiftly moving object. There can be no doubt that
the second is a finer passage than the first. In the first passage,
the idea as set out is complete and intelligible; the simile
plays the part which any good illustration might do in a piece
of prose. In the second, the idea cannot be separated out
without a grave loss of expressiveness; the idea is intrinsically

metaphorical and was not previously grasped abstractly by the poet. In it human life in its relation to the universe is apprehended in a wholly concrete way. So much so that it is misleading to describe the passage as an expression of an abstract idea.

CHAPTER IV

IMAGINATION, LYRIC, AND MORALITY

To be Good only, is to be
A God or else a Pharisee.

BLAKE—*The Everlasting Gospel*

I

In the perception of external objects, objects are
in strictness present only to the imagination; for what is given is
merely sensory, whereas what is prehended is a unity which
is more than sensuous. It is equally the case that the self in
self-consciousness is not a given datum, but is constructed
from a mass of given data which are wrought into imaginative
unity in varying degrees in different persons. It is generally
agreed by philosophers and psychologists that our awareness
of ourselves grows along with our awareness of the external
world of objects, and depends on that awareness of an external
world. We are not first of all aware of ourselves and of our
mental states, and then, at a later stage, aware of the outside
world; but become increasingly aware of ourselves as we become
increasingly aware of a system of objects represented as
independent of ourselves. That is to say, we become aware
of ourselves as one object among others, and are only aware
of ourselves in that way. We could never represent ourselves
to ourselves had not our imagination operated to evoke this
representation both of ourselves and of external objects. It
is true that the imagination of the child in prehending external
objects and people is aided at every step by his own inner
experience; it is equally true that his increasing awareness
of himself is dependent on his awareness of things and people,
and that, chiefly through imitation of his elders, he more and
more amplifies and clarifies his perception of himself. If it
is true that without what the psychologists call self-projection
he could never arrive at the prehension of objects, it is equally

true, paradoxical as it may appear, that without prehension of objects he could not arrive at self-prehension.

Hence the self in self-consciousness is no more 'given' than are external objects. It is of course the case that, as a basis or starting-point for self-consciousness, there is a great mass of sensation present to the mind as in the case of external objects; there is the mass of organic sensation and the sensational core of the self or coenaesthesia. Yet this mass of organic sensation *is* not the self which we know any more than the patches of colour present to our minds are the physical object. For the self in self-consciousness transcends the given body of sensation in a hundred and one ways; as we have said, it involves awareness of other things and people; in our idea of ourselves our relationship with things, people, their reaction to us, our social status, form indispensable elements. The unity of the self as we prehend it is woven from a very great number of elements, sensory and imaginative. For what is given to us in mere sensation is but a fragment of ourselves as we are aware of ourselves, in a way parallel to that in which sensation of external objects is but a fragment of the total object present to our minds. "The self of self-consciousness cannot be confined to what we immediately experience either in the way of sense or of active tendency. On the side of sense, it includes an extension of certain aspects of immediate sensation, which are relatively permanent, in contrast with those particular modifications in the sensory continuum which are perpetually coming and going and are properly called sense-impressions. In like manner what we immediately experience in the way of active tendency is only a partial ingredient in what we perceive as our own action, incapable of existing as being known by itself, but only as one continuous with a process which transcends and includes it."[1]

The growth of self-consciousness is a constant recasting and reconstruction of our mental life. Self-consciousness is

[1] G. F. Stout, *Mind and Matter*, pp. 309–10. Cf. Koffka, *The Growth of the Mind*, p. 380.

not a coming to be aware of what was already there. Paradoxical as it may seem, the way in which we represent ourselves to ourselves determines what we are. When the little girl plays with her dolls, adopting towards them a maternal and authoritative attitude, she is reconstructing and expanding her mental life; similarly, in adult life, my representation of myself as a person of a certain kind determines my action and my relationship to others, and thereby changes me. In this sense self-consciousness is creative of the self. It is not however the case that as we reach adult life we form for ourselves a clear, coherent, and stable prehension of the self. Indeed, it is notorious that we do not. We may fail to do so in two respects. First, it is our frequent experience that our self-consciousness may embrace a number of modes of self-prehension fairly discontinuous one with the others. In a given set of circumstances we may imagine ourselves in one way; in another environment in quite another way. And the immediate circumstances may induce a mode of self-consciousness which we may not trouble to relate to our other ways of representing ourselves to ourselves. Our self-consciousness may then be said to be a succession of patterns, existing in comparative disconnection, which we do not endeavour to relate and enclose within a single comprehensive pattern of self-consciousness.

In the second place, it is clear that our self-consciousness may be intensive in greater or less degree. We may be aware of our reactions in varying degrees. This is the text and theme of a good deal of modern psychology, of psycho-analysis and the theory of insanity. We may unknowingly decline to represent ourselves to ourselves as adopting or feeling a certain attitude, and shall therefore fail to effect a clear and acute self-awareness in that respect. We shall fail, in other words, to objectify that 'self'. As is well known, the whole theory of modern psycho-pathology has been built around this notion of failure to effect such objectification.

These two types of failure in self-consciousness are, of course, closely linked. Where the self in self-consciousness tends to be more a drift of differing patterns than a single self of inclusive pattern, failure of discrimination is natural. The mental life tends at once to be disorganized and a scene of repression and conflict. The root trouble in each case is a low degree of self-prehension and self-objectification.

At this low level of self-consciousness we find the parallel, in objective experience, to the comparative disorder of experience which marks the activity of the primary level of imagination. At the primary level, experience of the outside world is chaotic and poorly organized. Impressions of the outside world tend to come in isolation and without correlation to others; they take on no inclusive pattern. When this occurs, we find a similar failure of prehension of mental life; failure to relate to each other our experiences of the outside world and other people inevitably involves failure to relate the events of our own mental life. The coherence of our imaginative prehension of the outside world and of the self have the same foundation; or, clear prehension of the outside world and of the self are two aspects of a single process. In each case there is failure or success in forming a total prehension. The struggle to 'idealize and to unify' necessarily occurs both in ordering our imagination of the outside world and of the self.

We should expect therefore that at the level of what Coleridge calls the 'secondary' imagination, we should find a comprehensive self-consciousness of the inner life of the artist, corresponding in its unity to the pattern of unity which the poet endeavours to create in his imagination of the world. In the first place, the poet's self-consciousness is not a drift of selves, unrelated to each other; instead, while there must be variation in the selves present to the consciousness of the poet, these variations will not be merely suffered; they will take their place in a grasped pattern of total self-hood which embraces all such changes—a pattern at once stable and flexible. In this way, all the experiences coming to the poet are received not passively but actively, not chaotically but coherently. Each phase of the self as it is experienced is experienced in the light of the past and of the future; it is not a temporary occurrence only, but will have significance for the whole of experience which makes up the personality of the poet. This significance is acquired in and through the imaginative act whereby it is grasped in its relation to the rest of experience. And in the second place the powerful operation of secondary imagination must dissolve the obscurity in which, at a lower level of self-consciousness, mental reactions may be allowed to dwell. The attitudes of the poet, his emotional and conative responses to experience, are not merely experienced; they are present to his consciousness. The vague and distressing feeling of unrest and inner disturbance which such obscurely experienced reactions create is dissipated by a more adequate self-consciousness. And this, though it does not destroy the sources of unrest, brings them within the field of imaginative apprehension. The passion for order, wholeness, and unity, which is the mark of the imagination, demands that experience be clearly prehended in the light of a clear self-consciousness which seeks to leave no experience unrelated. The secondary imagination is therefore, in the inner life of the poet, a dissolvent of disordered and obscure self-perception; its activity is also an objectification of the self, a power of beholdment of it.

2

It is this objectification of the self, which implies a relating of emotional and conative experiences, which makes lyrical poetry possible. For poetry demands what Coleridge called 'restraint'; and above all, lyrical poetry, in which the poet sings his own experiences, demands 'restraint'. 'Restraint', however, is not a good word; it is too negative. It suggests a damping down or negating, at least to a degree. It would be better instead to refer to precisely this process of objectification to which we have referred, whereby, as it were, the poet 'distances' his emotional and conative reactions. It is not the case that they thereby differ in intensity; it is only that his self-consciousness seeks not to be diminished or swamped by strong emotion, or that his emotions are 'pushed out' from the centre of his mind. In this way his experiences are 'enjoyed' to a greater degree than otherwise would be possible. However impassioned those experiences may be, the condition of great poetry is that they do not wholly possess him. *He* must seek actively to possess *them*. They are but the material upon which his unifying imagination must work ; he must, therefore, to use a word of Mr. Santayana's, 'disintoxicate' himself from them. Their intensity may be great; yet they must be *his* emotions and *his* actions. They must, in all their intensity, be steadied by the practised stability of his imagination of himself. 'Restraint', therefore, there will be; but it is not a restraint of limitation and refusal placed upon his experiences, but a steadiness issuing from his act of self-imagination. It is an active 'enjoyment', not a passive 'suffering', of his experiences. Instead, therefore, of restraint of emotion, it would be better to speak of a strengthening of self-consciousness in proportion to the strength of the experience. Without this, lyrical poetry would never be possible; the lyrical poet must 'enjoy' his sorrows as well as his joys. In other words, behind all the emotional sensitiveness of the poet is the creative imagination operating on the 'material' of emotion. And for our present purpose, what we emphasize is not the strength or vividness of his emotional reactions, but the ordering activity of the imagination which gives significance to emotion. Mere emotion in itself is something and nothing; what is necessary for poetry is the imaginative command of this emotion. The life of art is in this sense a strenuous effort after release from emotion in the very act of experiencing it. There must go on a certain depersonalization, a quietness in the midst of the speed of passion. It is from the 'balance of those opposites' that poetry is born. Hence in lyrical poetry what is conveyed is not mere emotion, but the imaginative prehension of emotional states, which is a different thing. It is true that the object of imaginative prehension in this case is the poet himself; but it does not

follow that language as it is used in lyrical poetry is any more
'emotive' than in other kinds of poetry. Shelley's *Lines written
in Dejection* is as 'objective' as *King Lear* or *Othello*. It is
subjective only in the sense that it happens to be concerned
with an emotional state which actually occurred in the life of
the writer. Aesthetically, however, this fact is irrelevant.

It is necessary at this juncture to emphasize, with regard to
what has gone before, that this imaginative prehension of the
inner life which marks the level of the secondary imagination
is in itself not moral. The effort to obtain such clear self-
prehension is not inspired by moral idealism, nor does it arise
from any desire for self-improvement. It arises solely from the
effort of the imagination to relate, or to effect wholeness of
prehension; to get above the flux of experience and grasp it as
a unity. It is not the case therefore that the creative effort
of the artist as it manifests itself in his inner life is to change,
organize, harmonize his reactions; to reform his life in the
light of any pattern, or to impose any moral pattern upon his
life. Rather is it primarily an effort to transcend and be raised
above the life of passion and action and see it as a whole,
instead of experiencing a flux of selves and a succession of
obscurely felt reactions. In other words, it is not a harmony
of emotion and impulse which the poet endeavours to secure;
it is a singleness and clearness of prehensive grasp of the life
of emotion and impulse, which will leave no element in that
life unrelated and isolated. It is a struggle for unity of
prehension, not a struggle for moral unity and adequacy.
We must therefore deny any specifically moral characteristics
to the imagination. This denial is necessary at the outset in
order to realize the true relationship of the life of imagination
to the life of morality. It is true that the life of imagination
is of enormous importance for morality; indeed it may be said
to be a fundamental condition of fine moral achievement. Nor
is it the case that imaginative power and the moral life are in
the slightest degree inimical to each other, and that one must
necessarily diminish the power of the other. The detachment

from the life of emotion and volition which the imagination affords, the refusal to be immersed in feeling and action, is not to be confounded with a diminution of the life of feeling and action, a withdrawal, if such a thing were conceivable, from emotional experience and the strenuous practice of life. But, on the other hand, it does bring with it a diminution of the degree of disturbance which the changes and chances of life produce. And it is such a detachment which the poet is constantly endeavouring to achieve and to express in his work—the maintenance of his imaginative life in the face of everything which his personal experience and destiny may bring. There is a passage in an essay of Schopenhauer's in which, writing on genius, he says: "The brain may be likened to a parasite which is nourished as a part of the human frame without contributing directly to its inner economy; it is securely housed in the topmost storey, and there leads a self-sufficient and independent life. In the same way it may be said that a man endowed with great mental gifts leads, apart from the individual life common to all, a second life, purely of the intellect. He devotes himself to the constant increase, rectification and extension, not of mere learning, but of real systematic knowledge and insight; and remains untouched by the fate that overtakes him personally, so long as it does not disturb him in his work. It is thus a life which raises a man and sets him above fate and its changes. Always thinking, learning, experimenting, practising his knowledge, the man soon comes to look upon this second life as the chief mode of existence, and his merely personal life as something subordinate, serving only to advance ends higher than itself." He goes on to describe Goethe's inquiry into the theory of colour during time of war, and continues, "This is an example which we . . . should endeavour to follow, by never letting anything disturb us in the pursuit of our intellectual life, however much the storms of the world may invade and agitate our personal environment. . . . As our emblem and coat of arms, I propose a tree mightily shaken by the wind, but still bearing its ruddy fruit on every branch; with the motto *Dum convellor mitescent* or *Conquessata sed ferax. . . .* This intellectual life, like some gift from heaven, hovers above the stir and movement of the world; or it is, as it were, a sweet-scented air developed out of the ferment itself—the real life of mankind, dominated by will. . . . Thus genius may be defined as an eminently clear consciousness of things in general and therefore, also, of that which is opposed to them, namely, one's own self."[1] Schopenhauer is here writing of the intellect, by which he means the life of philosophy and science as well as of the imagination; but all that he says applies to the artist in his strenuous effort for imaginative command of experience. And in his poetry the artist expresses just his imaginative prehension of the world and of his own life. Thus, in conveying awareness of the world and his life, he also conveys his release from them in imagination.

In lyrical poetry (and by lyrical poetry we shall mean for the present such lyrical poetry as is frankly 'about' the poet— Shelley's *Lines written in Dejection* in an example) this process of depersonalization is wrought out. What is poetical in a lyrical poem is not the mere presence of strong emotion and feelings but the imaginative apprehension of them. Hence though we may usefully distinguish different kinds of poetry, lyrical, dramatic, etc., yet all kinds of poetry are poetical for the same reason, that they express imaginative apprehension of an object, whether that object be the poet's own feelings, or someone else's, or a tree, or the moon. The *Lines written in Dejection* are poetry for the same reason that *King Lear* is poetry. The fact that there was once an individual who actually felt as Shelley's poem records is of no *poetic* importance whatsoever. Our awareness that there was once a person who felt these emotions is as unimportant for our poetic enjoyment as the fact that there never was a person who actually spoke the lines

> To-morrow, and to-morrow, and to-morrow,
> Creeps in this petty pace from day to day.

[1] *The Art of Literature* (tr. T. B. Saunders), pp. 131–4.

For poetry, Shelley is no more a historical person than Macbeth; for the poetic consciousness simply is not concerned with history and actual sequence.

The distinction therefore between lyrical and dramatic poetry is primarily formal, and does not reveal any essential difference of poetic process. There is an impersonality which the lyrical poet must achieve in the singing of his joys and sorrows, a detachment from himself similar to that which the dramatist has from his characters; we may also view the tragic heroes of Shakespeare as lyrical poets who achieve the lyrical act of catharsis, which, as M. Brémond observed, is the liberation from his emotion which the poet must achieve and which makes his poetry. It is the depersonalization which the imaginative act accomplishes. And in the development of the doctrine of catharsis and its application to tragedy, it has been overlooked to what extent catharsis operates within the play and within the character of the hero. In each of the great tragedies of Shakespeare it is possible to point to a speech in which the catharsis, the release from immersion in the materiality of emotion, is effected. It is towards this process of deliverance that the tragedies move, and in it they find their consummation. And in this process, the achievement of this condition through suffering, the inner significance of the tragedies shows itself.

> Dost thou not see my baby at my breast,
> That sucks the nurse asleep?

is the most perfect expression of it. But it is also present in the others; and in them all the tragedy reaches its end at the point where Othello, Cleopatra, Macbeth speak as poets who have learnt to behold themselves as, what formerly they were, creatures of passion, weakness, and will. In their final achievement is a lyricism, a submission to catharsis, the stilling of passion through imaginative awareness. And we might add that unless this catharsis is accomplished in the play, it cannot be accomplished by the play. Where in Shakespeare it does not occur within the play, in *Troilus* and *Coriolanus*, for example, there is a failure of the tragic idea.

3

It is therefore of some use to bear in mind, in the discussion of poetry, and particularly of the type of lyrical poetry with which we are now concerned, the distinction between what we may call 'material' emotion and emotion which is the specific accompaniment of the desire for, and achievement of, vivified and adequate self-perception. When the poet sings his joys, sorrows, loves, despairs, these emotions may be said to be material; and, when imaginatively encompassed and related, they form the imaginative idea which the poem is concerned to express. For it is not, strictly, these emotions in themselves, but the poet's creative prehension of them, which makes the poem. It is, of course, the case that in the reading of the poem we must ourselves feel these emotions as did the poet himself. But our reading is truly poetic only if there occurs within ourselves also something of the poet's release from these emotions in the very act of experiencing them. We miss the purpose, for example, of Shelley's poem if we read it only as an expression of despair; for what is central to the poem is a certain terrifying impassivity, a freezing out or pressing out (taking 'expression' literally) of his dejection from the centre of his being; and the last lines bring to a high degree the excitement accompanying such an act of self-imagination. It is therefore of the utmost importance to distinguish poetic excitement or emotion from the 'material' emotions. It is usual to describe this truly poetic excitement as 'wonder'. But the word, although it is the best we have, has unfortunate associations. It is perhaps better to speak of imaginative excitement, the emotional response which in itself leads to no action other than renewed desire for more adequate perception. Hence, as we have said, it is misleading, even in regard to intensely personal poetry, to speak of poetry as using language 'emotively'. Poetry is never concerned primarily to awake 'emotion' and 'attitude'; its concern is to convey imaginative idea of, among other things, emotions.

Successful conveyance of such imaginative prehension will certainly be accompanied by excitement—but excitement of a unique kind, which is not itself part of the content of the poem, for it is that which accompanies contemplation of the object. This contemplative excitement is impersonal, as impersonal as that which may accompany intellectual comprehension. Poetry can be as impersonal as science—and in relation to matters in which impersonality is enormously difficult. This is not, of course, to say that Shelley does not effect a self-expression in his poetry. Of course he does; as also does Shakespeare for that matter in his plays. We have to be careful, in holding to the impersonality which poetry may achieve, not to go to the length of saying, as Mr. C. S. Lewis does,[1] that "at best—we meet the poet, even in the most personal lyric poetry, only in a strained and ambiguous sense"; and that it is, in fact, "quite impossible that the character represented in the poem should be identically the same with that of the poet". On the contrary, the 'character' and the 'poet' *are* one and the same; and Mr. Lewis' failure to see that this is so is due to his failure to see that self-expression is adequate only to the degree that it is creative. The 'man' is changed in and through the labour of self-expression, clear self-apprehension transforms 'character'; and the writer's 'character' and his poetry do not exist separately in watertight compartments. Style (which is another word for adequate expression) *makes* the man. Certainly Shelley's poem is a piece of self-expression. And we should not make the error of believing that perfection of self-expression is inconsonant with impersonality of the kind intended.

4

Poetry then is always the expression of the creativeness of the imagination and never merely of emotion. In this connection it is instructive to consider Wordsworth's celebrated passage on this subject: "I have said that poetry is the spon-

[1] *Essays and Studies*, English Association, 1933, p. 13.

taneous overflow of powerful feelings; it takes its origin from emotion recollected in tranquillity: the emotion is contemplated till, by a species of reaction, the tranquillity disappears, and an emotion, kindred to that which was before the subject of contemplation, is gradually produced, and does itself actually exist in the mind." In the first sentence we are told that poetry is the spontaneous overflow of powerful feelings; in the second that the origin of poetry is in the recollection and contemplation of the original emotional state. And it is clearly the second sentence which is important—'recollection' and 'contemplation' is that without which poetry could not occur. In the course of this contemplation there arises an emotion 'kindred to' the original one; but although Wordsworth goes so far as to say that the tranquillity as such disappears, the original emotion has become, so to speak, contaminated by 'tranquillity' and 'contemplation', and only in this condition can 'overflow' into poetry. And we may take Wordsworth to mean that it is this 'contaminated' emotion which is the actual source of composition. Probably, in writing the passage, Wordsworth wrote with an eye to lyrical poetry of a personal kind such as makes up the bigger part of his contribution to the Lyrical Ballads. And his thought is of the contemplation of emotion and not, as at first we might think, the mere occurrence of strong feeling. Wordsworth brought 'powerful feelings' and 'tranquillity' together by asserting the necessity of recollection as a link. It was indeed natural that one who was in *The Prelude* recounting his life should think of recollection as an indispensable element in poetic experience. But even if 'recollection' were a necessity to Wordsworth and is not to others, the passage utters the essential thought with which we are concerned— a meeting of tranquillity with emotion, of peace with agitation.

5

In the inner life of the poet then, as in his reaction to the whole of experience, an imaginative ordering of life occurs, a clarification of prehension. We may now go on to ask, if the poet thus develops a power of self-objectification which in itself is not moral, but is motivated only by a desire for fuller self-perception, what is the relation between this fuller self-perception and the moral life? It will be clear from what has gone before that there is an intimate and important connection. It is true that the life of imagination has no directly moral concern; it does not seek to 'contribute directly to the inner economy' of the life of action. But it is impossible to suppose that it can go on without an indirect influence upon the life of behaviour, which is of the greatest value. This influence arises on account of the creative character of perception—of the self as well as of the external world. As we have emphasized, self-consciousness is not an awareness of what is given any more than our consciousness of a world is of a world which is given. In each case there is construction from a given, and in the act of construction a transcending of initial data. Hence the growth of self-consciousness is not an increasing consciousness of a developing self; it is rather the transformation of the self through the act of self-perception. We have said that an acute self-consciousness is a necessary condition of lyrical poetry, a depersonalization effected through the imagination. But this is, of course, not only true of lyrical poetry of the frankly personal type; it is involved in all poetry whatsoever, since the external world and the life of the self are not cut off from each other; the life of the self is always apprehended as a part of a wider and enveloping reality. Hence the lyrical poet of the personal type who voices his joys and sorrows is never merely a personal lyrical poet; nor can the most 'objective' writer who creates fictitious character fail to effect such self-prehension as is more obvious in the personal lyricist. Awareness of the self and of the world grow together, and it would be impossible to suppose that the life of the 'secondary' imagination is different in this respect from the 'primary'. The dynamic in every poet, of whatever kind, is necessarily towards an imagination of himself as 'objective' as his imagination of the world. Now if this is so, we can say, in regard to all poetry whatsoever, that its effects upon the nature and quality of the moral life are great. For as surely as the success of one's behaviour in respect of an object will depend on one's power of perception of that object, so will the quality of behaviour depend upon adequacy of self-perception. Also, if it is true that the imaginative act of self-perception is creative, the self is changed through that act; and, as we have seen, the result of the act is that the emotional-conative activities of the self are reduced, in respect of their power of disturbance, in the total life of the mind.

It is a great misfortune that sincerity has always been regarded as a virtue. For sincerity is not a virtue but a quality of the imagination when the imagination is directed upon the life of the self. This error has arisen because we have confounded insincerity with deliberate deception. We condemn the insincere man, the hypocrite, because we think that he is practising a kind of fraud. But in fact he is doing nothing of the kind; his failing is not in his will but in his imagination, and is a failure of self-perception. Hence when it is said that art must necessarily have moral quality in some degree, that is, in so far as it must have sincerity, we go astray. The connection of art with morality is not here; for in speaking of sincerity and insincerity we are still speaking of the imagination. Insincerity arises only from confusedness and poverty of the imagination; or is an inability to relate each to the others, in a single inclusive prehension, the varied reactions of the mind. That this is so becomes abundantly clear from the wealth of evidence provided in recent years by psycho-analysis, which shows the degree to which failure in self-perception may extend, and the serious consequences which may result. And psychology has at least brought it about that we no longer view insincerity, at least when it is so developed as to have serious consequences, as a form of moral evil, but as a failure of perception, of imaginative vitality, which calls for treatment. To bring about clear self-perception is, in psycho-pathology, the vital step to the restoration of mental health, the doctor helping the patient to do that which the latter has failed to do, forming a single integrated view of the patient's mind.

Now the poetic mind is one in which such a process is constantly going on, a continuous catharsis as M. Brémond has seen and pointed out in his book *Prayer and Poetry*. Modern psycho-therapy has abundantly justified Aristotle's doctrine of catharsis, and shown that Aristotle was not talking the nonsense which many people, though devoted to the name and authority of Aristotle, have persistently attributed to him. The whole hygienic tone of the mind depends, at every step, upon such a continuous activity of self-imagination; and what is surprising is that it has taken the human mind so long to formulate a theoretical basis, in the study of psychology, for this reality. For it is apparent that it has always been the centre of the creativity of the greatest minds. And it is not, I think, an exaggeration to say that, in this sense, the poets have always been masters of psychology. For catharsis is a necessary accompaniment of the developed life of the imagination, and is known, if only implicitly, to all the poets. Nor need we go back to Aristotle for an explicit formulation of it. In the *Ethics* Spinoza points out that to form a 'clear idea' of a passion is to have dissipated its controlling power. But for this, it is power of imagination and not of will which is required. Sincerity the poet will necessarily have; but it springs from his imaginative, not his moral, life. It is necessary, in order to see the true connection between art and morals, to realize that this is so. The true connection rather lies in the fact that such self-imagination at once provides the will with a clear and lucid situation in which to act, and facilitates the action of the will by the diminution of the power of disturbance of emotional-conative activity. The action of the imagination is therefore twofold; on the one hand it saves the energy of the will from wastage, by virtue of the adequate awareness which it affords; it also increases the power of the will through the effects of objectivifying the emotional-conative reactions. These are the 'gifts' of the imagination to the life of morality.

They are not sought by the imagination directly, but nevertheless occur through imaginative activity and are a facilitation of moral effort. By its sense of proportion and wholeness it ensures 'judgment ever awake' and self-possession, and aids thus indirectly tenacity to a moral ideal.[1]

But there is a yet greater gift which the imagination makes to morality, a gift whereby morality is saved from itself and the dangers which encompass it, a gift which it is able to make because it is itself detached from the interestedness of morality. There are two dangers attaching to the moral life; first, that arising from what is necessarily present in moral struggle— the 'sense of inevitable failure'; secondly, that in its composition which threatens to transform it into a mere legalism or formalism. In the first case, morality is doomed to witness a constant receding of the ideal, and must, if it is to continue to exist, undertake a journey which it knows can have no end. It must maintain itself in existence while it also sees the ultimate hopelessness of its existence. From this position it cannot escape, or get release from this necessary contradiction. As the moral life advances, its ideal re-forms itself to represent, in the light of past progress, a further "ought-to-be"; and to this progression there is no end. It is not difficult "to put our finger on the central flaw of the ethical experience, the ultimate root of so much bitterness of heart. The nature of this flaw may be expressed . . . by the statement that the secret aspiration of the moral man is to obtain individual perfection—that is, to obtain a contradiction in terms. For perfection and *finite* individuality are incompatible. But morality is resolutely determined not only to have perfection, but to have it in the

---

[1] I do not mean to suggest that powerful self-imagination leads necessarily to a life of virtue. It might conceivably facilitate a life of heartless immorality. Such a state of affairs is portrayed in Dostoievsky's 'heroes' (e.g. Stavrogin), who deliberately pursue a life of evil with the fullest realization of what they are doing. But such men are not merely criminals; they are, in the deepest sense of the word, *serious* men, and are marked by extreme sincerity. I cannot imagine that great sincerity could occur along with immorality and vice of an ordinary kind.

form of individual and finite existence—a form which is really quite inadequate to the proposed content."[1] Endemic to morality therefore is a sense of hopeless discouragement and despair, a sense which found notable expression in some of Arnold's poetry. On the other hand is a still more sinister danger, the likely end of all morality which is not somehow saved from itself, that of conceiving virtue as submission to formal rules and of breeding thereby a kind of spiritual pride, and a hoarding and enjoyment of virtue as a miser hoards and enjoys his gold. Discouraged by the sense of an endless advance, it threatens to try to satisfy itself with the fulfilment of a number of rules and conventions which it feels it can adequately encompass. From these dangers morality cannot release itself; it can be saved only by an attitude of disinterestedness towards itself, an attitude which cannot possibly arise from within itself. What is required is an activity which, apprehending the life of will and moral effort in relation to its ideal, is not itself suborned to the errors of morality, and may thereby save it from the dangers which necessarily accompany it. And this the imagination is able to do; for standing outside the life of the will it is able to redeem it from itself with a due sense of proportion, criticism, and humour, and to look beyond morality to 'unknown modes of being', to tread what Mr. de la Mare calls the 'edge of life'. Of this transcendent exercise of the imagination we shall write in chapters to follow. Our present purpose is to observe that in this exercise, deriving from perception of the incompleteness of the life of will, the imagination gives release to the mind from that immersion in moral ends which may carry with it the great dangers which we have noted. The life of imagination strenuously lived is indeed naturally attended by the pursuit of virtue; the clarity of self-perception which it affords, and the detachment from the fanaticism of morality which is its essence, give signal occasion for lucid exercise of the will and the clarification of the moral ideal. Yet also, the life of imagination is no mere

---

[1] A. E. Taylor, *The Problem of Conduct*, p. 422.

affair of morality; indeed it carries with it, if it is not too strong a word, a certain fine contempt of mere morality. Yet this 'contempt' is a condition of a morality which may be healthy and vigorous, and saved, as it were, from itself. But such an attitude could occur only through the ability of the imagination dimly to perceive, as it were, the unknown; an unknown in which the reconciliation of perfection and individuality may somehow be effected in us, in which, that is to say, the difference between what is and what should be is lost and the life of morality ended. It is thus that, struggling to perception of a condition which morality cannot achieve, the imagination makes to the moral life its crowning gift, and ensures it against what is for morality alone its necessary weaknesses. And thus personality may be reconciled to the failure of the will and the bitterness of moral experience.

6

This is the greatest gift of the imagination to morality. And we may comment further upon it by contrasting what is above with the view of the relation of imagination to morals which is held by Mr. I. A. Richards. The substance of Mr. Richards' views will be remembered from an earlier chapter. I will briefly summarize that part of his doctrine with which we are here particularly concerned. 'The most valuable states of mind are those which involve the widest and most comprehensive co-ordination of activities and the least curtailment, conflict, starvation and restriction. States of mind in general are valuable in the degree in which they tend to reduce waste and frustration.'[1] This we may take as a statement of self-realization as the moral end. (But unlike certain philosophers, who have previously discussed self-realization, Mr. Richards does not take account of acts of self-sacrifice, or of extreme self-sacrifice, which may involve a total 'curtailment'.) Now poetry, we are told, is the outcome of such a harmonized

---

[1] *Principles of Literary Criticism*, p. 59.

inner condition; it is the expression indeed of states of
inner harmony, of exquisite poise, such as rarely occur in the
life of humanity. The condition of writing good poetry is
the occurrence, stimulated in some way, of such experience.
"Some system of impulses not ordinarily in adjustment within
itself or adjusted to the world finds something which orders
it and gives it fit exercise." In such a state of release from inner
conflict and ill-adaptation a greater vitality than is normal
occurs, and "then follows the peculiar sense of ease, of restfulness, of free unimpeded activity, and the feeling of acceptance,
of something more positive than acquiescence". The result is
poetry. Such experiences, we gather, are not the result of
moral struggle; 'something is found' which brings them about.
Such experiences are the most valuable we can have, and they
are therefore the most moral; and to read poetry, and as
a result to have such experiences ourselves, is to be given
a most valuable and moral experience likely to affect us
permanently for the better. Mr. Richards, therefore, claims
to have shown how precisely poetry is important; it is only
the development of the psychology of instinct and emotion
that has made this possible for us, 'and moreover, the wild
speculations natural in pre-scientific inquiry definitely stood
in the way'. Thus the doctrine is that poetry is the expression
of the most moral conditions in man's life, and the reading
of it likely to produce more moral living.

It will be seen that this view is very different from that which
we have tried to set out. I have already tried to argue that Mr.
Richards lays a false emphasis upon emotion and instinct for
the purposes of criticism at the expense of emphasis on
imaginative apprehension; our concern here is to observe
that in considering the relationship of poetry to morals, this
difference of emphasis leads to two radically different views
of that relationship, the one based on order and organization
among subjective responses, the other on order and clarity of
the imaginative apprehension of such responses. (For
convenience of the following discussion we may usefully keep

in mind the lyric of a personal kind; we can later generalize
for poetry as a whole.) For the one view, the poetic condition
is a state of the mind; for the other it is essentially an apprehension *of* a state of mind. For the former the poetic condition
is essentially moral; for the other it is a facilitation only of the
moral life. In considering the difference of view there are
three aspects of it upon which we can, perhaps, usefully
comment. (1) The general character of morality, and especially
its relation to such states of 'poise' as Mr. Richards designates
as most 'moral'; (2) the relationship between these states and
the writing of poetry; (3) the question whether in fact all
poetry does result from a release from inner conflict and, if
so, in what sense? (1) It is useful to have before us a statement
of what we mean by morality. The following is a statement
which I take from Professor A. E. Taylor's book *The Problem
of Conduct*, a statement with which I think no one can disagree.
"It is characteristic of the ethical attitude towards the world
that it never gets beyond the contrast of the actual and the
possible. It is assumed in all practical morality that the aim
of my conduct is to make real some state of things which
as yet exists only in idea, and further, that the realization of
this 'end' is to be brought about by the agency of myself and
other intelligent but finite and imperfect beings. Reduced
to its simplest elements this statement means—from the
psychological point of view,—that morality as such depends
for its existence upon two fundamental peculiarities of human
mental life,—the consciousness of time and the existence of
ideas as distinct from both sensations and perceptions."[1]
On this account the moral condition is one of conflict, an
opposition of a higher and a lower. No doubt Mr. Richards,
looking at the matter from the point of view of his naturalistic
and, so to speak, quantitative ethic, would prefer not to speak
of a higher and a lower; he would prefer to speak of more and
less comprehensive fulfilments. But it is certain that morality
is essentially a condition in which choice is made between a

[1] Pages 366–7.

I

number of alternatives which are factors in a situation which is one of conflict. Now Mr. Richards rightly points out that we enjoy from time to time states of mind in which we are not troubled by the difficulties of choice, but suffer a release to a condition of unimpeded activity. Such experiences we may have, varying greatly in the occasion which immediately gives rise to them. The company of congenial friends or the enjoyment of art may be marked by such a 'sense of ease, of restfulness, of free unimpeded activity'. Such experiences are, as it were, a temporary release from the life of choice; we are temporarily freed from inner antagonisms. The sense of time fades, and we enjoy an immersion in the experience of the moment, undistracted by past and future. To this degree we have risen above the moral condition, interpreted strictly as one of exertion of the will in the face of a number of opposing alternatives.

Now as we observed in the last section, the aspiration of the moral life must necessarily be towards such valuable states of mind in which moral effort may be superseded. Indeed we may say that morality, if it is to be saved from itself, can seek nothing less than a condition which is permanently removed from such inner antagonisms. Such a condition however, were it reached, would be one in which morality had been finally transcended—a non-moral condition. Morality must, that is to say, seek the supersession of itself by something other than itself. The most valuable state of mind conceivable, according to Mr. Richards' own showing, would be one in which free unimpeded activity, wholly released from conflict, would be permanently assured. Such a condition is, according to Christian teaching, the fruition in which the human soul may achieve its destiny, a condition of 'eternal life'. And Christian writers frequently use such experiences as Mr. Richards speaks of as a way of trying to convey the real meaning of 'eternity'. It is not therefore idle to comment that Mr. Richards' teaching exemplifies the impasse in which the moral life finds itself. Regarding such states as we have spoken of as the most valuable, he cannot fail to regard as the most 'valuable' individual one who might permanently enjoy such a mode of experience, which in its perfection would be a "whole, simultaneous and complete fruition of a life without bounds". Mr. Richards is not likely to accord credence to the conditions under which alone such perfect fruition is possible. But can he deny that "in the specific experience of the moral life we already have to do with endeavour which, from first to last, is directed upon the attainment of such a form of fruition, and yet, while it retains its specific character, can never finally reach its goal"?[1]

(2) It may be believed therefore that when Mr. Richards asserts a close relationship between poetry and morals, he is also asserting a relation between poetry and an aspiration which morality cannot satisfy. But putting aside this matter we may proceed to the second point. Let us for the present agree to say that poetry issues from a state of mind more than ordinarily free from conflict. We must then ask: Are such experiences confined to the poets? The answer is definitely in the negative. 'Although for most people these experiences are infrequent apart from the arts, almost any occasion may give rise to them.'[2] We must therefore ask: Why in certain cases do these experiences give rise to poetry and in other cases not? We may fairly assume that there come to most people, at some time or other, experiences marked by a diminution of conflict; but in comparatively few cases do such states issue in poetry. What is the power present in the mind of the poet which brings about poetry? Mr. Richards gives as an answer: "The greatest difference between the artist or poet and the ordinary person is found, as has often been pointed out, in the range, delicacy and freedom of the connections he is able to make between the different elements of his experience."[3] This is so, and is a statement of the activity of the imagination effecting or seeking to effect orderly and unified prehension, whether primarily of the external world or of mental responses. And what, we

[1] A. E. Taylor, *The Faith of a Moralist*, Vol. I, p. 93.
[2] *Principles of Literary Criticism*, p. 248.
[3] Op. cit., pp. 181–3.

should have thought, makes the difference between the poet and the ordinary person is precisely the possession by the former of such imaginative power, bringing about a heightened and unified awareness of the world on the one hand, and a vivified self-consciousness on the other. This greater imaginative grasp of the world and self is surely what makes imaginative creation possible. But Mr. Richards will not leave it at that. He says that the difference between understanding a situation (by 'understanding' he presumably means unified and inclusive imaginative apprehension) and 'the more usual reactions' is a "difference in the degree of organization of the impulses which it arouses. It is the difference between a systematized complex response and a welter of responses." Now admitting that people who do and people who do not write poetry enjoy 'experiences' free from conflict, the question arises, Why do some write poetry and others not? Both alike enjoy a state of poise, of inner balance—this is admitted. Mr. Richards begins by giving the right answer—there is a difference of imaginative power. But he goes on to add that this difference is equivalent to a difference in organization of the impulses; there is organization in one case, not in the other. But it is admitted at the outset that there is in each case a considerable degree of organization of impulses. Hence it must be agreed either that what explains the difference is the degree to which imaginative power is present, or that no one but poets have experience of inner poise. To believe the latter is absurd; to assert the former is to hold that what is required for poetry is not merely inner poise of impulses but imaginative grasp of the situation, whether the situation be external or subjective, as in the case of the personal lyric poet. Many people might and do experience such an inner balance without the power of making it (we have in mind again the lyrical poet of the 'personal' kind) an object of imaginative realization or apprehension. But it is precisely this power of depersonalization which is required if poetry is to result, a power which cannot be expressed in terms of balance or inter-inanimation of impulses.

(3) But we have finally to ask whether it is the case that poetry necessarily results only from 'freedom from conflict' as Mr. Richards holds? For this is apparently intended as a generalization covering all poetic creation whatsoever, and we are asked to believe that no poems express or embody a state of inner conflict. Agreeing that we may have experiences free from conflict, is it the case that all poetry arises from conditions of mind in which such comparative freedom occurs? Can we seriously believe that Shelley's *Lines* show Shelley free from conflict? On the contrary, Shelley's mind, as it is set out in the poem, is in a state of the greatest anguish. Or again in tragedy, we cannot persuade ourselves that our minds are rendered 'free from conflict'. Mr. Richards tells us that in watching *King Lear* we do experience such freedom. We are told that the two dominant impulses aroused are the impulse to approach (pity) and the impulse to retreat (terror), and that, alike aroused and in equal strength, they balance each other, and are thus reconciled.[1] But is this 'freedom from conflict'? When two such tendencies occur, directly opposed to each other, each checking the action of the other and denying each other expression, one would suppose that we have a state of conflict, not of reconciliation. In such a condition we are torn between two tendencies; and the tendencies being what they are can scarcely be *reconciled* to each other; they merely paralyse each other. It may be that in watching *Lear* we are suspended between love and revulsion. But surely this is not a state of ease, of repose, but of severe conflict. Mr. Richards is asking us to believe that the donkey equally inclined to go for the hay and for the carrots is in a state of repose. Apparently, also, Mr. Richards would have us believe that in Shelley's poem also there is such a reconciliation of impulses—Shelley's love of life and his longing for death, that these two tendencies were of equal strength, and left Shelley in a state of poise and inner reconciliation? But if to be suspended between two entirely opposed lines of action is to have inner reconciliation

[1] Op. cit., p. 245.

it surely would be better to do without reconciliation. Elsewhere Mr. Richards has said that what he calls valuable states of mind are those in which as many impulses as possible are involved, but with as little 'mutual interference' as possible between them; or again we are told that anything is "valuable which will satisfy an appetency without involving the frustration of some equal or more important appetency". But such a frustration is apparently precisely what happens in the tragic frame of mind, which yet is described as supremely valuable. We had thought that value attached to a mind in which the impulses each secured a maximum degree of satisfaction compatible with the satisfaction of the others. Now it appears that value attaches to that mind in which all the impulses succeed in thwarting all the others. We must conclude therefore that in the only instance which Mr. Richards gives of the reconciliation and harmony of impulses occurring as a result of poetry, he is describing precisely the opposite of harmony and reconciliation. Hence, if in the poetic experience there is any measure of stability and reposefulness, it does not occur in the way Mr. Richards would have us believe. We may indeed believe that some poems set out a state of mental being marked by such inclusive harmony of interests; the Comedies of Shakespeare, or *L'Allegro*, might be instanced. But surely all poetry does not occur from such states of mind.

7

It is true that in the writing of poetry there is release from conflict; but it is a release of a kind to which Mr. Richards gives no recognition. For the poet's adequate imaginative awareness is itself an extrication of himself from it in the process of experiencing it. The conflict is not eliminated; yet the poem could not occur if the poet were wholly immersed in that conflict. It is not the elimination of conflict, but the clear beholdment of it, which marks the greatest poetry; it is never the mere experience of a condition which characterizes poetry, but the ability, through imagination, to wrest that experience from obscurity and relate it to the whole of experience. Only thus can the experience be given expression. And it is for this reason that, in the reading of poetry, we obtain perception of the human situation as it has been real to a powerful imagination; it is because poetry sets out apprehension of human conflict in the act of suffering it, that it has its great interest for us. So far from being human life in release from conflict, the greatest poetry is most frequently the very embodiment of it. Yet by the very power of so embodying it, poetry is also a kind of transcendence of it, a catharsis whereby conflict is denied a power of controlling disturbance and is pushed out from the centre of personality; and whereby it is not merely suffered but beheld as from a 'central peace subsisting at the heart of agitation'. The act of self-perception is, as we have said, not merely awareness of a given; it is a changing, creative agency; and through it the inner situation is altered and becomes one, to the degree to which self-perception is adequate and inclusive, in which the major factor is a 'tranquillity'. Mr. Richards is therefore right in perceiving that in some sense poetry is the expression of an unusual peace of mind; but he is wrong in thinking that it necessarily arises from a sudden inner harmonization which dissolves conflict. He is right in thinking that somehow there is relief from the ordinary struggle and conflict of the moral life; but he is wrong in so far as he fails to recognize that the relief which arises from the steadiness of imaginative perception is not necessarily a mere cessation of conflict.

What the imagination does perceive increasingly as its power of perception becomes more adequate, is less the cessation of conflict than its enduring presence. The imagination fails to see in human life a wholeness in the contemplation of which it can rest. The moral experience, which is the human experience, is necessarily incomplete, and demands for its completion something other than morality. The imagination, we have seen, is not suborned to morality; it stands outside the life of the will and the endless conflict to which the will is bound. Only through it do we obtain deliverance from the hopeless task of morality, the failure in which the will is rooted, and stability whereby we are armed against the failures and chances of the life of action. And in its contemplation of human life and its unavoidable tragedy, it seeks also the perception of that which lies beyond the moral state. In its vivid apprehension of human life it fails to discover unity and harmony, and therefore carries within itself the dream of a perfection which is impossible to human life. In the greatest poets we can see how, perceiving the insoluble conflict of human life, they turn to the dream of 'unknown modes of being'. This transcendent activity of the imagination is, we have noted, a condition of health in the moral life and saves morality from the dangers natural to it. Yet morality itself cannot have enjoyment of that dream, for it is a dream of what is not a moral state. And the imagination in its turn can but enjoy it as a dream, though it be a dream of compelling power, and wait patiently upon it. 'Adam's dream', wrote Keats, 'will do here.'

Our conclusion therefore is a very orthodox one. The imagination is not a moral affair[1] but it has great importance for morality. First, by its penetration or attempted penetration

---

[1] Yet however much we may seek to deny any moral character to the imagination, there is, of course, an ultimate sense in which it is necessarily moral. For all human activity whatsoever is moral; and science and art and the enjoyment of science and art are therefore moral activities. In the last resort they must be judged good or bad. Hence it is impossible to draw any clear line of separation between imagination and morality, or to say here we are moral and there not. The activity of art has to take its place in a personality which as a whole we judge to be good or bad. Viewing it in this way, of course, the imagination is moral; and we might even speak of the moral imagination as that which keeps morality imaginative and therefore vital. If our morality is not imaginative, it fails, for the reasons we have indicated. The activity of imagination and the activity of morality go on in the same personality; and hence our imaginative life must be moral, as well as our morality imaginative. The imagination and morality alike cover the whole of life, and without each other there is an inevitable corruption of personality.

to what transcends morality, it keeps morality under constant criticism, and saves it from the humourless solemnity, the pessimism, and the legalism, which are only too natural to it. In seeking to represent to itself a state which is beyond good and evil it may indeed be but dreaming, only 'imagining things'; but the dream can exert power and keep before morality a recognition of its ultimate helplessness. Secondly, the self-perception which a strong imagination affords is vital to the moral life; without it we quickly become lost in the quagmires of self-ignorance and of humbug. And equally, the keen perception of the life of others, which marks the imaginative life, dissolves from them, as Coleridge says, the film of familiarity and selfish solicitude with which an unimaginative life quickly wraps them round. Such perception both of the self and of others is not indeed sought for moral ends; yet it becomes a factor of incalculable importance in the moral life, a vital condition of tenure of a moral ideal which seeks to maintain itself in vitality. These are the 'gifts' of the imagination to morality.

PART TWO

There one is on the edge of life, of the unforeseen, whereas our cities—are not our desiccated, faded minds ever continually edging and pressing further and further away from freedom, the vast unknown, the infinite presence. . . . I suggest that in that solitude the spirit within us realizes that it treads the outskirts of a region long since called the Imagination.

WALTER DE LA MARE—*The Creatures*

CHAPTER V

VISIONARY DREARINESS

> It was, in truth,
> An ordinary sight; but I should need
> Colours and words that are unknown to man,
> To paint the visionary dreariness
> Which, while I looked all round for my lost guide,
> Invested moorland waste, and naked pool,
> The beacon crowning the lone eminence,
> The female and her garments vexed and tossed
> By the strong wind.
>
> WORDSWORTH—*The Prelude*, Book 12

I

THE passage in Book 2 of *The Prelude* in which Wordsworth writes of the activity of the imagination in the life of the child clearly derives its substance from Coleridge. The 'first poetic spirit of our human life' is Coleridge's 'primary imagination', the condition of perception. The mind of the child, we are told, is 'prompt and watchful, eager to combine in one appearance, all the elements and parts of the same object, else detached and loth to coalesce'.[1] The 'else detached and loth to coalesce' rings indeed of associationism, as well as of the doctrine of the imagination creative in knowledge which Kant asserted and Coleridge adopted. Wordsworth, indeed, was not a philosopher, either by inclination or natural ability; and we can allow for confusion in whatever of philosophical theories he undertook to present. In any case, what Wordsworth, despite confusion in his thought, was most clearly concerned to assert was the activity of the mind in knowledge, not a bare receptivity to associated elements. And in speaking of this task of primary creation in perception,

[1] This is, of course, almost a travesty of Coleridge's view, which did not suggest that the child is a more or less conscious creator.

Wordsworth again follows Coleridge, for when he says that
the power of imagination

> Doth like an agent of the one great Mind
> Create . . .

we are hearing Coleridge's 'the primary imagination I hold
to be . . . a repetition in the finite mind of the eternal act of
creation in the infinite *I am*'.

Wordsworth, however, does not represent the imagination
as working alone in this act of creation; other parts of the
child's personality are involved; above all, his active response
to his mother and those around him. The child is not an
'outcast' working alone. His creation of a world of objects is
not his alone; the co-operation of society is necessary to complete the activity of his own original powers. The child 'claims
manifest kindred with an earthly soul'; the 'discipline of love'
is ever present; the flower 'to which he points his hand, too
weak to gather it' is plucked for him; and he quickly learns
the active and emotional responses to objects of those who
live with him. And in saying this Wordsworth no doubt gives
a fuller psychological account of the primary imagination than
Coleridge. He is quite right in insisting on the importance of
social co-operation, and in refusing to view the creativeness of
the imagination in the making of its world as the activity of
the isolated mind. It is in all strictness true that the child's
affections for and dependence on others are of the most vital
importance to the activity of the imagination. The entire life
of the child is involved in its creativeness, and not merely an
abstract faculty. The imagination, the primary organ of knowledge, is part and parcel of a personality reaching in a hundred
ways to an environment of people, in what psychologists are
accustomed to call 'intersubjective intercourse'. The knowledge of other minds and of objects as responded to by other
minds, is made possible only through the affectionate ministration of his mother and others; without this life of action and
emotional response the imagination could never obtain a

foundation for its activity. This point is of the greatest importance for Wordsworth's scheme; it means that he viewed the
imagination not as a power divorced from the full activities
of life, but as dependent on them, the flower of personality in
all its activities and responses, deriving its health from a total
well-being of mind. He says in the second book of *The Prelude*
that the imagination can only grow through the ministration
of affection and love; and at the conclusion of the poem he says
that intellectual love and imagination cannot act nor exist
without each other, cannot stand 'dividually'.

In human life, Wordsworth tells us, the imagination grows
from this humble beginning into the sublimest faculty of man,
a faculty which he describes at length in two famous passages
in *The Prelude*. Of imagination he says, at the end of the poem,
that it is

> but another name for absolute strength
> And clearest insight, amplitude of mind,
> And reason in her most exalted mood.
> This faculty hath been the moving soul
> Of our long labour: we have traced the stream
> From darkness . . .
> . . . follow'd it to light
> And open day, accompanied its course
> Among the ways of Nature, afterwards
> Lost sight of it bewilder'd and engulph'd,
> Then given it greeting, as it rose once more
> With strength, reflecting on its solemn breast
> The works of man and face of human life,
> And lastly, from its progress have we drawn
> The feeling of life endless, the great thought
> By which we live, Infinity and God.[1]

And it is of the imagination in this last sense that he speaks in
the other passage—

> Imagination! lifting up itself
> Before the eye and progress of my Song
> Like an unfather'd vapour; here that Power,

[1] This and all other quotations from *The Prelude* in this section
are taken from the text of 1805.

In all the might of its endowments, came
Athwart me; I was lost as in a cloud,
Halted, without a struggle to break through.
And now recovering, to my Soul I say
I recognize thy glory; in such strength
Of usurpation, in such visitings
Of awful promise, when the light of sense
Goes out in flashes that have shown to us
The invisible world, doth Greatness make abode,
There harbours whether we be young or old.
Our destiny, our nature and our home
Is with infinitude, and only there;
With hope it is, hope that can never die,
Effort, and expectation, and desire,
And something ever more about to be.

Wordsworth, then, with Coleridge, viewed the imagination as an essential unifying agency in all perception; but it was also something more. For it is the imagination, 'so called through sad incompetence of human speech', which also gives order and unity to life through its sense of an infinitude which is beyond 'the light of sense'. The imagination, failing to apprehend nature and man as a self-contained whole, beholds the world as pointing beyond itself to an infinite unknown. In its 'struggle to idealize and unify' the imagination, starting from its beginnings in the perception of the child, advances to the sense of an infinitude and of 'unknown modes of being'. The highest reaches of the imagination are of a piece with the simplest act of perception, and issue from the demand for unity which is the life of the imagination. There is a passage in *The Prelude* in which Wordsworth develops this thought. It occurs after his description of his ascent of Snowdon, in which he describes the moon 'naked in the heavens' shining upon a huge sea of mist 'through which a hundred hills their dusky backs upheaved'; while from below

> Mounted the roar of water, torrents, streams
> Innumerable, roaring with one voice.

In this scene Wordsworth beheld

> The perfect image of a mighty Mind,
> Of one that feeds upon infinity.

The resemblance between the scene and the 'mighty Mind' is then expounded. In the scene nature exhibited a 'domination upon the face of outward things'

> So moulds them, and endues, abstracts, combines,
> Or by abrupt and unhabitual influence
> Doth make one object so impress itself
> Upon all others, and pervade them so
> That even the grossest minds must see and hear
> And cannot chuse but feel.

The thought appears to be that in the scene before him the effect of the moon was to create so strange and 'unhabitual' a spectacle that the 'grossest mind' could not but be affected. The appearance of the moon created a new and astonishing world. Such a creation by nature of a strange and new world is the 'express resemblance',

> a genuine Counterpart
> And Brother of the glorious faculty
> Which higher minds bear with them as their own.

Here is Coleridge's 'secondary' imagination having expression in verse. 'Higher minds'

> from their native selves can send abroad
> Like transformations.

They are 'ever on the watch', 'willing to work and to be wrought upon';

> in a world of life they live,
> By sensible impressions not enthrall'd,
> But quicken'd, rouz'd and made thereby more apt
> To hold communion with the invisible world.
> Such minds are truly from the Deity.
> For they are Powers; and hence the highest bliss
> That can be known is theirs, the consciousness
> Of whom they are habitually infused
> Through every image and through every thought
> And all impressions. . . .

K

And hence, he adds, come 'religion, faith, sovereignty within, and peace at will'. The creativity of the imagination in perception, quickened in the life of the poet, leads on to, and is of a piece with, the sense of a transcendent world. It was clearly Wordsworth's view that the free development of the imagination is bound up with a perception of the world as in itself fragmentary and unified only in what is beyond itself. Such an imagination, operating in and through 'recognitions of transcendent power', is the condition of 'freedom' and 'genuine liberty', of an abiding reconciliation of emotion and peace.

2

Such was, we may believe, the essence of Wordsworth's doctrine of the Imagination. But he did not continuously enjoy such an imaginative life; for at the time of the Revolution he had not integrated into his imaginative scheme recognition of the world's suffering, pain, and evil. He responded to the Revolution with overwhelming enthusiasm; and the effect upon him of the attitude of the English Government, and then of the subsequent course of the Revolution, was catastrophic. It may appear surprising to us, when we consider the strongly religious character of his earlier imaginative life, that he should have been absorbed so completely in hopes of what he called

> Saturnian rule
> Returned,—a progeny of golden years
> Permitted to descend, and bless mankind.

Certainly his sense of life was not so clear-eyed as was that of Keats, who from the outset rejected any hopes of earthly happiness for mankind. Yet the fact remains that it seemed to Wordsworth that his view of life demanded, as a condition of its validity, 'Saturnian rule returned'. Shocked, therefore, by what happened, he felt that the failure of the Revolution was destructive of his imaginative life, and his confidence in what Keats was to call the 'truth' of the imagination. What happened, therefore, was a revulsion from the imaginative way of life and a search for a touchstone which could stand unshaken by circumstance. He therefore fell back upon the discursive intelligence, and endeavoured to create, by its exercise, a way of life and an attitude to the universe in which he might have a permanent confidence. Later, Wordsworth was to formulate what he came to think was the true relation of the discursive intelligence to the imagination. But this he did only after he had recovered his belief in the imagination. The faltering of his spirit before the facts of life which he experienced during the course of the seventeen nineties found him unprepared by reflection on the relation of the imagination to the intellect; and he was all the more inclined to abandon the imagination because of the respect which, when at Cambridge, he had felt for mathematical inquiry. From such studies

> I drew
> A pleasure quiet and profound, a sense
> Of permanent and universal sway,
> And paramount belief.

And he goes on to say,

> specially delightful unto me
> Was that clear synthesis built up aloft
> So gracefully.

He sets this 'clear synthesis' in opposition to the turgid condition in which the mind is

> beset
> With images, and haunted by herself.

Hence, when the passionate strength of his imagination was weakened, it was inevitable that his mind should revert to the clearness and certainty of intellectual inquiry which formerly he had most intimately known in the field of greatest abstraction, namely, mathematics. He turned naturally at this juncture to the exercise of the intelligence, but no longer to the intelligence in its activity of making

> an independent world
> Created out of pure intelligence,

but to the intelligence which seeks to discover a 'clear synthesis' of the world in its multiplicity, the concrete world of perception, feeling, will, and also to arrive at clear principles of knowledge and behaviour. In his first stage of doubt and despair he cheered himself by taking to mind

> those truths
> That are the commonplaces of the schools . . .
> Yet with a revelation's liveliness,
> In all their comprehensive bearings known
> And visible to philosophers of old.

But after the Terror he spoke

> with a voice
> Labouring, a brain confounded, and a sense,
> Death-like, of treacherous desertion, felt
> In the last place of refuge—my own soul.

And from this point on he could no longer cheer himself with the platitudes of ancient philosophy. If he was to recover, it would be, he then knew, by hard reflection compelled upon him by his own experience, by a philosophy sprung from the necessity of destroying, if might be, his sense of 'treacherous desertion' in his soul, and built up as a permanent bulwark against further collapse of his inner life.

> Evidence
> Safer, of universal application, such
> As could not be impeached, was sought elsewhere.

What he needed were

> speculative schemes
> That promised to abstract the hopes of Man
> Out of his feelings, to be fixed thenceforth
> For ever in a purer element.

The result of this incursion into philosophy was disastrous—
it gave him over, not to a 'clear synthesis', but to 'despair'.

> So I fared
> Dragging all precepts, judgments, maxims, creeds
> Like culprits to the bar; calling the mind,
> Suspiciously, to establish in plain day
> Her titles and her honours; now believing,
> Now disbelieving; endlessly perplexed
> With impulse, motive, right and wrong, the ground
> Of obligation, what the rule and whence
> The sanction; till, demanding formal *proof*,
> And seeking it in everything, I lost
> All feeling of conviction and, in fine,
> Sick, wearied out with contrarieties,
> Yielded up moral questions in despair.

This rejection of philosophy was absolute, and there was
no going back to it. No one ever had greater motive for philosophy than Wordsworth—it was a matter of life and death, an
intellectual search behind which a passionate need was present.
No doubt what training he had had in mathematics reinforced
his sense of need in endeavouring to extract from philosophical
reflection a degree of clarity, of 'clear synthesis' which philosophy is notoriously slow to supply, and set a standard of proof
which he found philosophy incapable of sustaining. The demand
for 'formal proof', arising both from his mathematical training
and from the insistence of his personal need, was inevitably left
unsatisfied. He might seek escape in abstract science

> Where the disturbances of space and time—
> Whether in matters various, properties
> Inherent, or from human will and power
> Derived—find no admission.

But this was merely escape, and he knew it. What certainties
abstract science could supply were irrelevant to his need.
Thus, with the total collapse of his belief in the 'holiness of
the heart's imagination', and the exasperation and despair
to which philosophy brought him, he was completely adrift.

A crisis had arisen in which he was helpless. The imagination carried within it no criterion of its truth; philosophy could supply no criterion of its truth or afford proof of that for which he hungered. All effort, all conscious direction of his energies, was stopped. There was nothing more he could do. He could but abandon effort; and in that abandonment remain.

In the third book of *The Excursion* Wordsworth retells this story, at least in part, in the character of the Solitary. The Solitary in *The Excursion* is the Wordsworth of his crisis, and is sharply set over against the Wanderer who is the Wordsworth who was afterwards matured and confirmed in his belief in the Imagination. In the Solitary, the rejection of life has gone to extreme lengths, paralysing action. Imagination and intellectual inquiry are not for him—

> Ah! What avails imagination high
> Or question deep?—

and with this goes the extreme of despair—

> Night is than day more acceptable; sleep
> Doth, in my estimate of good, appear
> A better state than waking; death than sleep:
> Feelingly sweet is stillness after storm,
> Thought under covert of the wormy ground!

The Solitary indeed, unlike Wordsworth, had known private grief; but it drove him to that state of agitated inquiry which was Wordsworth's after the Reign of Terror—

> Then my soul
> Turned inward,—to examine of what stuff
> Time's fetters are composed; and life was put
> To inquisition, long and profitless!
> By pain of heart—now checked—and now impelled—
> The intellectual power, through words and things,
> Went sounding on, a dim and perilous way!

From this condition he was restored by the hopes he fixed in the French Revolution; but the outcome was to plunge him

more deeply than ever into the condition from which he had
just escaped; a complete atrophy of his mental life set in.

                        My business is,
        Roaming at large, to observe, and not to feel
        And, therefore, not to act—convinced that all
        Which bears the name of action, howsoe'er
        Beginning, ends in servitude—still painful,
        And mostly profitless.

        3
        The Borderers is the one considerable work which
dates from this period in Wordsworth's life. It has, therefore,
a great significance as an additional comment upon his inner
life at this time. *The Borderers* is a tragedy, for these few
years were indeed Wordsworth's 'tragic period'; and that he
should have written what at no other period of his life he
attempted to do—a tragedy—offers us the possibility of an
illuminating comparison with those plays of Shakespeare
which convey the condition of Shakespeare's mind when he,
like Wordsworth, knew a sense of 'death-like, treacherous
desertion'. For our present purpose it is of more immediate
importance to notice how the story of *The Borderers* is connected with the story of Wordsworth's own life and of the
story of the Solitary. Both Oswald and Marmaduke are men
to whom a grave wrong has been done; the sense of 'death-like,
treacherous desertion' has been theirs. Oswald and Marmaduke
alike, through deception by others, have been made responsible
for an innocent man's death. And the words of Marmaduke

                the firm foundation of my life
        Is going from under me;

and those of Oswald when, narrating his story to Marmaduke,
he says   for many days
        On a dead sea under a burning sky
        I brooded o'er my injuries, deserted
        By man and nature—

alike spring from the same condition which was also Wordsworth's condition. In all 'desertion' is the key word; an unfair,
cruel blow had been struck at one utterly undeserving of it,
who trusted and believed his environment. The Solitary,
Oswald, and Marmaduke are all the Wordsworth of this time.
Indeed, Oswald uses words which are identical with those of
the Solitary after the death of his wife and children—

> three nights
> Did constant meditation dry my blood;
> Three sleepless nights I passed in *sounding on*,
> *Through words and things, a dim and perilous way.*

All three are men of nobility of imagination; all had known
'rainbow arches', 'highways of dreaming passion',

> What mighty objects do impress their forms
> To elevate our intellectual being.

Thence had they been brought back to

> The unpretending ground we mortals tread.

But while the Solitary, Marmaduke, and Oswald are one in
these respects, the response of each to this identical situation
is different. In the Solitary there occurs a revulsion from
feeling, and therefore from action, a permanent numbing of
sensibility; in Oswald it leads to deliberate evil; in Marmaduke
to resignation and the life of religion, 'in search of nothing
this earth can give'.

   There can be little doubt that it is Oswald who, though the
villain of the piece, voices most of Wordsworth's thought and
feeling of the time. In the play Wordsworth symbolizes his
own state as one suffering an unjust blow struck at a trusting
and confident nature. Sensitive to the forms of nature, Oswald's
disgust with humankind struck at his sense of our high 'intellectual being'; what he now knew of

> The world's opinions and her usages

could not be reconciled in one personality with the life of the
imagination and the contemplation of objects which 'impress

their forms to elevate our intellectual being'. The latter, 'a thing so great', must 'perish self-consumed'. Personality under these circumstances becomes split in two, a condition which, in Oswald's case, resolved itself, so far as it resolved itself at all, by a total rejection of moral sense. And though in part his treatment of Marmaduke was animated by resentment of a universe of experience which had betrayed him, a resentment which he vented on the conspicuous virtue of Marmaduke, it was also inspired by a certain inverted idealism, a pure assertion of the will, which sought to issue in an enlargement of 'Man's intellectual empire'. This pure, disinterested assertion of the will, concerned to maintain itself in disregard of good, became in the heart of Oswald a demand for pure freedom, free from the soft claims of shame, ignorance, and love.

>   We subsist
> In slavery; all is slavery; we receive
> Laws, but we ask not whence those laws have come;
> We need an inward sting to goad us on.

That 'inward sting' had come to Oswald as it had come to Wordsworth: In the Solitary, Wordsworth later envisaged a person whom the 'inward sting' had failed to goad into activity, leaving, after its first pain, a permanent numbness, a lasting extension of the chilling of life which he himself had for a while known. In Oswald, writing from the midst of this period of his life, he envisaged the other alternative, in which the sting became a 'goad'.

This condition of intellectual hate, of living in rebellion and a pure assertiveness, which was to be in later years a theme for the novels of Dostoievsky, never, it is probable, took considerable possession of Wordsworth's mind. It must, indeed, have occurred with unusual vividness to his imagination—*The Borderers* shows that it did. Yet over against Oswald is Marmaduke, embodying so different an attitude from that of Oswald that if what we have is what Wordsworth actually wrote in the years 1795 and 1796,[1] we are compelled to believe either

---

[1] And we have Wordsworth's word for it that in all essentials it is.

that Wordsworth was never in the gravest danger of the pure
rebellion of Oswald, or that, at the time of writing, he was
recovering in some degree the previous condition of his mind.
It is true that Marmaduke, believing, at Oswald's prompting,
in the depravity of Herbert, reacted as Wordsworth at the time
of the Terror had done, with a despair which believed the
'world was poisoned at the heart'; yet he was able to say

> there was a plot
> A hideous plot, against the soul of man;
> It took effect—and yet I baffled it,
> In *some* degree.

Which he can say, a little priggishly indeed, because he killed
Herbert, not with his sword but by leaving him exposed to cold
and hunger, out of regard for a higher judgment than his own.
And, instead of a goad to enraged activity, his action becomes an
inducement to the way of religious humility and expiation—

> A man by pain and thought compelled to live
> Yet loathing life.

There are three issues of this experience which is represented
differently in the guise of fiction in *The Borderers* and *The
Excursion*, yet in essence identical with that which Wordsworth
himself suffered—first a lasting atrophy of the imagination and
intellectual life, secondly a fierce effort to live a life in the
greatest degree lawless, and thirdly the way of religious
humility. Wordsworth was to re-discover the last. But, inevitably, he could not be the same; although, in all essentials,
he was to find again the attitude to life which he asserted in the
famous passage in Book VI, it had now become an attitude far
more inclusive, an imaginative grasp of life richer and more
comprehensive than formerly it was. For where formerly it
was a vision of life irrelevant to and without knowledge of evil,
crime, and suffering, it must now incorporate that knowledge
into itself and be reconciled with it. Wordsworth now knew the
unmitigated reality of evil and pain. Somehow, before he could
be a man again, these facts must become part of a single

imaginative grasp of things. He had known the bitterness of mind of a Stavrogin, the extremity of revolt; to forget this and to ignore the facts and realities from which such a condition takes its origin would necessarily mean a loss of integrity and self-respect. If his imaginative life, as formerly he knew it, was to return, it must be inclusive of all his experience and to that degree must be changed. To be led back

> through opening day
> To those sweet counsels between head and heart
> Whence grew that genuine knowledge, fraught with peace—

was what was necessary to him, a 'genuine knowledge' which might occur out of, and as a reconciliation of, the conflict of head and heart. Formerly his strong imaginative life was a natural growth, unimpeded by perplexity and conflict. That condition, indeed, could not last; it was too simple, too easily come by. Terror in some form was bound to come. And having come, it destroyed, or at least overcast, the vitality of his imaginative vision; and his head, saturated with realizations which in his youth did not exist for him, was unable to give liberation. Out of this condition he could not release himself. The vitality and energies of the imagination do not operate at will; they are fountains, not machinery. And from his intellectual inquiry came no knowledge. Such a condition is, in a sense, final. There was no more that Wordsworth could do. Life was cut off from him,

> inwardly oppressed
> With sorrow, disappointment, vexing thoughts,
> Confusion of the judgment, zeal decayed,
> And, lastly, utter loss of hope itself
> And things to hope for!

Here is the nadir of descent from that view of the imaginative life of which he said

> With hope it is, hope that can never die
> Effort, and expectation, and desire,
> And something ever more about to be.

4

After reviewing the restoration of his imaginative vitality, Wordsworth, although he has paid tribute to Dorothy and Coleridge for all they meant to him, insists upon the loneliness in which the imagination is nourished—

> Here keepest thou in singleness thy state:
> No other can divide with thee this work:
> No secondary hand can intervene
> To fashion this ability; 'tis thine,
> The prime and vital principle is thine
> In the recesses of thy nature, far
> From any reach of outward fellowship,
> Else is not thine at all.

This 'singleness of state' Wordsworth must have felt to an extreme degree during this period of his life, exhausted as he must have been by a sense of his own helplessness. Yet, in his helplessness, it was his early imaginative life which stood him in greatest stead; and what returned to him was not, at first, the joyous and abounding vitality of his earlier years, but recollection of two incidents which from this time on were to be a type of symbol very frequent throughout his poetry. It is worth while pausing to comment at length upon them; for, in looking back, he realized, through the memory of these incidents, that his imagination in years gone by had been acquainted with something of the desolation which in greater degree he had since known. Both the incidents relate to death, and to a natural scene associated in each case with death. In the first he describes how he had stumbled upon an old and mouldering gibbet, and saw, clearly preserved upon a stone, the name of a murderer who had been hanged there. He fled 'faltering and faint, and ignorant of the road'. In his terror he climbed to a point whence he saw

> A naked pool that lay beneath the hills,
> The beacon on the summit, and, more near,

> A girl, who bore a pitcher on her head,
> And seemed with difficult steps to force her way
> Against the blowing wind. It was, in truth,
> An ordinary sight; but I should need
> Colours and words that are unknown to man
> To paint the visionary dreariness
> Which, while I looked all round for my lost guide,
> Invested moorland waste, and naked pool,
> The beacon crowning the lone eminence,
> The female and her garments vexed and tossed
> By the strong wind.

The second incident, of identically the same quality, describes his ascent to a crag from which he could see two roads, along either of which he was feverishly and impatiently awaiting horses whereby he might return home.

>   'twas a day
> Tempestuous, dark, and wild, and on the grass
> I sate half-sheltered by a naked wall;
> Upon my right hand couched a single sheep,
> Upon my left a blasted hawthorn stood.

Some days afterwards his father died; the event at once carried back his imagination to

> The single sheep, and the one blasted tree,
> And the bleak music from that old stone wall.

And his imagination of the scene became for him a fountain whence he drank. Wordsworth clearly attaches an enormous importance to these two incidents; and to his recollection of them at this period of his life. Recalled from a time when his imagination was strong and growing, they had a peculiar significance for him now. They contained, he came to see, a dissolvent of his present condition, a 'renovating virtue'. They had left 'power behind', and

>   feeling comes in aid
> Of feeling, and diversity of strength
> Attends us, if but once we have been strong.

'If but once we have been strong.' Wordsworth recalled that not once, but twice, he had been strong, and had found imaginative vision in which strong feelings of revulsion and pain had been absorbed or had purgation. What, then, was the secret of the power of these incidents upon his troubled mind?

In the second incident, the scene came to have 'visionary dreariness' only after his father's death; his response to it while waiting for the horses was negligible—he was merely impatient to be gone. It became, in all truth, an object to his imagination only after sorrow had come. In the first, the desolate scenery had stirred him as he fled in terror from the thought of the hanged murderer. In both cases the scene was bare, wild, swept with wind and mist, untouched by gentleness or softness of colour; in both were features marked by a curious stillness; in the one, the naked pool, the beacon, the girl bearing a pitcher on her head; in the other, the sheep, the tree, the stone wall—all set around with tempest and vast expanse. It is this which, in each case, held his imagination, reconciled peace with tempest, calm with emotion, an 'emblem of eternity', an overwhelming sense of 'something ever more about to be'. It is no wonder that in the revulsion and numbness of mind at the time he recalled this experience—

> I should need
> Colours and words that are unknown to man
> To paint the visionary dreariness.

Here, we may be sure, more than even the ministrations of Coleridge and Dorothy, were places of power which on revealing themselves in the 'recesses of his nature', renewed his imagination. He knew then that he was no further changed

> Than as a clouded and a waning moon.

His past had reappeared to succour him. And from this time on his imagination, in all its variety of activity, centred around, as its highest objects of contemplation, images of a like type, men and women who knew the extreme of desolation and suffering, creatures of curious impassivity, who in the midst of

'dreariness' seem to be almost terrifying intimations of 'otherness'. In speaking of the restoration of his imaginative life he
made special mention of the two incidents which we have
quoted, incidents dating back to early years; but it is to be
noticed that in the poem are recounted two other incidents, of
a like kind, incidents which no doubt had been brought back
vividly to his mind when he had realized the significance of the
incidents relating to the gibbet and his father's death. They
are to be found in Book IV and Book VII. That in Book IV
describes a soldier whom he met on a road, in moonlight—

> He was alone,
> Had no attendant, neither Dog nor Staff,
> Nor knapsack; in his very dress appear'd
> A desolation, a simplicity
> That seem'd akin to solitude. Long time
> Did I peruse him with a mingled sense
> Of fear and sorrow. From his lips meanwhile
> There issued murmuring sounds, as if of pain
> Or of uneasy thought; yet still his form
> Kept the same steadiness; and at his feet
> His shadow lay, and mov'd not.[1]

Here, again, is desolation, and again a terrifying acquiescence:

> and when, erelong,
> I ask'd his history, he in reply
> Was neither slow nor eager; but unmov'd
> And with a quiet, uncomplaining voice,
> A stately air of mild indifference,
> He told, in simple words, a Soldier's tale. . . .

and throughout the telling of his story there was in all he said

> a strange half-absence, and a tone
> Of weakness and indifference, as of one
> Remembering the importance of his theme,
> But feeling it no longer.

[1] This and the three following quotations are taken from the 1805
version of *The Prelude*.

In the seventh book Wordsworth describes a beggar whom he saw in London, on his chest a label telling who the man was and his story—

> My mind did at this spectacle turn round
> As with the might of waters, and it seem'd
> To me that in this label was a type,
> Or emblem, of the utmost that we know
> Both of ourselves and of the universe;
> And on the shape of the unmoving man,
> His fixed face and sightless eyes, I look'd
> As if admonished from another world.

So it is with the Leech Gatherer 'from some far region spent'; in all alike is the extremity of suffering and desolation coupled with composure, unmoving and awful.

There can be no doubt that it was in the contemplation of such scenes and personages as this that Wordsworth's imagination reached its highest limit. He could never, to reiterate Keats, have seen these scenes and these men as he describes them had he not "committed himself to the Extreme"; and certainly his ability to recall them from his past and to contemplate them mark the full restoration of his powers. It was not, indeed, that he effected such a restoration; his restoration was a gift to him from his early imagination which in its young strength had been able to encompass and grasp all that the scenes described in Book XII represented. In them sweet counsels between heart and head are re-established; a finality of desolation is incorporated into a supreme object of imaginative contemplation, reconciled with vision, and suggestive 'of unknown modes of being'. There is a sense in which, humanly speaking, such imaginative vision is final. It is the stage to which Keats' young Apollo had come when he cried—

> Names, deeds, grey legends, dire events, rebellious
> Majesties, sovran voices, agonies,
> Creations and destroyings, all at once
> Pour into the wide hollow of my brain
> And deify me.

In all these passages the greatest dreariness and dereliction is melted into the visionary, and lost in it; suffering, known in the extreme, is invested, more than aught else could be, with the sense of something 'ever more about to be', so that the soldier, telling the story of his life, spoke as one who, 'remembering the importance of his theme', yet felt it no longer.

Once Wordsworth had reached this phase in the growth of his imagination, it became true of him that knowing too well the importance of the story of human life and suffering, he felt it no longer. For over the abyss hung the world of vision. It was not that he became insensitive to the spectacle of human evil and pain, but that over it lay suspended the firmament of otherness. The overwhelming sense of the unknown, the unforeseen, which visited him when he had crossed the Alps, was now with him in his contemplation of the deepest suffering and apparent dereliction. And in the attainment to this sense in the face of pain and destitution lay the full restoration of his imaginative power. His imagination had now encompassed with the feeling of Infinity not only the world of nature, but the world of man. The importance of that world he could never indeed deny, or wish to deny; but he could 'feel it no longer' in the same degree. 'So still an image of tranquillity, so calm and still' could he now maintain in himself that

> —What we feel of sorrow and despair
> From ruin and from change, and all the grief
> The passing shows of Being leave behind,
> Appeared an idle dream.

In other words, Wordsworth had come to see the error which he had made in thinking that his early view of the life of imagination was bound up with a return of 'Saturnian rule'. Actually, as he came to see, in recollecting those early days, his experience had contained within itself the answer to the questions which in his time of crisis he asked and could not answer. And

L

indeed it was not that his early imaginative powers were inadequate to meeting that crisis; instead, he had allowed himself to become absorbed in a passionate social idealism to a degree which blinded him to the power and adequacy of his imagination to include in its synthesis the whole world of human suffering. He thought, overwhelmed by a disappointment accompanied by a sense of human evil greater than anything he had known before, that his life was destroyed, and all foundations for the future destroyed. But in reality, all that was necessary was the exploration in memory of his former days of imaginative vitality. 'The days gone by return upon me'; and those days proved 'hiding-places' of his power. It was not that his imagination had failed him, but that he had failed his imagination. Natural as it was that, when a very young man, he had abandoned himself to revolutionary ardour, yet it was the recollection of his imaginative experiences, above all those which were vitally associated with pain, terror, and sorrow, which saved him. Then he was able to see that his imagination, which in his younger days could invest dreariness with vision, might do so again. It was not that his revolutionary ardour had been misplaced or mistaken; no one, I think, would judge that it was. What had been misplaced was the effort, however unconsciously made, by his imagination, to circumvent the fact of evil and suffering—the refusal to see them as inevitable to human life. But the result of his revolutionary experiences was more than ever to thrust them before his eyes, even to the point of paralysing his powers. Then there was no escape; and he was delighted and surprised to find that in himself and 'days gone by' lay the power to encompass all the degradation of human life with his imagination. He was thus able to see the French Revolution as the 'weak functions of one busy day' set over against the 'slowly moving years of time, with their united force', the years of effort and suffering which even no return of 'Saturnian rule' could blot out for an imagination which in its contemplation of life seeks to maintain its integrity.

> Within the soul a faculty abides,
> That with interpositions, which would hide
> And darken, so can deal, that they become
> Contingencies of pomp; and serve to exalt
> Her native brightness.

What had come to him was an extension of the power of imagination which he had enjoyed in his youth. If he rejected that power for a while, the circumstances of that rejection proved but 'contingencies of pomp'. 'The sense of possible sublimity', which he had known in the presence of nature, to which he felt the soul aspires

> With faculties still growing, feeling still
> That whatsoever point they gain, they still
> Have something to pursue,

he now felt with, if possible, a still greater force, his mind 'swept, as with the might of waters', in the presence of what is, humanly, a total dereliction. The infinity of the soul's aspiration, so that however far it moves and grows there is always a 'something', the vast unknown dimly apprehended before it, became now the 'main theme of his song'; a 'something' so real that in comparison sorrow, despair, ruin, change, and grief are but 'the passing shows of Being', an 'idle dream'. The triumph of his imagination, or better, the restoration to him of imaginative power, was the apprehension, however dim, of 'Infinitude' as the necessary complement and completion not only of the beauty of nature, but of the extremity of suffering. Now that this realization, or this imaginative grasp of reality, had been made in his mind, it was natural and indeed inevitable that the dogmas of Christianity should increasingly appear to his mind as a consummate conveyance of all that he had learnt; and his increasing humility before Christianity is surely a mark not of the decay, as is so often rashly thought, of his imagination, but of the consummation of it. His gratification in realizing that all that he had learnt, by 'proof upon the pulses', in the loneliness of his imagination, 'in singleness of state', was embodied in the tradition of Christianity must indeed have been tempered with a sorrowful and healthy humiliation. He was, indeed, no longer

> Voyaging through strange seas of thought, *alone*;

he was no longer

> sounding on,
> Through words, a dim and perilous way;

he had found community. His greatest poetry is indeed the story and expression of his lonely voyaging. But if his imagination in those later days found adequacy and rest in forms of expression not his own, it is not for critics to assume, as they have been so quick to do, that his life degenerated at its source.[1]

5

Of the relation of poetry to religion we shall try to speak in a later chapter, and we shall have occasion to recur again to the effect upon his poetry of Wordsworth's Christianity. There is occasion, however, at this point to observe the attitude which, after the restoration of his mental health, Wordsworth adopted towards science, an attitude which showed that Wordsworth never arrived at a harmonized view of human experience. Holding the view of the imagination which I have tried to set out earlier in this essay, Wordsworth never tired of setting over against the direct creativity of the imagination

> that false secondary power
> By which we multiply distinctions, then
> Deem that our puny boundaries are things
> That we perceive and not that we have made.

[1] Some time after the above was written, a reference in an article on A. C. Bradley in *The Times Literary Supplement* (May 23, 1936), led me to read (what, to my shame, perhaps, I had not formerly read) Bradley's lecture on Wordsworth in *Oxford Lectures*. The reader who feels that in the above section I have over-emphasized one aspect of Wordsworth's imaginative life may be advised to read Bradley's remarkable lecture.

In the same passage, immediately preceding that in which he writes of the imagination in the earliest years of the mind, we find the following lines, in which Coleridge is addressed—

> to thee
> Science appears but what in truth she is,
> Not as our glory and our absolute boast,
> But as a succedaneum, and a prop
> To our infirmity.

It is difficult not to be puzzled by these lines, written by one who at a time of the greatest 'infirmity' sought a 'succedaneum' and a 'prop' in intellectual and scientific inquiry, and signally failed to find one. During that time he despaired, as we have noticed, of philosophy; science, by its very security 'from disturbances of space and time', might be an escape; but by its very irrelevance to his life, 'to human will and power', it could not conceivably help him. Whether, therefore, in the passage quoted he means by 'science' the discursive intelligence in all its operations, or physical science in a strict sense, it is difficult to see how he could write of it as a 'succedaneum' or 'prop'. For it was precisely as a succedaneum, something we fall back upon, a substitute source of power, that it had failed him. If his experience was an adequate guidance, it was neither our glory, absolute boast, succedaneum nor prop. Yet he continued to cleave to this sentimental view of science. In the fourth book of *The Excursion*, in other respects one of the very greatest pieces of Wordsworth's work, his attitude to intellectual inquiry is childish and condescending, mistaken in thought and false in feeling. Go, he says,

> demand
> Of Mighty Nature, if 'twas ever meant
> That we should pry far off yet be unraised;
> That we should pore, and dwindle as we pore,
> Viewing all objects unremittingly
> In disconnexion dead and spiritless . . .
> waging thus
> An impious warfare with the very life
> Of our own souls!

Certainly, if the exercise of the intelligence necessarily implied an atrophy of imaginative powers, one could understand such an outburst. But it is only a superficial view of the intellectual life which implies that this is so. Wordsworth writes in resentment of the life of intellectual inquiry. But why? Wordsworth should surely have seen that there is as urgent a practical and moral necessity to exercise the intelligence to the full extent of its powers as to exercise the powers of the imagination. And later, we find the following—

> Science then
> Shall be a precious visitant; and then,
> And only then, be worthy of her name:
> For then her heart shall kindle; her dull eye,
> Dull and inanimate, no more shall hang
> Chained to its object in brute slavery . . .

nor—

> Shall it forget that its most noble use,
> Its most illustrious province, must be found
> In furnishing clear guidance, a support
> Not treacherous, to the mind's *excursive* power.

This is the height of nonsense. Such a condescending attitude to science is merely silly; and condescendingly to justify science at all by holding that it can, if it behaves itself nicely, give evidence and support to the 'excursive power' is not only utterly mistaken but false to Wordsworth's own experience. It is monstrous to seek to justify science and philosophy by any other than intellectual values; it is still more monstrous that Wordsworth should thus ignore all that his experience had most clearly taught him. Had he reflected a little more he would have seen, what indeed he should have seen from his own experience, that science is simply irrelevant to the problems of life. Wordsworth no doubt was right to give pride of place to the imagination; but it is merely an insult to science patronizingly to offer it second place, and that on condition that it furnishes 'clear guidance' and 'a support not treacherous' to the creative imagination. The fact is that science can no more offer clear guidance or reliable support to the imagination than it can offer false guidance or doubtful support to the imagination; and there was a time in Wordsworth's life when he saw this, compelled on him as it was by the very anguish of his experience. And equally his enjoyment of mathematics should have saved him from such mistaken condescension to the intellectual life. The Arab of his Cambridge dream was concerned to save mathematics as well as poetry from the general deluge. And there was no reason why Wordsworth should not combine in his reflection both a knowledge of the essential irrelevance of science and mathematics to the problem of life, and a recognition of their worth and joys. This, however, he failed to do, however nearly we may judge, in reviewing his story, he came to succeeding. He was right in his perception that what knowledge science can give is 'secondary' and abstract. But he was not true enough to his own experience to conclude with a recognition of what is, from the point of view of the imaginative life, the unimportance of scientific knowledge.[1] Had he gone the whole length of this realization he would not have been tempted to such a pompous patronage of science nor sought from science 'aids and supports'. The imagination he tells us in the Preface to the *Lyrical Ballads* is, in contrast to the detachment of science, part and parcel of our life "as enjoying and suffering beings", the apprehension by personality, in action and emotion, of the world. "If the time should ever come", he goes on to say, "when what is now called science—shall be ready to put on, as it were, a form of flesh and blood, the Poet will lend his divine spirit to aid the transfiguration." This is, indeed, eloquent; but such a transfiguration is as undesirable as it is impossible, an absurd fiction created for an eloquent argument more passionate than

[1] That this is so is shown by the fact that the issue between a mechanistic and purposive view of the universe stands to-day precisely where it did when Socrates read the works of Anaxagoras. Similarly, despite a widespread illusion to the contrary, it is absurd to suggest that Freud's psychology has in the slightest degree affected the agelong conflict of freedom *versus* determinism.

careful. He says rightly that science must seek to view all objects unremittingly

> In disconnexion dull and spiritless;

but this 'deathly and bloodless' condition is for science a condition of its life; and to resent it, or wish it changed, is the merest peevishness. And equally foolish is it to expect science to offer 'props and stays'; for as Wordsworth himself recognized, science simply is not concerned with the values which are 'flesh and blood' to the life of personality. Though one hesitates to quarrel with a statement which has won such universal quotation and respect, it is nevertheless difficult to see how poetry is the 'breath and finer spirit of all knowledge', and how it is the 'impassioned expression which is in the countenance of all science'. At a later date Wordsworth was to deplore the viewing of things in 'disconnexion, dead and spiritless' and to urge that to do so is to "wage an impious warfare on the soul". The countenance of activity such as that would hardly bear the 'impassioned expression' which Wordsworth claims poetry to be. And Wordsworth cannot have it both ways. It is merely rhetoric to say that science is really a poetical affair. On the other hand, it is equally absurd to say, as Wordsworth says in *The Excursion*, that science is a kind of demoralizing 'prying'.

Wordsworth's mature view of human nature failed to embrace a clear comprehension of the relation of the imaginative to the intellectual life. But on the other hand, his perception of the relation of imagination to morality was clear and sure. Here at least he stood on sure ground. He grounded his moral sense in the contemplative life which gives release from immersion in action and emotion. And in *The Prelude*, at least (and he did not see fit to change it in the later version), it is the discipline of the contemplative life lived in intimacy with nature which he sets over against the formal discipline of religious observances as the condition of moral health. It is in the potency of 'a mere image of the sway' of solitude that the self which is the seat of true morality finds itself. The moral life, that is to say, flows naturally from the discipline of quietude. In such a discipline, he held, is the condition of a true morality, springing not from imposed precept, and proof therefore against 'shock of accident'. Such morality therefore cannot be sought for itself; it is a product of a life animated by

> The universal instinct of repose
> The longing for confirmed tranquillity

which is, indeed, the life of the imagination, craving peace

> Not as a refuge from distress or pain
> A breathing-time, vacation, or a truce
> But for its absolute self.

And in such a life the forms of nature, a world of life at peace, are the paramount and lasting influence. Sought for their own beauty, they give the imagination freedom from the urgency of will and emotion, creating thereby 'stability without regret or fear'.

CHAPTER VI

ADAM'S DREAM

The Imagination may be compared to Adam's dream,—
he awoke and found it truth. . . . Adam's dream will
do here. . . .
KEATS—*Letter to Benjamin Bailey*, Nov. 1817

I

THE frequent irritation which Wordsworth aroused
in Keats did not prevent Keats from judging *The Excursion*
to be one of the three finest things of the age—"I am convinced that there are three things to rejoice at in this Age—*The
Excursion*, your pictures, and Hazlitt's depth of taste", he
writes to Haydon. And there is no reason to believe other than
that, despite occasional annoyances and irritations, he felt
throughout his life a profound reverence for Wordsworth's
work. To-day, indeed, *The Excursion* is only rarely read; it is
the work of the later Wordsworth whose imaginative power
was, it is said, waning under the influence of more sober political
views, and still more, of Christianity. In addition, there is the
fact that for later generations it has become outshone by *The
Prelude*, in which the standard of poetry is no doubt consistently
higher. But it is nevertheless of enormous and striking interest
to read Keats' judgment on Wordsworth's later poem, the
most extensive embodiment of the mind of the later Wordsworth. And it is all the more interesting if we recall the story
of Wordsworth's judgment on the *Hymn to Pan*, that it was
a 'pretty piece of paganism'. It is difficult not to smile at the
picture of the youthful Keats modestly declaiming his poem
to the austere poet whom he admired so passionately, only to
receive so contemptuous a rebuke. The incident, indeed, called
forth one of Keats' sharp criticisms of Wordsworth, in a letter
to Reynolds. But it reveals sharply the contrast between the
two men, the younger of whom had sought the older as the
creator of one of the finest things of the age. And if Words-

worth severely patronized the *Hymn to Pan*, the poem had yet
been written by a very young man who was yet old enough
to rise to the heights of Wordsworth's argument in *The Excursion*, and to recognize its 'grandeur'. The rebuke, we feel, was
extremely unfair and regrettable; it was pathetic that Wordsworth should ever have thought of Keats as a 'pretty pagan'
who was without seriousness. Keats indeed had, from the days
of his earliest poetry, a seriousness which could match Wordsworth's, though he had (what saved him from the Words-
worthian solemnity) a capacity for mere enjoyment which
Wordsworth always and conspicuously lacked. And had
Wordsworth listened carefully to the *Hymn to Pan* he would
have detected in it something more than what he called pretty
paganism. No doubt Wordsworth had wearied of the luxurious
descriptiveness of the earlier stanzas; otherwise he could hardly
have failed to hear the last stanza of the hymn, a stanza which
brings Keats, to our minds, so near to Wordsworth, and which
is expressive of what was always at the centre of Keats' poetic
excitement and activity.

> Be still the unimaginable lodge
> For solitary thinkings; such as dodge
> Conception to the very bourne of heaven,
> Then leave the naked brain; be still the leaven,
> That spreading in this dull and clodded earth
> Gives it a touch ethereal—a new birth:
> Be still a symbol of immensity;
> A firmament reflected in a sea;
> An element filling the space between;
> An unknown—but no more.

This may indeed be paganism; but it is not pretty paganism;
it is very high and serious paganism. And it is kind to Wordsworth's memory to think that he failed to hear; that he maintained his interest long enough to hear of the Pan who is
pleased to tumble
> into Naiads' cells,
> And, being hidden, laugh at their out-peeping;
> Or to delight thee with fantastic leaping
> The while they pelt each other on the crown
> With silvery oak-apples.

then gave it up, and did not hear of the Pan who is the

> Dread opener of the mysterious doors
> Leading to universal knowledge.

Wordsworth, we must regret, like many critics after him, saw only what has always been called the luxurious sensuous imagination of Keats, and failed to become aware of the centre of Keats' imaginative life, in agitation about that to which the world of perception is but a mysterious door.

Keats' imagination was indeed of what Wordsworth called the contemplative kind; it sought to achieve the contemplation of the world from a point outside it, 'from the pillowy silkiness that rests full in the speculation of the stars'. And it was so from the start. From Keats' first published poem *I Stood Tip-toe Upon a Little Hill*, in which he recounts some of the 'lovely mythology of Greece' as embodying the sense of that which the imagination cannot encompass, we can see that this is so. Poetry, he represents, in the making of myth, as the pursuit of that which is beyond capture, as the aspiration for the possession of that which cannot be commanded. It is the love of Psyche, known and enjoyed only in darkness, for what is mysterious and undisclosed, and which can have fruition only in 'realms of wonderment' before Jove's throne; or it is the love of Narcissus, dying of an impossible passion; or it is the love of Endymion ('that sweetest of all songs') for her who 'brought him shapes from the invisible world', Endymion who 'sought to burst our mortal bars'; or it is the love of Pan for Syrinx, who was nought

> but a lovely sighing of the wind
> Along the reedy stream; a half-heard strain,
> Full of sweet desolation—balmy pain.

It is the sweet desolation and balmy pain of all these loves which had caught Keats' imagination; and, indeed, his poetry was to find its chief theme in the love which embraces these two different qualities, of sweetness and desolation. And when he came to make his first lengthy poem it was to one of these stories that he turned for a subject—the story of Endymion.

But in the last of the poems in his first volume he writes at greater length, and not through the symbolism of Greek mythology, of the 'height for which his spirit was contending'. Here he sets out his view of poetry; but he begins his poem with the praise of sleep, in which, he says, is gentleness, soothing, tranquillity, health, secrecy, serenity, vision. Yet what, he asks, is 'higher beyond thought' than sleep, that which having these qualities, with all of strangeness and beauty, is yet unimaginably greater? The following lines seek to set out the answer:

> No one who once the glorious sun has seen
> And all the clouds, and felt his bosom clean
> For his great Maker's presence, but must know
> What 'tis I mean, and feel his being glow:
> Therefore no insult will I give his spirit
> By telling what he sees from native merit.

We are reminded of the passage in *The Prelude* in which Wordsworth describes his experience after crossing the Alps. Keats has not, indeed, at his command the poetry with which Wordsworth could express what he felt, the sense of what Keats was to call 'the unimaginable lodge for solitary thinkings' and what Wordsworth called the sense of 'unknown modes of being'. But Wordsworth, when he wrote the sixth book of *The Prelude*, was writing in retrospect, a poet matured by practice and wide experience; Keats when writing *Sleep and Poetry* was a young man, only two years older than Wordsworth at the time of his visit to Switzerland, and eight years younger than was Wordsworth when he wrote *The Prelude*. But if Keats' poetry be weak and unpractised, it is sufficiently inspired for us to know the quality of the experience which he is seeking, however inadequately, to convey.

> What is it? And to what shall I compare it?
> It has a glory, and nought else can share it:
> The thought thereof is awful, sweet, and holy,
> Chasing away all worldliness and folly; . . .

> So that we look around with prying stare
> Perhaps to see shapes of light, aerial limning,
> And catch soft floatings from a faint heard hymning.

And it is at this point that he begins to speak of poetry. At once we see the evidence, as has frequently been said, of a conflict in Keats' mind between his exquisite sense of the luxurious and a more strenuous spiritual life—what he here calls the 'teazing' of his spirit. For if he begins by asking for

> some clear air,
> Smooth'd for intoxication by the breath
> Of flowering bays, that I may die a death
> Of luxury,

he has not reached the end of his paragraph before he writes of an 'awfuller shade' in which he would record on his tablets

> all that was permitted,
> All that was for our mortal senses fitted.
> Then the events of this wide world I'd seize
> Like a strong giant, and my spirit teaze,
> Till at its shoulders it should proudly see
> Wings to find out an immortality.

In these lines is the perpetual theme of Keats' greatest poetry —the violent contrast between what is human and what is immortal, and the achievement by the human of an immortality. The Psyche of *I Stood Tip-toe*, Endymion, and Apollo in *Hyperion* all embody this aspiration and its fulfilment, a fulfilment with which the narratives abruptly end. And here, in the volume of 1817, imagination of this metamorphosis is already at work in Keats' mind, the penetration into that which is for humanity an 'unimaginable lodge for solitary thinkings', an 'unknown but no more'. Then suddenly possessed by a sense of the passing of time, he asks for ten years in which to

> do the deed
> That my own soul has to itself decreed.

First, a period of luxurious enjoyment, and then, repeating the antithesis he has already stated, a period in which to 'teaze his spirit' with the contemplation of human life in its pain and struggle. This world he would 'seize as a strong giant'. And in the ensuing passage he represents this effort of the imagination to contemplate and encompass the world of human suffering as of divine origin, coming from and returning to the divine. The imagination is here a charioteer, first having converse with nature, and then contemplative of

> Shapes of delight, mystery, and fear,

passing through a 'dusky space' which we may probably take for a symbol of death:

> some, clear in youthful bloom,
> Go glad and smilingly athwart the gloom;
> Some looking back, and some with upward gaze.

The car returns 'into the light of heaven'. And Keats feels the fear that he may lose the imaginative power capable of such contemplation, and his soul be 'borne to nothingness'.

> But I will strive
> Against all doubtings and will keep alive
> The thought of that same chariot, and the strange
> Journey it went.

To make himself this journey, to learn what his charioteer learnt—

> O that I might know
> All that he writes with such a hurrying glow—

is the end and aim of poetry. But this end and aim has terror for him; he has no illusions concerning its 'widenesses and desperate turmoil'. He would unsay his vow always to keep alive the thought 'of that same chariot', yet knows it is impossible that he should do so.

What is striking in this poem is the clarity with which Keats envisages to himself the 'end and aim of poetry'; and so much that his later poetry was to express has here an expression, inadequate yet unmistakable. His main idea—'there ever rolls a vast idea before me, and I glean therefrom my liberty'—is already expressed, his sense of the achievement of immortality which must succeed the impassioned enjoyment of the beauty of the human world. Of such achievement he has no doubt—

> 'Tis clear
> As anything most true; as that the year
> Is made of the four seasons.

His reason, indeed, does not sort out

> the dark mysteries of human souls
> To clear conceiving.

But before his imagination is present, with an overwhelming power, the possibility of 'unknown modes of being', to be realized after the teasing of the spirit in the face of the world's sufferings. To convey the sense, however dim, of such a possibility is the end and aim of poetry. In doing so, he claims, it 'soothes the cares and lifts the thoughts of man'. For the goal of the imagination is not to be strong in itself, merely to find the resources whereby it may contemplate

> Darkness and worms, and shrouds and sepulchres.

Nor ought it to feed 'upon the burrs and thorns of life'. To do so may, indeed, show 'strength'. But mere strength is like a 'fallen angel' which has forgotten its high destiny, its 'being's heart and home'. And we may observe incidentally that if Keats was later to complain of Wordsworth 'having a design on us', he was not himself above saying that poetry must 'soothe the cares and lift the thoughts of man'.

2

As we have suggested, it is surprising that so young a poet, in his first volume of verse, should thus be certain of his purposes, and of the goal of poetry. We have not, in Keats' poetry, any more than in Wordsworth's, a 'chamber of maiden-thought', a period in which the 'burden of the mystery' was not present. Like Wordsworth and unlike Shakespeare, his poetry begins, with however strong a sense of the luxurious, with a still stronger sense of the reality of evil and suffering. His imaginative life was from the start overwhelmed with a sense of 'glorious fear'. This phrase, which he uses to describe the mental state of his charioteer as he begins his journey, is also descriptive of his own. Such a 'glorious fear' arose from two causes: the fear resulting from the feeling of oppression and dismay which must accompany the contemplation of human life in its squalor, suffering, and defeat; the glory from the possession of a vast idea, from which liberty is gleaned, and with which that suffering may be faced, an idea, moreover, of the adequacy of which he had no doubt—' 'tis clear as anything most true'. This confidence in the journey of the imagination is noteworthy; for Keats had, from the outset, a notion of his goal, and therefore a sense of 'glory' which Shakespeare in his tragic period lacked. In Shakespeare's tragedies we are aware of the imagination of the poet stumbling in darkness and uncertainty, on a voyage of the purest dis-covery and unaware of his goal, knowing the extremity of 'fear' without any dissolving sense of 'glory'; but we observe from the beginning of Keats' work the presence of an idea of the destination of the imaginative journey. And this idea he managed to 'keep alive' throughout his life of suffering; the mass of his poetry is the record of the journey which, following his charioteer, he made. Nor was it a mock journey. The bitterness of his own experience ensured that it should not be so; yet the journey was made under the inspiration of seeking to establish the idea which from the start was present to his imagination.

But though Keats says of his 'idea' that it is 'clear as any-thing most true', it is yet rooted in a sense of the mysterious and unknown.

> No great ministring reason sorts
> Out the dark mysteries of human souls
> To clear conceiving.

M

And, to quote again the passage from the *Hymn to Pan*,

> Be still the unimaginable lodge
> For solitary thinkings; such as dodge
> Conception to the very bourne of heaven,
> Then leave the naked brain; be still the leaven,
> That spreading in this dull and clodded earth
> Gives it a touch ethereal—a new birth:
> Be still a symbol of immensity;
> A firmament reflected in a sea;
> An element filling the space between;
> An unknown—but no more.

The relevance of this passage to the "vast idea" can scarcely be doubted, for Pan is described in the preceding stanza as the

> Dread opener of the mysterious doors
> Leading to universal knowledge—

an apostrophe more suited, we may think, for utterance by the poet than by the simple shepherd folk, and rather out of keeping with the sportive Pan who has been described in the previous stanzas. Here, without doubt, it is the voice of Keats which speaks, turning the shepherd's hymn to his own need for self-expression. And if we agree that this is so, the passage is of the greatest importance for our purpose.

We may notice the way in which Keats speaks of the intelligence. Pan, represented as the power who can give "universal knowledge", the realization in the full of Keats' "vast idea", is sought by human thought as its end and aim, yet eludes it. There is here, as in "the dark mysteries of human souls", no "clear conceiving". The aspiration to the knowledge of Pan mounts beyond the reach of conception; thought is "dodged", and finally left behind, the brain left naked. We recall "the dull brain perplexes and retards" of the *Nightingale* and the "dost teaze us out of thought as doth eternity" of the *Grecian Urn*. For these latter poems are, after all, expressive in different ways of what Keats is trying to express in this stanza. But here he is using no concrete symbol; he is rather seeking to make, so to speak, a negative expression of his theme. For it is notable that not only does Pan and the knowledge which Pan alone can afford elude conception, "clear conceiving"; Pan is also enjoined to remain

> the unimaginable lodge
> For solitary thinkings.

And in this Keats is at one with Wordsworth. In *The Excursion* Wordsworth wrote

> That 'tis a thing impossible to frame
> Conceptions equal to the soul's desires.

But also, that to which the mind aspires remains an "unknown mode of being"; or at best we have an "obscure sense of possible sublimity". And what Keats is emphasizing here is similarly the bafflement which the imagination knows in its pursuit of vision; it has but an obscure sense; the end to which the imagination labours, and the sense of which conditions its life, is yet unimaginable, cannot be encompassed by it as an object— "an unknown but no more". That this "obscure sense" of the imagination of that which is beyond its reach is yet the condition of our being more than "dull and clodded earth", Keats goes on to say in the next few lines; it is the condition of our being more than earthly, of our having a "touch ethereal—a new birth". Pan is a 'firmament' (a favourite symbol of Wordsworth's, it may be remembered), an 'immensity', that which we cannot encircle with our mind; yet he is also an 'element filling the space between' the 'firmament' and 'immensity' of his life and our mind, bridging a gap which uncrossed would leave us 'dull and clodded earth'; but which, if crossed, leavens the imagination with an aspiration and a hunger which yet can ask of Pan "Be still an unknown—but no more". At work in Keats' mind is a sense of a necessary limit to the imagination; there is at once the demand of the imagination for what is beyond the world, and a sense of imaginative frustration, a frustration which, however, is necessary, and must be accepted. "I know no one but you," he writes to Haydon in May 1817, "who can be fully sensible of the turmoil and anxiety, the sacrifice of all that is called comfort, the readiness to measure time by what is done and to die in six hours could plans be brought to conclusions—the looking upon the Sun, the Moon, the Stars, the Earth and its contents, as materials to form greater things—that is to say ethereal things—but here I am talking like a Madman,—greater things than our Creator himself made!"

3

Endymion, too, talks 'like a madman', as had also for that matter the Shepherds in their Hymn. Endymion is a 'contemplative sort of person', Keats writes in a letter; and the first book in the poem shows him in contemplation. The long conversation which Endymion has with his sister (of which Keats said that the 'whole thing', though it might appear to some as a thing 'almost of mere words', was to him as he wrote it 'a regular stepping stone of the imagination towards a truth'), shows the subject and manner of his contemplation, and with the *Hymn to Pan* contains the core of the poem.

> Brother, 'tis vain to hide
> That thou dost know of things mysterious,
> Immortal, starry,

says Peona. And in reply Endymion tells his dream, such a dream

> That never tongue, although it overteem
> With mellow utterance, like a cavern spring,
> Could figure out and to conception bring
> All I beheld and felt.

Then follows the description of Cynthia—

> with such a paradise of lips and eyes,
> Blush-tinted cheeks, half smiles, and faintest sighs,
> That, when I think thereon, my spirit clings
> And plays about its fancy, till the stings
> Of human neighbourhood envenom all.

Here, as in the earlier poem, we have the conjunction of sleep and poetry, with the vision emerging from a dream within a dream. And Endymion goes on to explicit statement—

> Wherein lies happiness? In that which becks
> Our ready minds to fellowship divine,
> A fellowship with essence; till we shine
> Full alchemiz'd, and free of space. Behold
> The clear religion of heaven!

This, he says, is the highest destiny we may know. First, indeed, is the happiness coming from the enjoyment of the world's beauty, the coolness of a rose leaf to the lips, and the music of the winds—

> Feel we these things?—that moment have we stept
> Into a sort of oneness, and our state
> Is like a floating spirit's.

But higher than the delicious life of the senses are richer entanglements, enthralments far more self-destroying—love and friendship. In these is a still richer and higher unity known—

> Nor with ought else can our souls interknit
> So wingedly.

And men who might have towered in 'the van of all the congregated world'

> Have been content to let occasions die,
> Whilst they did sleep in love's elysium.

Such an arrest of the life of action by human love does not seem wrong to Endymion; such love has the same justification as the 'bloom of flowers or the bright mail of fish'—it is a 'thing of beauty'. But if this be so, how much more justified is he in relinquishing all 'poor endeavour after fame', who keeps 'within his steadfast aim a love immortal'. Upon this 'love immortal' his life depends—

> My restless spirit never could endure
> To brood so long upon one luxury,

> Unless it did, though fearfully, espy
> A hope beyond the shadow of a dream.

"My having written that argument will perhaps be of the greatest service to me of anything I ever did." Keats knew after the writing of it, not indeed with the force of an entirely new discovery but as a confirmation of all his previous thought, that his 'restless spirit' could not endure except in the pursuit of what was not a mere perfection of luxury, but rather a ground for a 'hope beyond the shadow of a dream'. And when, in the same letter to Taylor, he said that the writing of the dialogue 'set before me the gradations of happiness' it is natural to recall—"He should begin by loving earthly things for the sake of that absolute loveliness, ascending, as it were, by degrees or steps"; for the Gods, says Endymion, keep

> Mercifully, a little strength of heart
> Unkill'd in us by raving, pang or smart;
> And do preserve it like a lilly root,
> That, in another spring, it may outshoot
> From its wintry prison.[1]

All this is repeated, in the finest poetry, in the long speech in the second book. And we especially notice the lines in which the imagination, now envisaged as an army, undertakes the siege and capture of 'cities', the last of which is human life—

> and then he foams,
> And onward to another city speeds.
> But this is human life: the war, the deeds,
> The disappointment, the anxiety,
> Imagination's struggles, far and nigh,
> All human; bearing in themselves this good,
> To make us feel existence, and to show
> How quiet death is.

Here human life, lit up by the imagination, is represented as at once giving us a vigorous sense of 'existence', and a know-

[1] From a rejected passage. See Gowans and Gray edition, Vol. 1, p. 100.

ledge of the 'quietness' of death. Again and again Keats brings together in his poetry the greatest intensity of life and the 'quietness of death'.

It is not to our present purpose to recount in detail the story of the poem. The remaining books are filled, but for certain irrelevant episodes such as that of Venus and Adonis, with the story of the preparation of the soul of Endymion for translation to the life of a God, a story enlivened by occasional visits from the Goddess. The value of attempting to find spiritual significances in all the detail of the story is doubtful. But its main purpose is clear, and shown forth in the course of the poem:

> 'twas fit that from this mortal state
> Thou shouldst, my love, by some unlook'd for change
> Be spiritualized,

says the Goddess, and abruptly Endymion is carried away, a God, his 'immortality' won. It is won after his rejection of the world, and a failure of hope—

> I did wed
> Myself to things of light from infancy;
> And thus to be cast out, thus lorn to die
> Is sure enough to make a mortal man
> Grow impious.

Then, after such a dereliction, the Goddess declares herself; and the 'stings of human neighbourhood' are finally destroyed.

4

Endymion may therefore be viewed as an explication or development of what had been more vaguely present to Keats' mind in the writing of *Sleep and Poetry*. "How much toil!" he wrote there, of his "vast idea"—

> How many days! what desperate turmoil!
> Ere I can have explored its widenesses.

Desperate turmoil and the exploration of some of its wideness
is to be found in *Endymion*. It is wrong to regard *Endymion*, as
is frequently done, as the product of a 'luxurious' and 'sensuous'
imagination; all the rich and lavish description in the poem
gathers around a central agitation of the imagination about
something other than "all that was for our human senses
fitted". And though, in *Sleep and Poetry*, he had anticipation of
the creative pain his poetry must undergo, in *Endymion* he
underwent that pain to an incomparably greater degree, and
forced his imagination to a fuller contemplation of it. This
was not easy. "He is the only man", he writes to Bailey, "who
has kept watch on man's mortality, who has philanthropy
enough to overcome the disposition to an indolent enjoyment
of intellect, who is brave enough to volunteer for uncomfortable
hours." And *Endymion*, so far from being a riotous indulgence
of pleasurable imaginative activity, is the product of many
"uncomfortable hours", or as Keats would say, "a search for
truth". And it was not only that in Endymion's speech he wrote
'stepping-stones to truth', and thereby clarified his imaginative
idea; it was also that, as the book proceeded, he explored in
detail the bitterness and suffering which the advance, in actual
living, towards that idea must involve, 'the thought, the deadly
feel of solitude', the sense of desertion, of loss of both ideal
and reality, the extremity of dereliction which has cast off the
world in an ecstasy but which has lost all sense of another.
Indeed, so far from seeing Keats' poem as an indulgence of
sensuousness, the poem is more truly seen as a shedding of
it, as a testimony to his transcendence of it, as a sense of his
loss of it—

> A homeward fever parches up my tongue—
> O let me slake it at the running springs! . . .
> O let me hear once more the linnet's note!
> Before mine eyes thick films and shadows float . . .
> If in soft slumber thou dost hear my voice,
> O think how I should love a bed of flowers!
> Young Goddess! let me see my native bowers!
> Deliver me from this rapacious deep!

Endymion springs, not from a passion for sensuous beauty, but from an aspiration towards what the sensuous can at best vaguely suggest.

"You tell me", he says in a letter to Haydon, "never to despair—I wish it was as easy for me to observe the saying— truth is, I have a horrid Morbidity of Temperament which can show itself at intervals—it is, I have no doubt, the greatest Enemy and stumbling-block I have to fear—I may even say that it is likely to be the cause of my disappointment. However every ill has its share of good—this very bane would at any time enable me to look with an obstinate eye on the Devil himself—aye to be as proud of being the lowest of the human race as Alfred could be in being of the highest. I feel confident I should have been a rebel angel had the opportunity been mine."

Yet, for that matter, there was nothing to stop him being a rebel, and giving his mind over to hate, even though he had had no 'opportunity' of being a rebel angel. Indeed, his letters give us reason to believe that such hate, such a corruption of his spirit, did frequently and intensely lay hold upon his mind. The above quotation shows that this was so. The Hamlet mood was often his, if we may judge from this letter. Yet only a few lines later he is 'talking like a madman' seeing the sun, the moon, the stars, the earth, and its contents as 'materials to form greater things—ethereal things'. And his Endymion has both these elements in his experience. The 'impiety' which tempted him he seeks to overcome, with an unbreaking endurance, by persistency in his 'madness'. "I must think that difficulties nerve the spirit of a man—they make our Prime Objects a Refuge as well as a passion." So that, as we remarked earlier, if Keats, unlike Shakespeare and like Words- worth, never knew during his poetic life a period of 'maiden thought', yet, unlike both Wordsworth and Shakespeare, he never knew a period in his life that was wholly given over to despair and revulsion. He might, indeed he did, know short seasons of despair—"I could be as proud of being the lowest

of the human race as Alfred could be in being of the highest."
Yet such seasons were intermittent and of short duration in a
life which as a whole was dedicated to 'keeping alive the thought
of that same chariot'. His 'vast idea' steeled him for difficulties,
saving him from such crisis as is shown in *Troilus and Cressida*,
and such as Wordsworth recounts in *The Prelude*. "Why don't
you, as I do, look unconcerned at what may be called more
particularly Heart-vexations? They never surprise me—lord!
a man should have the fine point of his soul taken off to become
fit for this world." And again, "the first thing that strikes me
on hearing a misfortune having befallen another is this—well,
it cannot be helped; he will have the pleasure of trying the
resources of his spirit".

5

As we might expect, Keats never believed in the
possibility of mankind achieving perfect happiness. We should
expect this from our reading of Endymion's speech in the
first book.

> Wherein lies happiness? In that which becks
> Our ready minds to fellowship divine,
> A fellowship with essence; till we shine
> Full alchemiz'd, and free of space.

The word 'essence' here is striking and unusually abstract
for Keats; it gives the passage a Platonic ring. We can only take
it in its meaning of 'spiritual existence', into the knowledge
of which, 'full alchemiz'd' and 'free of space', we escape from
'harsh mortality's dull net'. It is not in human life but in a
transformation from the human that the hope of happiness lies;
Keats clearly envisaged humanity as caught in a 'net' and a
'prison', from which a deliverance is necessary. It is the sense
of a world which is not human which was central in Keats'
imagination. And in that attitude death is seen as the necessity
which conditions life. The best that humanity can know is

'sweet desolation', 'balmy pain', the pain which is part of its
aspiration towards what is yet beyond its reach. "You perhaps
thought at one time there was such a thing as worldly happiness
to be arrived at, at certain periods of time marked out. . . . I
scarcely remember counting upon any happiness—I look not
for it if it be not in the present hour." And in a famous letter
written in April 1819 he develops his argument further, and
bluntly denies that human life was cradled in a state of perfection and happiness, or is destined to arrive at such perfection in the future. 'Mischances', 'hardships', and 'dis-
quietudes' are man's necessary lot; and even if happiness could
be 'carried to an extreme', "what must it end in?—Death—and
who in such a case could bear with death? The whole troubles
of life which are now frittered away in a series of years, would
then be accumulated for the last days of a being who instead
of hailing its approach would leave this world as Eve left
Paradise". "If", he says again, man "improves by degrees his
bodily accommodations and comforts—at each stage, at each
ascent there are waiting for him a fresh set of annoyances—he
is mortal, and there is still a heaven with its stars above his
head." Keats, indeed, never needed to suffer the disillusion
about 'Primeval Nature's child' which was necessary for
Wordsworth. The Solitary, in his journey into the west of
America, hoping to find primitive man

> Free as the sun, and lonely as the sun,
> Pouring above his head its radiance down
> Upon a living, and rejoicing world!

dismally realized that that 'pure archetype' of human greatness was not to be found. He found instead what Keats calls
a 'poor forked creature'. Wordsworth had to be bereft of his
dream of human happiness; Keats never indulged such a dream.
He never indulged it because he saw that in the face of death
the hope of happiness is a sentimental dream; if the approach
of death cannot be 'hailed', it is a misery that cancels out all
of happiness the world might give. It is for this reason that the

pleasures of the senses and the enjoyment of human love could not satisfy Endymion; though human love have the justification of a lovely flower, and bless

> The world with benefits unknowingly;
> As does the nightingale, upperched high
> And cloister'd among cool and bunched leaves;

yet it cannot avoid the annoyances of the world and above all the annoyance of death. "The point at which Man may arrive is as far as the parallel state in inanimate nature and no further. For suppose a rose to have sensation, it blooms on a beautiful morning, it enjoys itself, but then comes a cold wind, a hot sun—it cannot escape it, it cannot destroy its annoyances—they are as native to the world as itself—no more can man be happy in spite, the worldly elements will prey upon his nature."

In the letter in which he speaks of misfortune affording the pleasure of 'trying the resources of the spirit', written when he was engaged upon the last book of *Endymion* (November 1817), there is a long passage in which Keats writes of the nature of the imagination which we may appropriately notice here.

I am certain of nothing but the holiness of the heart's affections, and the truth of imagination. What the imagination seizes as Beauty must be Truth—whether it existed before or not,—for I have the same idea of all our passions as of love; they are all, in their sublime, creative of essential Beauty. . . . The Imagination may be compared to Adam's dream,—he awoke and found it truth; I am more zealous in this affair because I have never yet been able to perceive how anything can be known for truth by consecutive reasoning—and yet it must be. Can it be that even the greatest philosopher ever arrived at his goal without putting aside numerous objections? However it may be, O for a life of Sensations rather than of Thoughts! It is a 'Vision in the form of Youth', a shadow of reality to come—and this consideration has further convinced me . . . that we shall enjoy ourselves hereafter by having what we call happiness on Earth repeated in a finer tone. . . . Adam's dream will do here, and seems to be a conviction that Imagination and its empyreal reflexion is the same as human life and its spiritual repetition.

It is to be noted in the first place that Adam's dream is similar to Endymion's. Here is the passage in *Paradise Lost* which recounts Adam's dream—

> Mine eyes he closed, but open left the cell
> Of fancy, my internal sight; by which
> Abstract as in a trance, methought I saw,
> Though sleeping, where I lay, and saw the Shape
> Still glorious before whom awake I stood. . . .
> Under his forming hands a creature grew,
> Man-like, but different sex, so lovely fair
> That what seemed fair in all the world seemed now
> Mean, or in her summed up. . . .
> She disappeared, and left me dark; I waked
> To find her, or for ever to deplore
> Her loss, and other pleasures all abjure:
> When, out of hope, behold her not far off,
> Such as I saw her in my dream. . . .

The parallel to the narrative in *Endymion* is clear; for after Endymion has narrated his dream, and Peona has sought to bring him back to a sense of reality—

> how light
> Must dreams themselves be; seeing they're more slight
> Than the mere nothing that engenders them!—

he goes on to relate how in his waking life he met the Goddess, and knew that his dream had yielded him 'truth'. Adam's words,

> She disappeared, and left me dark; I waked
> To find her, or for ever to deplore
> Her loss, and other pleasures all abjure—

apply as well to Endymion as to Adam. Imagination, then, is likened to a dream, a dream of a transcendent 'essence'; and that this dream is not merely dream or illusion, is the 'conviction' upon which Keats depends.

The 'imagination' of which Keats is here writing is not the imaginative enjoyment of earth, which gives a luxurious acuteness to the senses, and invests all things with remote and

romantic suggestiveness and association. This is the first
'gradation' of happiness which Endymion spoke of—

>   Fold
>   A rose leaf round thy finger's taperness
>   And soothe thy lips,

and

>   Bronze clarions awake, and faintly bruit,
>   Where long ago a giant battle was.

Nor is it the imaginative life which springs from love, the
influence of which

>   Thrown in our eyes, genders a novel sense,
>   At which we start and fret.

It is the imagination which craves an unconditioned reality in
the knowledge of which alone fulfilment and the last 'gradation
of happiness' may be achieved. In choosing what he calls
'sensations' rather than thoughts, he says of the object of
imagination that it is a 'shadow of reality to come'. 'Adam's
dream will do here'; the conditions of human life make it
indeed but a dream. And Keats' thought appears to be that
we must 'awake' before we know it to be 'true'. Whatever
'conviction' we may have is not, when all is said, a belief
which we can know, once and for all, to be true. All we have
is the demand of the imagination for an unconditioned and
ideal Beauty, a demand and a dream which the imagination
cannot relinquish. It is not that the imagination can help itself,
or merely choose to dream, or not to dream. The 'dream' is
inevitable to the imagination and cannot be shaken off.

'I am more zealous in this affair, because I have never
yet been able to perceive how anything can be known for
truth by consecutive reasoning.' Keats thus looks for no
support from philosophy and science. He cannot see how
they can help to make the dream known 'for truth'. If the
imagination can afford itself no certainty of knowledge, neither
can philosophy supply it. The imagination is left, and left
alone, with its dream, a dream which it cannot know for

'truth'. Such is the human lot, and here is the burden of the mystery. The imagination can but have faith or hope that it will 'awake' and find that dream 'true'. But again, such a faith, or hope, or conviction is not an adoption of the will; it is not a chosen basis for pragmatic and experimental living. For just so long as Endymion's dream cannot be known for truth, no more can it be known for falsity. It must therefore command the imagination and suffer it no release. There is nothing to do but wait for the 'awakening'. We can only say, as Keats said, 'it must be truth'; but the 'must' is the 'must' of a 'glorious fear' which must know the utmost of despair as well as of hope.

The title of Keats' poem *Sleep and Poetry* was no whim or accident. Throughout his poetry sleep and imagination are in close conjunction. The imagination strives to its highest reaches when we 'are laid asleep in body', and forgetful of the known, seek the unknown in dream. We may awake back into humanity, and then the 'thoughts of self' come on,

> how crude and sore
> The journey homeward to habitual self!
> A mad pursuing of the fog-born elf,
> Whose flitting lantern, through rude nettle-briar,
> Cheats us into a swamp, into a fire,
> Into the bosom of a hated thing.[1]

What Keats' poetry labours to suggest is an awakening, not backwards into humanity, but forward into something that is not human at all.

6

There has been a good deal of discussion concerning Keats' identification, in the *Ode on a Grecian Urn*, of beauty and truth. No doubt so bald an identification is meaningless,

---

[1] This theme of course recurs in the *Nightingale*—
> Forlorn! the very word is like a bell
> To toll me back from thee to my sole self!
> Was it a vision, or a waking dream?
> Fled is that music;—Do I wake or sleep?

certainly too crude an expression for the purposes of his poem. But it is doubtful, if we may judge by the letter from which we have quoted, if what Keats had in mind was what Mr. A. C. Bradley has suggested in his well-known essay.[1] "The central article of the faith of Keats", writes Mr. Bradley, "is given in the words Beauty is Truth, Truth Beauty. These two are reached, apprehended, and expressed in different ways; beauty in or through sense and imagination, truth in or by thought, 'knowledge', or 'philosophy'. But the two are none the less one and the same; so that whatever is felt, perceived, imagined as beautiful would, if adequately expressed in intellectual form, be found in reality truly conceived; and truth, adequately transformed into the shape of 'sensation' or imagination, would have turned into beauty." Even this, it is to be noted, does not save the face of Keats' identification, for, after all, it would not be truth that would be beautiful, but the world truly conceived. But apart from this, it is more satisfactory to think that the clear explication of the saying is in the statement—'The imagination may be compared to Adam's dream—he awoke and found it truth'. (We may notice that he says 'found it truth', not, as we might expect, 'found it true'.) Is it likely, therefore, that in saying that Beauty is Truth, Keats is doing other than repeating, in more enigmatical form, what his remark about Adam's dream clearly conveys? —than saying that the dream of a transcendent object which commands the imagination is not an illusion? Surely this is the obvious interpretation to be derived from the letter. The dream, when Adam wakes, is found to be '*truth*'; and the puzzle as to what Keats really meant has occurred because of his curious preference for the noun rather than for the adjective. The 'truth' for Keats was that 'essential beauty' which he calls the 'prototype' of all lovely things. Hence, when he says in his poem that Beauty is Truth he is not, I think, attempting to express anything so abstract as Mr. Bradley suggested. He is merely expressing his faith that

[1] *Keats and Philosophy* in *A Miscellany*.

'Adam's dream' is a manifestation, however obscure, of the highest reality. But to call it a faith is to say no more than that this ultimate hunger of the imagination can neither be satisfied nor eradicated.

This is so because, as we have said, the imagination is unable to satisfy itself as to the reality of its supreme object. The 'dream' may indeed be only a dream. Nor can philosophy, Keats thought, decide the issue for us. He was never able to see how anything could be known for truth by consecutive reasoning. (When he says 'anything' we may presume he means metaphysical doctrine; he clearly cannot be thinking of abstract inquiries.) 'Can it be that even the greatest philosopher ever arrived at his goal without putting aside numerous objections?' Wordsworth, it will be remembered, 'yielded up' philosophy 'in despair'. Keats never did so for the reason that he never placed reliance on philosophy. There is no reason to believe that, at this time at least, Keats had read philosophy; he simply felt, without any philosophical knowledge, that metaphysics is never a merely intellectual affair, but is actuated, by factors other than intellectual, to choose reasons rather than be controlled purely by reasons. He could not see, he says, that it could be otherwise. Yet he also felt that he must be wrong, for immediately after saying that nothing can be known for truth by consecutive reasoning, he at once says 'and yet it must be'. He clearly felt a hesitation in thus rejecting the power of the intellect to know truth. But his own preference is for the life of imagination; and his confidence in the imagination never failed to such a degree as to compel him, as in Wordsworth's case, to philosophical inquiry. Yet we may believe that Keats felt a strong urge towards philosophical study. For one thing, it would have been of enormous interest to him to submit his failure to perceive that consecutive reasoning could arrive at truth to the test of severe thought. Yet, although in one letter he told Reynolds that he would ask Hazlitt the 'best metaphysical road to take' we have no reason to believe that he read philosophical works with application.

N

It is worthy of notice at this point that Keats frequently used the word 'philosophy' to mean the maintenance of a disciplined life whereby the activity of the imagination might be facilitated even in the face of bitter experience. Using the word in this sense, it is set over against the sense of the luxurious, and means the 'teazing of the spirit' of which he spoke in his first volume of poems; and it was with this sense of the word in mind that he quoted, "How charming is divine philosophy", and that he wrote in one of his anguished letters to Fanny "I must make myself as good a philosopher as possible". Thus philosophy became for him not a body of doctrine, but simply humility towards the 'Eternal Being, the Principle of Beauty, and the memory of great men'; not an acceptance of opinion but a way of living. Yet it was, as Keats knew very well, a way of living which is surrounded by darkness, or at best by the light of a 'dream'. For if nothing can be known 'for truth', the imagination can but follow its deepest impulse. Hence, though this be wisdom, it is also sorrow. "As Byron says, 'knowledge is sorrow'; and I go on to say that 'sorrow is wisdom', and further for all that we can know for certainty, 'wisdom is folly'." 'Philosophy' comes more and more to be the passionate quest for certainty, for 'knowing for truth', though not by intellectual inquiry; and he even sets it over against poetry "which is not so fine a thing as a philosophy—for the same reason that an eagle is not so fine a thing as a truth". By poetry here he seems to mean the detached contemplative attitude of the imagination in so far as it is content to see 'fineness' in the things and events of the world, and is not led to a strong sense of what is beyond them. Similarly, by philosophy here he seems to mean the reaching of the imagination to the unknown, and the hunger to 'know for certainty'. The sonnet 'Why did I laugh to-night?' is the expression of this hunger—

No God, no Demon of severe response,
Deigns to reply from Heaven or from Hell.

The sonnet, Keats says in a letter, "was written with no agony but that of ignorance; with no thirst of anything but knowledge".

7

There is a very interesting passage in Keats' notes on Milton in which he writes—

The Genius of Milton . . . calculated him . . . for such an 'argument' as *Paradise Lost*; he had an exquisite passion for what is properly, in the sense of ease and pleasure, poetical Luxury; and with that it appears to me he would fain have been content, if he could, so doing, have preserved his self-respect and feel of duty performed; but there was working in him as it were that same sort of thing as operates in the great world to the end of a Prophecy's being accomplish'd: therefore he devoted himself rather to the ardours than the pleasures of song, solacing himself at intervals with cups of old wine; and those are with some exceptions the finest parts of the poem. With some exceptions—for the spirit of mounting and adventure can never be unfruitful or unrewarded: had he not broken through the clouds which envelope so deliciously the Elysian field of verse, and committed himself to the Extreme, we should never have seen Satan described as

> But his face
> Deep scars of thunder had entrenched . . .

This is throughout as perfect a comment upon Keats' own work as upon Milton's. Indeed, Keats must have known this when he wrote the passage—it reflects so much that we find in his letters. And Keats, too, 'solaced himself with cups of old wine'. There is hardly a poem in which such solaces do not occur; of *Isabella* and *The Eve of St. Agnes* we may say that as entire poems they are 'solaces'. We might be tempted to say the same of *Lamia*, only that there are some aspects of the poem that give us pause. For example, we find in it a view of philosophy which occurs nowhere else in Keats' work. In the letters, as we have seen, he writes of metaphysics with the greatest respect, even if he fails to see that it can give truth, and suggests that his failure is due to weakness in himself. But in *Lamia* he does what Wordsworth was too fond of doing, and views intellectual inquiry as a form of degenerate "prying", destructive of beauty.

> Do not all charms fly
> At the mere touch of cold philosophy?
> There was an awful rainbow once in heaven:
> We know her woof, her texture; she is given
> In the dull catalogue of common things.
> Philosophy will clip an angel's wings,
> Conquer all mysteries by rule and line. . . .

We might think, or at least hope, that in writing this Keats was not serious; only that a note which Mr. Buxton Forman appends gives ground for thinking this is not so. And, indeed, the point of the poem is an opposition between Beauty and Thought in which Thought is represented as a destroying agency. And, if we believe that Keats in *Lamia* is serious, this is foolish and regrettable, and not in consonance with the sanity of Keats' general attitude. Indeed, it is difficult not to feel, in the reading of the poem, that fine as it is in many respects, as a whole it suffers from uncertainty of intention. And in this respect at least it is inferior to *Endymion*, the central idea of which is clear, even if, in the working out of some aspects of it, it is obscure. In *Lamia*, on the other hand, the poetry throughout is clear and sharp, the central idea obscure, if indeed there is one at all. But to return to what Keats says of philosophy and science in *Lamia*, we may contrast with so sentimental and thoughtless a view a passage in the letters where he writes

> Were I to study physic . . . again, I feel it would not make the least difference in my Poetry; when the mind is in its infancy a Bias is in reality a Bias, but when we have acquired more strength, a Bias becomes no Bias. Every department of Knowledge we see excellent and calculated towards a great whole. . . .

Again, *Lamia* is reminiscent of *Endymion* in certain respects. When Lamia first appears to Lycius lost in fantasy

> where reason fades
> In the calm'd twilight of Platonic shades,

she appears to him as a goddess whom to lose is to die. We have here the dream of Adam once more. Further, Lamia represents herself as a goddess to Lycius—

> Thou canst not ask me with thee here to roam
> Over these hills and vales, where no joy is,—
> Empty of immortality and bliss! . . .
>   . . . Alas! poor youth,
> What taste of purer air hast thou to soothe
> My essence?

So far we have the *Endymion* situation. But there is an important difference. In reality Lamia is not divine—

> I was a woman, let me have once more
> A woman's shape, and charming as before,

and her desire is for the "ruddy strife of lips and hearts". And moreover, in so far as this is so, the situation is the reverse of that in the last book of the *Endymion*, in which the goddess appears as the Indian maid tempting Endymion to human life and marriage; she is in reality divine, but represents herself as human. Lamia is human and represents herself as divine. Endymion, refusing earthly love for the maid, is taken from "this mortal state" into immortality by the maid, then revealed as the goddess; Lycius, accepting earthly love for Lamia, is brought to a disastrous end by her, revealed as anything but divine. The opposition of the two situations is complete. But what is Keats' purpose? We can only assume that, in order to give the poem's intention clarity, the poet's sympathy is with Apollonius, not with Lycius and Lamia—

> "Fool! Fool!" repeated he, while his eyes still
> Relented not, nor mov'd; "from every ill
> Of life have I preserv'd thee to this day
> And shall I see thee made a serpent's prey?";

for Lamia is evil and a deception; and Apollonius seeks to save Lycius from a false love, a love human and not spiritual "in the calm'd twilight of Platonic shades". But if this is so, Keats has certainly obscured his purpose; and the explanation may be looked for in Keats' attempt to run together the dramatic and the symbolic, a fusion which must necessarily lead to obscurity. But we may reasonably assume that in Keats' mind in writing *Lamia* was an aspect of what he sought to convey in *Endymion*— its reverse side, so to speak.

Keats' last considerable work, *Hyperion*, reiterates and carries farther what he had said in *Sleep and Poetry*. Here he endeavours to be more signally the 'strong giant' seizing the events of the wide world and 'teazing' his spirit to an 'immortality'. Apollo in *Hyperion* 'seizes the wide world'

> Names, deeds, grey legends, dire events, rebellions,
> Majesties, sovran voices, agonies,
> Creations and destroyings. . . .

and so becomes immortal. The 'vast idea' present in *Sleep and Poetry* remains to the end. Certainly, he had not forgotten the chariot's 'strange journey'. The Apollo of *Hyperion* is the Keats of *Sleep and Poetry*, of the *Ode to a Nightingale*, of the *Ode on a Grecian Urn*; he is the Keats who would worship Psyche as a Goddess—

> Latest born and loveliest vision far
> Of all Olympus' faded hierarchy!

and he is Endymion. Apollo cries to Mnemosyne

> "Surely I have traced
> The rustle of those ample skirts about
> These grassy solitudes. . . .
> Goddess! I have beheld those eyes before,
> And their eternal calm, and all that face,
> Or I have dream'd." "Yes," said the supreme shape,
> "Thou hast dream'd of me. . . ."

The greater part of Keats' verse is the attempt to shadow forth that dream; and is also therefore written 'with no agony but that of ignorance, with no thirst of anything but knowledge'. Apollo, re-echoing this sentence asks,

> Whose hand, whose essence, what divinity
> Makes this alarum in the elements,
> While I here idle listen on the shores
> In fearless yet in aching ignorance?

Yet it is to be observed that the Mnemosyne of *Hyperion* and the Moneta of the second version are not intended to be merely further versions of the Goddess of *Endymion*. From the last quotation but one we might think so. But actually the relationship between Apollo and Mnemosyne and between the Dreamer and Moneta is not the relationship of lovers; it is nearer to being the relationship of mother and son. Apollo is a foster child to Mnemosyne; and of some of Moneta's words to the Dreamer we are told that

> As near as an immortal's sphered words
> Could to a mother's soften were these last.

Moreover, in the first version, Mnemosyne is represented not only as the object of Apollo's dreaming and of his love; she is represented as an ancient power

> Who hath forsaken old and sacred thrones
> For prophecies of thee, and for the sake
> Of loveliness new born;

by her sacrifice of 'old and sacred thrones' she is creating a new loveliness—hers is the creative power which makes possible the immortality of Apollo. And in the second version it is of importance to notice that Moneta is wholly strange to the Dreamer, where Mnemosyne is familiar to Apollo from his dreams, the Dreamer has no recollection—he must ask "And who art thou?" Thus in the second version the Goddess does not play a double role; she is only a Goddess at once of desolation and calm, of the extremity of suffering and of perfect vision, and a foster-mother creative of new loveliness in her son; and in this she is in contrast to the Goddess of the first version who is both the object of Apollo's dreaming and love (another Cynthia) and his foster-mother. The second

version is at least superior in this, that Moneta is not, like
Mnemosyne, a double symbol, combining two significances,
and therefore confusing to the imagination.

It is the mother in Mnemosyne and the 'motherly' Moneta
who are our present concern. Both Mnemosyne and Moneta
are creative by virtue of a great sacrifice, and for a 'prophecy'
have abandoned their thrones. They combine in themselves
desolation and creation, suffering and fulfilment. There can
be no doubt that thus Keats sought to represent them; and that
in them he sought to represent the creativeness of God. The
importance of *Hyperion*, in both its versions, is that in them
Keats' imagination took on a more metaphysical character than
in any other parts of his work. "I have not the slightest feeling
of humility . . . to anything in existence—but the eternal
Being, the Principle of Beauty and the Memory of great Men."
And if his earlier poems were concerned with the Principle
of Beauty, and the expression of the hunger of the imagination
for a transcendent object of contemplation, in *Hyperion* he
sought to set out his imagination of the 'Eternal Being'. In
the first version it is the 'eternal calm' of Mnemosyne's face
which is given emphasis, though from her face Apollo derives
'enormous' knowledge of the 'wide world'; in the second the
face of Moneta (freed from contamination with that part of
Mnemosyne who is Endymion's Cynthia) is described as

> Not pin'd by human sorrows, but bright-blanch'd
> By an immortal sickness which kills not;
> It works a constant change, which happy death
> Can put no end to; deathwards progressing
> To no death was that visage. . . .
> But for her eyes I should have fled away;
> They held me back with a benignant light,
> Soft, mitigated by divinest lids
> Half-clos'd, and visionless entire they seem'd
> Of all external things; they saw me not,
> But in blank splendour beam'd, like the mild moon,
> Who comforts those she sees not, who knows not
> What eyes are upwards cast.

Such a description hardly calls for comment; and alone it justifies the second version—it gives a fuller expression to Keats' intention than anything in the first version. The mind of Moneta encompasses the tragedy and suffering of the universe along with the perfection of Eternity—a divine desolation, the eternal suffering of God, in which the 'love of good and ill' is present, and which makes possible the new loveliness of Apollo and his immortality.

The poem was never completed, as indeed we could hardly expect it to be. The rejection of the first version may very well have been due to his feeling that his symbolism was complex and confusing. No doubt, too, the fact that he was attempting an epic which in its content and theme might suggest comparison with *Paradise Lost* was strongly in his mind, and, coupled with his passionate admiration of Milton, made him a victim to unintended imitation of Milton's language; and against this he rightly rebelled. But even more important is the following factor. *Hyperion* resembles *Paradise Lost* not only in its 'inversions' but in its plot. The first two books of *Hyperion*, like those of *Paradise Lost*, are a description of fallen divinities and their conclave. But the third book of *Paradise Lost* shows God and Christ planning the gift of grace to a creature fallen, and the main concern of the poem is the narrative of the fall of man; in the third book of *Hyperion*, on the contrary, we are shown not the fall, but the achievement of immortality. Thus early in his third book Keats has, so to speak, completed his *Paradise Regained*. Hence the poem had to stop—with the gift of immortality, as *Endymion* had necessarily ended at that point. It is difficult to see what more Keats could write. His essential idea, which should have been given expression as the climax of his story, was already, in the third book, expressed, and whatever he might subsequently write would necessarily lose in interest. He therefore recast his plans, decided to avoid the epic manner as much as possible, wrote in 'cantos' instead of 'books', and attempted a more modest and probably shorter poem. He avoided epic suggestiveness by the more subjective manner of the second version; but again he failed to work out a narrative which would be preliminary to the expression of his essential idea. We may notice the contrast here with *Endymion*. Endymion becomes a God at the end of four considerable books; but admittedly, the narrative of the last three books is diffuse and difficult. Apollo becomes a God at the beginning of Book Three of *Hyperion*; and the Dreamer receives his 'universal' and 'enormous' knowledge in the first canto of the second version. Keats' problem was to find a suitable narrative which, unlike the narrative in *Endymion*, would be clear and vigorous, which might precede the culminating event, or which, though succeeding it, might throw light upon it and thereby maintain interest. But this he failed to do.

8

Finally, let us return to the letters, and to a famous letter which connects with the theme of *Hyperion*, in which Keats sketches his 'scheme of salvation'. In the relevant portion of the letter Keats rather crudely describes the Christian 'scheme of salvation'. "The common cognomen of this world among the misguided and superstitious is a 'vale of tears' from which we are redeemed by a certain arbitrary interposition of God and taken away to Heaven. What a little circumscribed straightened notion!"[1] Certainly, if that were the Christian scheme of salvation, it would be open to such a charge. But Keats goes on to recast it, and to do so in a way which is virtually a statement of the true Christian view. "Call the world

[1] It is worthy of notice that in a later passage in the same letter, he expresses the view that his view of 'soul-making' underlies the making of all important religious 'mythology': "It is pretty generally suspected that the Christian scheme has been copied from the ancient Persian and Greek Philosophers. Why may they not have made this simple thing even more simple for common apprehension by introducing Mediators and Personages in the same manner as in the heathen mythology abstractions are personified? Seriously I think it probable that this system of soul-making may have been the Parent of all the more palpable and personal schemes of Redemption. . . ."

if you please", he writes, " 'the vale of soul-making'. Then
you will find out the use of the world (I am speaking now
in the highest terms for human nature admitting it to be
immortal which I will here take for granted . . .). I say
'soul-making'—soul as distinguished from an Intelligence.
There may be intelligences or sparks of the divinity in millions
—but they are not souls till they acquire identities, till each
one is personally itself. Intelligences are atoms of perception—
they know and see and they are pure, in short they are God.
How, then, are souls to be made? How, then, are these sparks
which are God to have identity given them—so as ever to
possess a bliss peculiar to each one's individual existence?
How but by the medium of a world like this?" Keats' idea
appears to be that the world affords opportunity to the bare,
pure identity of the child to evolve into individuality and self-
possession—a process only possible through pain and suffering.
The soul which is finally brought into being has the wholeness and perfection of the child, but combines such wholeness
with a sense of identity and individual being; the soul at this
level becomes 'God' again, though at a higher level of creation
than the 'intelligence' of the child. This is Keats' formulation
of the doctrine of the Fall, and upon this fundamental idea in
Keats' work, *Endymion* and *Hyperion* may be read as commen-
taries, as recording the movement of the mind, by constant
self-abandonment, to an immortality and 'fellowship with
essence'.

Keats never seems to have doubted the immortality of the
soul. 'I have scarce a doubt of immortality of some nature
or other . . .' he writes; and goes on, writing of the 'grandeurs
of immortality'—"There will be no space, and consequently
the only commerce between spirits will be by their intelligence
of each other—when they will completely understand each
other, while we in this world merely comprehend each other
in different degrees. . . ." Later on, as he moved towards
and entered his last terrible suffering, his hope of immortality,
as we might expect, deserted him, or at least did so in part.

"I long to believe in immortality", he writes; and again, "Is there another life? Shall I awake and find all this a dream? There must be; we cannot be created for this sort of suffering." The terror that this world was the only reality, and that he would not 'awake'—'to find truth'—was natural at this time; for it was a time of dereliction, when he was swung between two worlds. "I have an habitual feeling," he wrote to Brown from Rome, "of my real life having passed, and that I am leading a posthumous existence."

CHAPTER VII

THE FAILURE OF THE BALLAD-MAKERS

> Such a deal of wonder is broken out within this hour
> that the ballad-makers cannot be able to express it.
> SHAKESPEARE—*The Winter's Tale*

I

.SHAKESPEARE'S development was different in important ways from that of both Wordsworth and Keats. In the case
of Wordsworth we have seen how 'the works of man and
face of human life' as he became aware of them during the
Revolution, temporarily destroyed his imaginative life; and
how with the passing of time, by the uncovering of 'hiding-
places of power' in his earlier days, imagination

> rose once more
> In strength, reflecting from its placid breast
> The works of man and face of human life.

Keats, on the other hand, as we can see from his earliest poems,
was forearmed against any such crisis and derangement; indeed
his imaginative life centred around a knowledge that human
life is necessarily crisis from beginning to end, and cannot
shake itself free from it. And therefore, though he knew from
time to time the true temper of despair and rebellion, such
states of mind occurred in a life which as a whole was with

> hope that can never die
> Effort and expectation and desire.

The difference between Keats and Wordsworth was that
Keats knew, with extraordinary clearness, the necessity of
permanent crisis in human life, whereas Wordsworth, though
he had powerful intimations of this truth, was by no means
so surely grounded in it. He therefore allowed himself to
indulge hopes of the earthly happiness which Keats from
the outset viewed as simply impossible; and the French

Revolution was the occasion which took Wordsworth into paths which inevitably led to his despair. Wordsworth had to learn his lesson; somehow or other, Keats had no need to learn it—he had always known.

On the other hand Shakespeare knew to a degree in which neither Wordsworth nor Keats did, a period of 'maiden thought', of brilliant and tender secularity from which he only slowly emerged into the storm and stress from which Wordsworth and Keats were never very far. No doubt the intense and human joy of Shakespeare's earlier work, in which human love, unclouded by the metaphysical and transcendent, is portrayed in such perfection, was a phenomenon of the unique time in history in which Shakespeare lived. But however that may be, it is certain that Shakespeare knew a time of satisfying human enjoyment which the later poets never possessed. Set in the midst of a civilization rapidly growing old, they could not be expected to know the simplicity of the younger Shakespeare. The 'simplicity' and the 'genial sense of youth' of which Wordsworth spoke were apprehended and desired by a sophistication 'keeping watch o'er man's mortality'; but the sophistication which is in Shakespeare's comedies and histories is the sophistication of a simplicity and genial sense of youth such as Wordsworth never knew or was to know. Hence, when Shakespeare's time of crisis came, it came with a shock for which he was strikingly unprepared. And in this he was different from the later poets. Keats indeed was beyond such shock and prepared against any such possibility. The shock to Wordsworth's imagination came only because he allowed himself to be deflected from the comprehensive labours of his imagination previous to the time of the Revolution; and it was a shock which was overcome when he turned to discover what power was hidden away in the hiding-places of his earlier imaginative life. Hence Shakespeare was not armoured against the world as they were; his was a completeness of derangement which, being what they had been and were, the later poets could not suffer.

It is not within the purpose of this essay to consider the detail of Shakespearean tragedy. Our chief concern is with what is beyond the tragedies, that is to say, with what happened after the failure of Shakespeare's imagination to 'idealize and unify' the world of human experience as he faced it in the tragedies. For Shakespeare's 'tragic period' ended as Shakespeare became, like Wordsworth's soldier, one

> Remembering the importance of his theme
> But feeling it no longer.

He had failed to solve the 'problem' which he 'presented' in his tragedies, to apprehend unity and harmony informing human affairs; he had seen the necessarily tragic character of human life. In that apprehension lay, for Shakespeare, as for Keats and Wordsworth, peace of mind. And it was this peace of mind which gave us the last plays. But these last are not among the greatest of Shakespeare's plays, for the simple reason that they are not plays; they are no longer, that is to say, of the order of imagination which is 'human and dramatic' —they are of the order of imagination which is 'enthusiastic and meditative.' In them he is no longer interested in humanity —his interest is elsewhere. It is a platitude of criticism that the later plays are the writings of a man careless of what he is doing; poetry is no longer a passion or a necessity to him, and he finally gives it up and goes home. And it is not an accident that Shakespeare's last plays are tortured by a sense of inexpressiveness and failure, that Wordsworth's poetic powers declined, that Keats gave up *Hyperion*. The source of failure in all three is one and the same.

Though Keats from the start anticipated the labours of an imagination which seeks to be comprehensive, he had to wait for that 'teazing of his spirit' of which he wrote until his own experience brought him a realization of suffering greater than any mere recognition of the existence of suffering could afford; and the poetry of Keats records an increasing realization of that kind, for his experience was increasingly painful. All his poetry is therefore a poetry of crisis; for if he was, from the outset, beyond such an extremity of shock and derangement as came to Wordsworth and Shakespeare by virtue of his early realization of the hopelessness of earthly happiness, he yet lived in an ever-deepening knowledge of suffering; and this kept his imagination extended to its full creativeness if it was not to be overborne. His poetry is the record of an enormous courage, a hope that was built on hopelessness; and his own experience never released him from the effort which that courage demanded. He clung to his dream of immortality and gave perfect expression to it in his Odes, his greatest poetry. And in the midst of his suffering he sought to do more than express his 'Adam's dream'; he sought also to express his 'conviction' that Adam's dream is truth and for this purpose sought a mythology, as Shakespeare and Wordsworth in their later days sought a mythology. But if the *Ode to a Nightingale* and *Ode on a Grecian Urn* are perfect, *Endymion* and *Hyperion* are not. *Endymion* is not a great poem; at least, it is great and contains fine things, but it is a failure; and he 'gave up' *Hyperion* —he could not use it as he sought, and even abandoned a second attempt. His great poems are the lyrics of aspiration and dream. *Endymion* is obscure and prolix, and the symbolism of *Hyperion* vague and fluctuating; both fail through lack of air in which the human imagination can breathe. His failure in these poems was indeed inevitable; inevitable because there are limits to the imagination, or if we will, because the transcendent region to which the imagination seeks to penetrate cannot be suborned to the detail of poetic expressiveness. It was the very 'vastness' of Keats' idea, though that idea was the dynamic and centre of his verse, which made *Hyperion* impossible. And quickly, his life, hurrying to its end with its weight of intolerable suffering, cast him into a finality of crisis, a dereliction, his 'posthumous' existence, in which poetry was impossible.

But such an extremity of suffering did not fall to Wordsworth's lot; after his period of crisis came restoration in which he could write the story of his youth and disillusion. But,

though he wrote it in retrospect, he was still near enough to it
to feel its pressure and anguish; and the expression of it in
The Prelude is amongst the greatest poetry. But increasingly,
as time went on, he used the dogmas of Christianity which
slowly were becoming central to his imaginative life. By 1805
the greater mass of his poetry had been written, and had been
written in acute recollection of his disillusion and suffering,
and of his release from it. And the poetry he wrote up to the
year 1805 is admittedly his greatest. But from then on his
imagination, no longer 'voyaging through strange seas alone',
found adequate conveyance in Christian dogma, a change
which, I have suggested, was in accordance with all that was
fundamental in his earlier imaginative life. Once he had seen
the inevitability and the justice of his disillusion, he found
peace of mind such as he had never formerly known in such
degree. And in that peace of mind he came slowly to the
perception that Christianity expressed through its dogmas all
that he had come to apprehend human life as being. This
perception reduced his poetic vitality. And it did so because
it released him from the necessity of attempting to convey
in his own language what he saw to be adequately expressed
in Christianity. The urge to personal creation therefore
weakened; and weakened not because he distrusted his own
imagination, but because he saw in Christianity the consummation of his own imaginative life. His own personal poetry was,
as it were, silenced in the face of a greater poetry. The difference
therefore between Wordsworth, on the one hand, and Keats
and Shakespeare on the other, is this: that Keats and Shakespeare endeavoured themselves to create a mythology and failed
in the task, while Wordsworth, accepting Christian dogma,
was not under the necessity to attempt the task to which
the other poets had addressed themselves. Hence while the
later phases of the poetic lives of Shakespeare and Keats are
marked by a strenuous effort of the imagination to create
adequate mythology, the later Wordsworth rested his imagination more and more in an imaginative scheme, ready-made,

so to speak, for him. Hence if the poetry of Keats and Shake-speare in their efforts to formulate adequate expression of their final apprehension of the world failed, as was indeed natural, the poetry of Wordsworth shows a withdrawal of energy from any such attempt, and an acceptance of forms of expression supplied him by Christianity. Such an acceptance lessened the demand on his own poetic expressiveness, and made the decline of his poetic powers natural.[1]

Shakespeare, having failed to see human life as a neat, orderly, and satisfying unity, had resort to myth for the convey-ance of his new imaginative apprehension of life. But his mythology was not Christian; as long as he wrote poetry he tried to maintain its independence of traditional forms. Yet he must quickly have come to see the impossibility of what he was trying to do. Several times he tried to recast the essential symbols which are present in all the later plays. But however highly we may praise the plays, they exert, as attempted mytho-logies, little of the sheer compulsion exerted by the comedies and tragedies as conveying Shakespeare's former sense of life. No doubt Shakespeare's instinct in endeavouring to avoid a frankly mythical form which would use the language of religion was a sound one; he wanted a poetry which would, as far as possible, show forth his final attitude to life and death, without surrendering to traditional religious language. But the result is necessarily unsatisfactory. The plays are comparatively formless (with the exception of *The Tempest*, in which he made his last supreme effort), and thereby show a failure of expressive-ness. The symbols are there; but they rarely liberate compulsive significances. We hover between apprehension of momentous significances, of a luxurious imagination, and of absurdities. And if we need a sign that Shakespeare was aware of this failure of expressiveness, we need only observe the ways in which he repeatedly used a single theme for his purpose—a curious lack of versatility for the man who wrote the comedies and tragedies with all their great variety of plot. Labouring,

[1] I return to this subject in the next chapter, Section 4.

with the true instinct of the great artist, to avoid direct expression of belief, he failed nevertheless to create a mythology of adequate expressiveness. The making of a mythology is too great a work for one mind, though that mind be Shakespeare's. Moreover a mythology implies an accompanying belief; and Shakespeare sought to keep his symbols pure, uncontaminated by assertion. Wordsworth bowed to what he came to feel was the superior expressiveness of Christian dogma, and his imagination became dominated by forms of expression which did not flow from himself; the autonomy of his poetry, so to speak, was destroyed. Keats and Shakespeare, avoiding that path, sought to create their own symbols, and failed in the effort. All alike exhibit the limits of poetry, Wordsworth by accepting modes of expression which his own poetry did not create, Shakespeare and Keats by attempting the impossible task of creating original forms of expression for 'unknown modes of being'.

> It is a flaw
> In happiness to see beyond our bourn

Keats wrote. It also makes for flaws and failures in poetry. Of Shakespeare, Wordsworth, and Keats we can say that we can see in them the passing of the poetic mind into the philosophic mind,

> In the faith that looks through death,
> In years that bring the philosophic mind.

The concern of all three became for something more than poetry; we feel that this is so in the last plays of Shakespeare and in *The Excursion*; and we read it stated in Keats' remark: "Poetry is not so fine a thing as a philosophy—for the same reason that an eagle is not so fine a thing as a truth."

2

But we are anticipating what we have to say of Shakespeare's last poetic days. To consider what are called the 'problem' plays, and the tragedies as leading up to the last group, is beyond our present scope. It is enough for us to say here that the problem plays are plays of revulsion and cynicism— *Troilus*, *Measure for Measure*, *Hamlet*; the tragedies are plays in which that sense of revulsion is still present but no longer unredeemed—the suffering of the tragedies, as has been said, is creative. They do not indeed bring us reconciliation or acceptance; but no more do they bring a predominant sense of loathing. In *Antony* indeed there is, for the first time, a sense of triumph—

> My desolation does begin to make
> A better life;

even in *Timon*, the strongest impression is one of nobility, and Timon's most famous utterance is heavy with prophecy of things to come—

> my long sickness
> Of health and living now begins to mend
> And nothing brings me all things.

From this time on Shakespeare left tragedy for myth and symbol. When in *Timon* Alcibiades asks

> How came the noble Timon to this change?

Timon replies

> As the moon does, by wanting light to give:
> But then renew I could not, like the moon;
> There were no suns to borrow of.

Yet the last plays are a renewal; a new light had somehow been borrowed, a light difficult of conveyance, but which Shakespeare nevertheless struggled to shed. But the light was not merely the destroyer of tragic darkness; it was not the light which the comedies shed. And its difference demanded a new kind of artistic creation, unique in drama, so unique that it can hardly be called drama. For it is not concerned with expression of imagination of the human situation. And its uniqueness may be said to consist in this, that for the first time in his poetic life, Shakespeare seems to be concerned to *say* something with a degree of explicitness greater than ever before. For if we are right in believing that in the later plays there is an essential mythology; and if a mythology be a mode of saying something which evades lucid and intelligible expression in the prose of statement; then we may believe that in the last plays is a degree of explicit significance and meaning which is not present in the comedies or the tragedies. It may be that it is possible to extract from any poem or play whatsoever some tatter of meaning, however impoverished or worthless; and that we can, if we wish, state the meaning of the tragedies, as for example Mr. A. C. Bradley did in his famous *Shakespearean Tragedy*. But in the last plays we feel Shakespeare is no longer primarily concerned to show forth a human situation, from which we can, if we will, extract a meaning; we feel rather that while what is set forth is done in a way to capture our imagination, the plots yet contain a direct significance which is intended to be released in the course of imaginative effort. For myth is essentially the point at which dream and exposition, imagination and conviction, meet; the two aspects are essential to its existence. And if therefore there is myth in these plays we cannot fail to be sensitive to them both. The purpose of myth is the showing forth of that which cannot be set out by the representation of a merely human situation; its function is the conveyance, to whatever degree possible, of the divine as well as the human. Yet it is the case that to try to extract its significances, and to convey them in the prose of statement, is at once a desecration of the work of art, and, in any case, an impossibility; for the justification of the work of art is that it is only thus that an adequate conveyance of the writer's mind can be made.

Nevertheless, we are under compulsion to attempt judgment on the adequacy of myth to its purpose and significance; and if it be said that to do so is to carry out desecration and to attempt the impossible, the only reply must be that we cannot help ourselves. The critic can no more avoid trying to explicate and draw out the significances of Shakespeare's last plays than the theologian can help seeking to draw a philosophical theology out of the structure of Christian dogma. It is true that the attempt to evolve a satisfactory philosophy out of dogma is impossible; and that the results of the effort are a poor thing in comparison with that from which it set out. It is true that we cannot reduce the last plays to a neat system of significances; and that in trying to do so, we are in constant danger of losing sight of what, after all, is the important thing, namely, the plays. Yet the compulsion to try to do so remains. The theologian and the critic stand, in this matter, under a necessary self-condemnation. And the critic can but claim that what he tries to do is a necessary means whereby the adequacy of the poet's myths may be judged and the appreciation of them heightened. If such a process may at all facilitate a grasp of the author's intention and thereby facilitate judgment on the effectiveness of the author's symbols, the critic may, though under condemnation, find a measure of assurance.

3

The essential myth which runs throughout the last plays, *Pericles*, *Cymbeline*, *The Winter's Tale*, and *The Tempest*, is the finding of what is lost. Pericles loses and finds Marina; Cymbeline loses and finds his sons; Leontes loses and finds Perdita; Alonso loses and finds Ferdinand. This myth, however, is complicated in certain ways. There is throughout the plays another myth, which is run into the first, namely, the bringing to life of what is dead. Thaisa is literally raised from the dead; Imogen revives from what is taken for death, and Posthumous too had been thought to be dead; Hermione comes to life, and Ferdinand had been thought dead by Alonso. So closely run together are the two myths that it is difficult, if at all possible, to pick them apart. Thus Pericles finds Marina after thinking she had died; the sons of Cymbeline were thought to

have been dead; Perdita was thought to be dead, as was
Ferdinand. These two myths, essentially one in idea, are again
fused with a third, namely, that of the recovery of a lost royalty.
Pericles is compelled to relinquish his throne, but later returns;
the sons of Cymbeline live as wild huntsmen, but finally are
restored to royal estate; Posthumous too in a measure fits in
here, for he was of noble descent, at one time favourite of
the court, is banished, and returns to Imogen; Perdita lives
as a shepherdess; Prospero and Miranda are outcasts from a
kingdom but are finally restored. This again, it will be seen,
runs into the former mythical elements and becomes an integral
part of it. Again, there is a fourth element, namely, that of
the seeking of what is lost by a royal personage; if what is
lost be royal, a royal person seeks it out, or is at least instrumental in its recovery. Thus, in *Pericles*, Pericles is brought
back through the agency of Helicanus who has refused the
princedom of Tyre in the absence of Pericles; Marina is restored
to Pericles largely through the help of Lysimachus, the governor
of Mytilene; Posthumous is sought by Imogen, and it is she
who falls in with Belarius and the sons of Cymbeline; Perdita
is sought out by Florizel and Miranda wooed by Ferdinand.
Between these pairs are ties of strongest attachment, even
when, as in the case of Imogen and her brothers, they are
ignorant of each other's identity; and Lysimachus finally
marries Marina, Florizel Perdita, and Ferdinand Miranda.

The mythical situation is however not yet fully described.
There is constant repetition of situations in which a lost person
is placed in a position of peculiar helplessness. Marina is
born at sea and, her mother dead, is parted from her father;
the sons of Cymbeline are stolen as small children, and no
mention is made throughout the play of their mother; Posthumous' name is significant; Perdita is carried away and exposed,
and her mother is powerless in prison; Miranda, motherless,
is also exposed to the greatest danger. Such is their condition
as little children; and on growing up further grave dangers
await them. In *Pericles* Marina's life is threatened by Dionyza,

and on her coming to Mytilene is taken to a brothel; in *Cymbeline* evil takes on a vile form in the Queen and Cloten who are the enemies of Posthumous and Imogen; Perdita, in *The Winter's Tale*, is indeed threatened by no such terrible evil, though she must face the anger of Polixenes and lifelong poverty, as she believed, with Florizel, a permanent loss of royalty; in *The Tempest* Miranda is threatened by Caliban. Yet from these dangers they are rescued. Moreover about them all is an essential royalty of character; indeed the praises of them, sung by other characters, seem to throw about them something of divinity.

Finally, we must observe that in these plays all the disturbing events recorded are, by the hatred, suspicion, jealousy which give rise to them, a striking contrast to an original condition of peace, harmony, love and friendship, which is suddenly disrupted. *Pericles* indeed begins with Antiochus; but immediately and in contrast appears the friendship of Pericles for Cleon and Dionyza and theirs for Pericles. But this strong and confident friendship is suddenly broken in upon by Dionyza's hatred of Marina. In *Cymbeline*, the original condition, though not actually represented in the play, is one in which Posthumous enjoys the admiration and friendship of the entire court; but the play opens with the disruption caused by the Queen and Cloten. In *The Winter's Tale* such disruption of friendship quickly occurs with the freakish jealousy of Leontes. And Prospero and Miranda endure their sufferings subsequent to a time in which Prospero loved Antonio next only to Miranda. The stories of the plays issue from a state of peace and love into which, after suffering and disloyalty, they again pass.

4

Such is the essential mythical situation which is presented in each of the four plays; and upon it the following comments may be made. In the first place, it is worth emphasizing the theme of the loss of royalty. In *Pericles* there is in

Pericles and Marina an acute sense of such a loss. Pericles, at the court of Simonides, a wandering and unknown knight, says

> Yon king's to me like to my father's picture,
> Which tells me in that glory once he was;
> Had princes sit, like stars, about his throne,
> And he the sun, for them to reverence;
> None that beheld him, but, like lesser lights,
> Did vail their crowns to his supremacy:
> Where now his son like a glow-worm in the night
> The which hath fire in darkness, none in light.

And this speech is matched when later Marina, speaking to Pericles who does not yet know her identity, says

> I am a maid,
> My lord, that ne'er before invited eyes,
> But have been gazed on like a comet: she speaks
> My lord, that, may be, hath endured a grief,
> Might equal yours, if both were justly weigh'd.
> Though wayward fortune did malign my state,
> My derivation was from ancestors
> Who stood equivalent with mighty kings:
> But time hath rooted out my parentage,
> And to the world and awkward casualties
> Bound me in servitude.

The identical significance of the two speeches is unmistakable, a significance derived from what we feel to be high metaphysical symbol. And when Pericles asks

> What countrywoman?
> Here of these shores?

Marina replies

> No, nor of any shores:
> Yet I was mortally brought forth, and am
> No other than I appear.

And elsewhere in the play the world appears to Marina a 'lasting storm' denying her her heritage, 'whirring me from my friends'. There is a sublimity in Marina which gives her an

unhuman greatness, a gigantic stature. She is described by
Pericles in lovely poetry in two speeches in the last act:

> Prithee, speak:
> Falseness cannot come near thee; for thou look'st
> Modest as justice, and thou seem'st a palace
> For the crown'd Truth to dwell in. . . .

And later,

> Tell thy story;
> If thine consider'd prove the thousandth part
> Of my endurance, thou art a man, and I
> Have suffer'd like a girl: yet thou dost look
> Like Patience gazing on kings' graves, and smiling
> Extremity out of act.

We are taken back to the hopeless love of *Twelfth Night*—

> And what's her history?
> A blank, my lord, she never told her love . . .

And so Marina

> never would tell
> Her parentage; being demanded that
> She would sit still and weep.

But if it takes us back to *Twelfth Night*, the 'smiling extremity
out of act' also takes us back to the terrible figures that haunted
Wordsworth's imagination and to the face of Moneta; and
when Marina says—

> Time hath rooted out my parentage
> And to the world and awkward casualties
> Bound me in servitude,

we think of

> the glories he hath known
> And that imperial palace whence he came.

Of her we read that

> She sings like one immortal, and she dances
> As goddess-like to her admired lays.

And, as Mr. Wilson Knight has pointed out,[1] arguing his belief in the high significance of music in these plays, the reunion of Pericles and Marina is touched with more than human significance. "Give me my robes", cries Pericles, recalling an act of Cleopatra at the greatest moment of her life; and the 'notable passion of wonder' of which we read in *The Winter's Tale* is in his words 'I am wild in my beholding'.

Now it is to be observed that it is in *Pericles* that we have the most perfect representation of the myth of lost and recovered royalty; in none of the three later plays is it set out with the same simplicity and single-mindedness. This simplicity is achieved by the careful avoidance of a love story. Lysimachus does not become Marina's lover until after she is known for what she is. Indeed Lysimachus, if we look at him through the eyes of Florizel and Ferdinand, has a chilliness and conscious sense of royalty which is distasteful—

> She's such a one, that, were I well-assured
> Came of a gentle kind and noble stock,
> I'd wish no better choice and think me rarely wed.

This is not the attitude of Florizel and Ferdinand; and though Lysimachus helps Marina, they do not 'change eyes'. Lysimachus does not gain our admiration, as do the later heroes. And he does not do so because Shakespeare is strenuously keeping the issue of the play to Marina's restoration to royal status. For in the other plays the love interest is contradictory to the myth of royalty. In them, though the essential myth is retained for the framework of the plays, and in all of them is a restoration to royalty, there is that which threatens it. Imogen, we feel, would have been happy in exile, were she with Posthumous; Florizel would have sacrificed his crown, not Perdita; Ferdinand was content with his prison, could he but see Miranda. In other words, the introduction of the love stories acts against the significance which Shakespeare is attaching to his symbol of royalty. And in the last three plays

[1] *Myth and Miracle*, pp. 12–13.

we have situations in which Imogen, Florizel, and Ferdinand, so far from suffering a loss of royalty, would gladly yield it up. To this extent is the efficacy of the myth weakened; in *Pericles* alone did Shakespeare maintain the myth of royalty uncontaminated. And in the succeeding plays he had to run together his myth of royalty, of its loss and recovery, with another element, namely, that of willingness to abandon royalty in the presence of eclipsing beauty. This gives to them a lack of the simple significance which we derive from *Pericles*.

But this complication was inevitable. It was inevitable because the symbol of royalty was inadequate to embody all that was present in Shakespeare's imagination, and he was therefore driven to be unfaithful to it. So external a symbol could not hope to express the spiritual supremacy, 'with a more than mortal seeming', with which he wished to endow his heroes and heroines. For he endows them with a transfiguring beauty which the symbol of kingship fails to convey, though no doubt it was the most appropriate he could find. In the face of such beauty princes willingly abandon their thrones; kingship is as nothing to such love. Hence, where in *Pericles* it is kingship and not love which dominates the play, in the later plays, though there remains the restoration to royalty, it is a love greater than thrones which is paramount. And so we have in these plays the exercise of a myth which shows its inadequacy, and to which, in the interests of conveying what is in his mind, Shakespeare is unfaithful. For he is concerned with that for which no earthly symbol is adequate, a beauty which, so far from being conveyed in the symbol of kingship, is one for which kingships are well lost.

This does not of course mean that he discontinued the use of the myth of royalty. But it is clear throughout the four plays that in describing his heroes and heroines he endows them with an incomparable beauty for which royalty is only a partially adequate symbol. Cloten is a prince, and as such gains the reverence—'that angel of the world'—of Belarius. But in the heroes and heroines is a sublimity which is their own and which is recognized unfailingly. And in all these plays it is this perfection which holds our imagination, and which is only reinforced by the symbol of royalty.

Of Marina we read that others are to her as 'crows to the dove of Paphos'—

> She sings like one immortal, and she dances
> As goddess-like to her admired lays.

Posthumous

> Sits 'mongst men like a descended god:
> He hath a kind of honour sets him off,
> More than a mortal seeming;

he is

> such a holy witch
> That he enchants societies unto him.

Belarius says of Guiderius and Arviragus

> O thou Goddess,
> Thou divine Nature, how thyself thou blazon'st
> In these two princely boys! They are as gentle
> As zephyrs, blowing below the violet,
> Not wagging his sweet head; and yet as rough
> Their royal blood enchafed, as the rudest wind,
> That by the top doth take the mountain pine
> And make him stoop to the vale. 'Tis wonder
> That an invisible instinct should frame them
> To royalty unlearn'd.

And they are worthy, he says elsewhere, 'to inlay heaven with stars'. Imogen, to Belarius, is 'divineness no elder than a boy'; and the two boys to Imogen are beyond peer. Perdita is no shepherdess

> but Flora
> Peering in April's front,

or, if she be a shepherdess,

> the Gods themselves
> Humbling their deities to love, have taken

> The shapes of beasts upon them . . .
>   . . . their transformations
> Were never for a piece of beauty rarer.

Miranda might call Ferdinand

> A thing divine; for nothing natural
> I ever saw so noble.

And Miranda to Ferdinand is a goddess upon whom music attends. Throughout these plays the heroes and heroines, whether or not they have suffered loss of royalty, take on 'a more than mortal seeming'. If in the tragedies the leading characters be kings, princes, leaders of state who show in the course of the play a certain and frail mortality, in these last plays the heroes and heroines are princes and princesses who, whether or not they bear the robes of royalty, are royal; who in poverty and suffering take on a divine bearing, and, so far from suffering death and disaster, are given at the close the full attributes of royalty. But in the reading of them it is the perfect beauty of these men and women in contrast to all others, not their mere royalty in contrast to the humble condition of all others, which occupies the eye of imagination. The external royalty is seen as an inadequate symbol to a superlative spiritual beauty. Of them all, whether or not aware of high descent, whether or not they have lost their kingly standing, it is true that

> they are worthy
> To inlay heaven with stars.

In *Pericles* everything turns on the restoration of Marina to Pericles; without that there is a complete desolation. But in *Cymbeline*, in *The Winter's Tale*, in *The Tempest*, we should be content if Imogen can be with Posthumous; content if Florizel remains a shepherd with Perdita; content if Alonso had indeed suffered his sea-change and Ferdinand be left, though in poverty, with Miranda. Thus we see that the myth of royalty, though it is retained, is no longer the adequate conveyance

of significance which it was in *Pericles*. In *Pericles* the symbol
and significance are one; we are aware of the high destiny
of the soul in and through the symbol of royalty. But in the
later plays symbol and significance have fallen apart; the symbol
is manifestly inadequate.

The reason why the myth of royalty fails to make, in these
last three plays, a clear and single conveyance of significance
is not far to seek. If, in *Pericles*, royalty is a symbol for what is
spiritual, and even if Shakespeare used it strenuously for
that purpose alone, he also found it useful in the later plays for
another purpose. For what marks these heroes and heroines is
the completeness of their 'dedication' to each other. And
Shakespeare could not more fitly express the degree of this
'dedication' than by showing them willing to yield up their
royalty. In *Pericles* what seems paramount is the necessity of
restoration to royal status in which the fulfilment of the soul
is symbolized. But in the later plays the complete self-dedication
of these 'more than mortal seeming' men and women to each
other in love is paramount; and to express such self-dedication
royalty is used as that which, in the presence of beauty, is of
no account. It is a value and human value which these 'gods'
and 'goddesses' lay aside. Hence royalty is here a symbol
for a different significance from that which it had in *Pericles*,
and which it has in the last three plays, in so far as restoration
to royalty is the framework of the plot of these also. The
symbol therefore has two significances; the first as a signification
of the divine destiny of the soul, and secondly, of all worldly
values which the royalty of the pure spirit discounts. Thus
there is a confusion in the symbolism, for in the last three
plays at least royalty is used to symbolize the merely worldly
as well as the purely spiritual. Thus whereas in *Pericles* the
world which does not give recognition to Marina's royalty
is a storm, or a bondage, to her; in *The Tempest* bondage is
enough if it be bondage with Miranda. And it is to be noted
that this double significance does not merely mark a difference
in the usage of the symbol in *Pericles* on the one hand, and in

the last three plays on the other. It is present in the last three plays themselves. For Shakespeare took over from *Pericles* the myth of royalty; it remains in all three essential to the plot of each. Yet in all three royalty is used to indicate something other than what the myth demands. And this confusion of symbolism arises because the myth of royalty was inadequate to Shakespeare's purpose, though it was the best that he could find. For Shakespeare sought to convey not only the assertion by the soul of its high descent; he sought also to convey the abandonment and self-dedication of perfect love. And relatively to these two purposes he uses the symbol of royalty differently. Yet, though royalty in the plays becomes two symbols, which are in contradiction, it is difficult to doubt the nature of Shakespeare's essential purpose; for it was one essential purpose which thus used royalty as a double symbol.

5

Let us now consider another strand in the skein of mythology which makes up these last plays, namely, what seems to be Shakespeare's way of showing the tragic character of human life. He does this by representing many of his heroes and heroines as tiny children, parentless, who are committed to danger and tempest. He thus expresses a sense of the infinitesimal smallness of human life and affairs, of the helplessness of human life, and of its terrible trials. This piece of symbolism is surely clear in its intention. Yet these infants are preserved. And they are preserved too from the terrible dangers which befall them in later years, Marina from the brothel, Imogen from Iachimo as well as from Cloten and the Queen, Miranda from Caliban. In these three instances at least Shakespeare does not fail to represent forms of evil of the extremest vileness. The scene in the brothel is surely the most repulsive in the whole compass of Shakespeare's work. In *Cymbeline* Iachimo, Cloten, and the Queen are irredeemably bad; they rival, if they do not eclipse, anything to be found in the tragedies,

the very embodiment of evil. And in *The Tempest* there is
Caliban. Yet from these also there is a complete deliverance.
It is noteworthy also that in *Cymbeline* there is a repetition,
as Mr. Wilson Knight has pointed out, of the theme of *Troilus*.
Posthumous, believing in Imogen's faithlessness, speaks as
Troilus did. And we hear an echo of it and of the Hamlet
mood in the speech of Antigonus when Leontes insists on
Hermoine's faithlessness—

> If it be so,
> We need no grave to bury honesty:
> There's not a grain of it the face to sweeten
> Of the whole dungy earth.

Yet Imogen was not unfaithful, and Posthumous can spare
Iachimo's life and forgive him—

> Kneel not to me:
> The power that I have on you is to spare you;
> The malice towards you to forgive you.

And Hermione was not unfaithful and can forgive Leontes.
Thus in the world which Shakespeare is in these plays portray-
ing, the sense, 'death-like, of treacherous desertion, felt in
the last place of refuge', is indeed present but only to be
shown to be without foundation and to be dispelled. This
world is one in which all the terrors of the tragedies are overcome, dissolved in a new birth of the spirit; and tempest,
as Mr. Knight says, gives place to music. If a part of Shake-
peare's purpose was to show the tragic nature of human
existence, it was also a part of his purpose to show its deliverance
from danger, evil, and despair. This double purpose made
his work difficult and gives again a complication to the plays,
a complication which is shown in two ways. In the first place
Posthumous, though he sat 'mongst men like a descended
god', is also a mortal; he is at once a god, Troilus, and Hamlet,
rolled into one, and hence a symbol of two things, of the human
and tragic, and of the more than human spirit. His symbolic
significance thus loses simplicity. And in the second place,

P

though Shakespeare seeks to present, in all the plays, the very extremity of evil and depravity as instrumental to his purpose of displaying the tragic quality of human life, yet that evil must not, if he is to set out his sense of deliverance, be shown as merely evil. Hence he has at once to create completest embodiments of evil whereby he may drive home the sense of the human tragedy; yet he has in so doing to contradict that extremity of evil even in those very characters. Of Boult Marina says

> Thou hold'st a place, for which the pained'st fiend
> Of hell would not in reputation change:
> Thou art the damned doorkeeper to every
> Coistrel that comes inquiring for his Tib;
> To the choleric fisting of every rogue
> Thy ear is liable; thy food is such
> As hath been belcht on by infected lungs.

Yet it is Boult who gives her deliverance from the brothel. There is nothing viler in Shakespeare's work than Cloten and the Queen; and yet Shakespeare cannot leave them wholly unredeemed. It is indeed only after their deaths that good is spoken of them.

> He was a Queen's son, boys:
> And, though he came our enemy, remember
> He was paid for that: though mean and mighty rotting
> Together have one dust, yet reverence—
> —That angel of the world—doth make distinction
> Of place 'tween high and low. Our foe was princely.

And Belarius commands that he be buried, 'his head to th' east'. The 'angel of the world' which is abroad in these plays takes regard even of Cloten, who at least lay 'to th' east'. And even of the Queen, who on her death bed made unrepentant confession of her evil, Cymbeline strives to speak well—

> it had been vicious
> To have mistrusted her.

In *The Winter's Tale*, the only play of the four in which Shakespeare does not present an image of the greatest evil, we have indeed Autolycus, who is enough to reconcile the hardest heart to thieving, if thieves be such as he. And in *The Tempest* Caliban is endowed with a sense of glory which opened the clouds to him. Hence we have again a complication of sym- bolism. These figures of evil, spirits of evil, are not simple; they too bear a double significance.

6

We may pass at this point to the theme of finding that which is lost. The circumstances in which the characters in each of the four plays are lost differ in each case. In *Pericles*, Marina is lost through the action of the murderous Dionyza, and of the robbers who sell her to the brothel; Guiderius and Arviragus are lost through the revenge of Belarius on the injus- tice of Cymbeline; Perdita is lost through the 'jealous sickness' of Leontes; and Ferdinand is lost to Alonso through the action of Prospero which arises in the last resort out of the action of Alonso and Antonio years before. In each case therefore the loss occurs as a direct result of the evil doings of other charcters; these other characters are in three cases parents of the lost child, and in the other case Dionyza has been foster-parent to Marina. What actuates Dionyza in occasioning the loss of Marina is a jealousy in the interests of her own child; in *Cym- beline* the sin is of injustice and of revenge; in *The Winter's Tale* it is a wild unreasoning sexual jealousy; in *The Tempest* it is the love of power and possession. It is, it need hardly be said, dangerous to seek a precise symbolism in all that is to be found in these plays. Yet here again, where a situation is repeated, in essence, four times, it is difficult to avoid the conclusion that in it is a clue to an important element in what Shakespeare was, in his last work, labouring to convey. We may believe therefore that in this part of his mythology, he is seeking to body forth his sense of the loss by man, through his own evil, of his most treasured possession, 'the jewel of his soul'. It is impossible to avoid the parallel with the constant

use of the theme in the Gospels, the theme of the finding
of that which is lost.

But let us in the first place concentrate on the loss. The loss
is due to man's evil, which in each case is a sudden, inexplicable
evil arising out of a former state of happiness, love, and loyalty.
In *The Winter's Tale*, which unlike the other plays has not such
figures of extreme evil as Cloten and Caliban, what of evil is
shown is concentrated, but for Autolycus, in Leontes. Here
Shakespeare elaborately portrays the state of perfect love which
precedes Leontes' fatal jealousy. It is emphasized repeatedly
in the most beautiful language; it is described by Camillo in
the opening scene. And again by Polixenes, when he says

> We were as twinn'd lambs that did frisk i' the sun,
> And bleat the one at the other: what we changed
> Was innocence for innocence; we knew not
> The doctrine of ill-doing, no, nor dream'd
> That any did.

And equally is the previous love of Leontes and Hermione
stressed, only to be followed at once by the first signs of the
jealousy of Leontes. From that time on his jealousy burns like
a disease. Indeed it is repeatedly described as a 'sickness.'
'Good my lord', says Camillo,

> be cured
> Of this diseased opinion, and betimes.

And again

> There is a sickness
> Which puts some of us in distemper; but
> I can not name the disease.

Again it is a 'madness'; Leontes has a 'weak-hinged fancy'.
There can be little doubt that Shakespeare is setting out the
evil of Leontes as a sudden eruption into disease of what
originally was healthy. And although this theme has an emphasis
which it has not in the other plays, it is present in them also.
It is from outbursts of sheer evil, on the part of characters
who in their former nature were otherwise, Dionyza and
Cleon Cymbeline, Leontes, Antonio, that the loss occurs.

And where, as in *Pericles* and *Cymbeline* the loss of Marina and the exile of Posthumous are not due directly to Pericles and Cymbeline, it is yet due to evil in someone closely related to themselves; Pericles entirely trusted his friends Cleon and Dionyza; Cymbeline thought it 'vicious to have distrusted' his Queen. Similarly with Prospero and Antonio. The originating evil in these cases issued from persons who, by their intimacy with them, were identified with Pericles, Cymbeline, and Prospero.

In each case what is lost through the agency of this evil is a person of the greatest beauty and incomparable worth. And that person is in each case restored; and with that restoration comes the recovery, to those who have lost them, of their true nature. Pericles has no active evil to be purged from his nature; but he is brought out of desolation, and also sees the characters of Cleon and Dionyza in their true light. Cymbeline similarly has not the record of a Leontes or an Antonio; yet he is disintoxicated from his love for the Queen and sees her for what she was. And all four, Cleon and Dionyza, and the Queen and Cloten, are destroyed by death. Leontes, though the gods have destroyed his jealousy, knows fulfilment only with the return of Perdita; and Antonio and Alonso are changed by the finding of Miranda and Ferdinand. Clearly, the most satisfactory interpretation we can place upon this striking repetition, in four plays, of a single theme, is Shakespeare's imagination of human life as a descent into a necessary tragedy and evil which is seen as a sudden irruption into what is originally perfect, and as a sudden loss of innocence; and as the recovery of a lost perfection, the achievement of a condition which is not merely an innocence but which, in its achievement, is an 'affliction' having

> a taste as sweet
> As any cordial comfort.

'They seem'd almost', it was said of the King and Leontes after the return of Florizel and Perdita, 'with staring on one another, to tear the cases of their eyes; there was speech in their dumbness, language in their very gesture; they lookt as they had heard of a world ransom'd, or one destroy'd: a notable passion of wonder appear'd in them; but the wisest beholder, that knew no more but seeing, could not say if the importance were joy or sorrow,—but in the extremity of the one, it must needs be.'

And again, describing the scene,

'Then have you lost a sight, which was to be seen, cannot be spoken of. There might you have beheld one joy crown another, so and in such a manner, that it seem'd sorrow wept to take leave of them,—for their joy waded in tears.' 'Such a deal of wonder is broken out within this hour that the ballad-makers cannot be able to express it.'

Such restoration, occasioning so 'notable a passion of wonder', does not however occur by accident. It is, in each case, however indirectly, brought about either by a royal personage or by a child of royal personage—a child who has not been lost. In all the plays royalty seeks out royalty, or, if it does not seek it out, recognizes it for what it is. It is the offices of Lysimachus, a royal person, which restore Marina to Pericles; and though Lysimachus does not love Marina at first sight, he recognizes her all-excelling worth. Imogen goes out to seek Posthumous, and falls in with the sons of Cymbeline; they

> at first meeting loved;
> Continued so, until we thought he died;

and she, well or ill, is "bound to them". It is Florizel who sees Perdita's beauty and seeks her, though it cost a crown.

> —were I crown'd the most imperial monarch,
> Thereof most worthy; were I the fairest youth
> That ever made eye swerve; had force and knowledge
> More than was ever man's,—I would not prize them
> Without her love; for her employ them all;
> Commend them, and condemn them, to her service,
> Or to their own perdition.

And it is Miranda who sees in the lost Ferdinand 'a thing divine'. In each case such meetings, and the love which springs immediately from them, are vital to the plot; and in *The Tempest* it is Prospero's will and plan that such meeting and such love should be. And in all but *Pericles* it is child who discovers child; it is the child of the older order, wracked with evil, which discovers the lost and so is the means whereby there breaks over that older order 'a notable passion of wonder'. The older order seeks out, in the form of its child, the lost beauty which is embodied in the form of another child lost, and so redeems itself. The story of the discovery of child by child is the story of the search by what is fallen for what it knows it has lost, but which, when it is found, comes with a fine and wonderful surprise. 'Comes with a surprise' because the finding comes at a time of hopelessness, of a despair which precedes the finality of discovery.

7

Finally, we must notice the constant repetition of situations in which the dead return to life. Thaisa alone is literally ʻrecovered from death; yet Marina, the sons of Cymbeline, Posthumous, Imogen, Perdita, Hermione, Ferdinand, all reappear as if, to those who thought them dead, from death to life. Mr. Wilson Knight has rightly emphasized the story of Thaisa,[1] for it is unique in the four plays. Buried at sea and in a great storm, her body washed ashore is brought to Cerimon. In the scene in which Cerimon is introduced, he is thus addressed:

> Your honour has through Ephesus pour'd forth
> Your charity, and hundreds call themselves
> Your creatures, who by you have been restored:
> And not your knowledge, your personal pain, but even
> Your purse, still open, hath built Lord Cerimon
> . . . strong renown.

Here, as in other respects we have noticed in *Pericles*, the symbolism is clearer because less human. There is in *Pericles*

[1] *Myth and Miracle*, pp. 11–14.

a transparency of religious signification which Shakespeare, with a true instinct, sought to avoid in the later plays. But here it cannot be mistaken; and the name *Cerimon* is significant. Immediately before, Cerimon has said

> I hold it ever,
> Virtue and cunning were endowments greater
> Than nobleness and riches: careless heirs
> May the two latter darken and expend;
> But immortality attends the former
> Making a man a God.

And Thaisa is revived while viols play and there ensues a conversation which recalls the 'notable passion of wonder' in *The Winter's Tale:*

> *First Gentleman:* The heavens
> Through you increase our wonder and set up
> Your fame for ever.
> *Cerimon:*   She is alive; behold,
> Her eyelids, cases to those heavenly jewels
> Which Pericles hath lost, begin to part
> Their fringes of bright gold; the diamonds
> Of a most praised water do appear,
> To make this world twice rich.

Shakespeare never again repeated this situation; in future he confined himself, and more safely, to 'resurrection' from what was *thought* to be death. This he repeats with astonishing frequency. So frequent is it that indeed it takes on something of absurdity, and is introduced with a strange arbitrariness. It is absurd, for example, that Imogen should have mistaken the dead body of Cloten for that of Posthumous, even though his head was off and he was wearing the clothes of Posthumous; yet Shakespeare, no doubt aware of the weakness of what he wrote, by insistence makes matters worse by making Imogen say

> I know the shape of's leg: this is his hand;
> His foot Mercurial; his Martial thigh . . .

Again the 'death' of Imogen is quite unnecessary though it occasions one of the loveliest things in literature; Paulina's deception of Leontes and imprisonment of Hermione is preposterous, as also for that matter was Thaisa's segregation in a temple for a long period when she could very well have sought out Pericles; Marina also might have done so. But in this, as in other respects, what Shakespeare was anxious to convey he attempted to convey at the expense of his art, about which he seems in these plays to have cared little. And the coming to life of the 'dead' obsessed his imagination to the point of making his work silly to a degree it never had before been. And the effect of his repetition of it was enormously to weaken the power of his symbol. Unless we believe that in writing these last plays Shakespeare was merely making pretty stories, we must believe that these 'resurrections' were the vehicle of a momentous significance in his mind. Yet, at the same time, by his frequent and artistically irrelevant repetition of them, he makes them trivial.

This primary myth fails him as he uses it, and for the good reason that it was, by virtue of the limitations he set on his expression of what was in his mind, inadequate to his purpose. In *Pericles* he literally resurrects Thaisa; but he resurrects her into the incredible stupidity of not attempting to find Pericles. Had she sought and found Pericles his plot would have been ruined, for she would have also sought Marina who would then never have been lost. Having been saved from tempest and transfigured by death, she at once becomes a more than usually silly mortal and is stored away in a temple. Imogen is restored from 'death' to behave with an almost equal foolishness. Such situations, which he was under necessity to create, cut across the expression of his momentous purpose in these plays. And if we ask why he was under such necessity, the answer is because, although concerned primarily to convey his sense of the more than human, he struggled, as hard as he could, to do so without resorting, as Wordsworth and Keats in differing degrees did, to a mythology which frankly involves religious belief and language. He was right in refusing to do so. Yet by not doing so, he set himself the impossible task of conveying a sense of what lies beyond humanity through the use of human symbols. The dogmas of Christianity weakened Wordsworth's poetry, and Keats failed in his efforts to use the 'divine mythology' of Greece. It was inevitable that Shakespeare, seeking to use a 'human' mythology, should also fail. So long as he was using men and women characters his purpose in seeking to convey imagination of something more than mortal was necessarily obscured. We alternate throughout the plays between a sense of Shakespeare's high metaphysical symbolism and a sense of the silly. His purpose and his art were in conflict, and there was no resolution of it. For if his purpose was to command our imagination with a sense of 'worlds unrealized', he had also to write a story about men and women who, to serve his purpose, must at once be symbolic of 'worlds unrealized' and behave with an almost more than mortal silliness. Refusing to use, for by far the greater part, a frankly religious imagery and language, he has to use his symbol of resurrection in a trivial way, so that though we feel his purpose, his means of expressing it are inadequate, and pathetically so. When we read the story of the resurrection of Thaisa we feel the greatness of Shakespeare's significance and so far it becomes adequately symbolic. But when we view the incident from the point of view of Thaisa's later behaviour it is a piece of tawdry magic. And when, in the later plays, Shakespeare refused to repeat so frank a piece of symbolism, he has to resort to a form of it in which characters are 'resurrected' from what was only thought to be death. But this enfeebles the symbolism; and it is still more enfeebled if, as sometimes happens, the assumption that they are dead is made on little or no grounds, or when their 'death' has a complete artistic irrelevance.

It is not wholly true that Shakespeare, apart from the incident of the raising of Thaisa from the dead, avoided the use of incidents and language of a religious kind. For it is in the temple of Diana at Ephesus, where Thaisa has become a high priestess and where Cerimon 'than whom the Gods can have no mortal officer more like a god' attends, that the re-union in *Pericles* occurs. In *Cymbeline* there is the apparition of his father, mother, and brothers to Posthumous, and then also of Jupiter. It comes at a time when Posthumous, thinking Imogen dead, longs for death and freedom

> —take this life
> And cancel these cold bonds.

Sicilius, on appearing, chides Jupiter with cruelty to Posthumous:

> I died whilst in the womb he stay'd
> Attending nature's law:
> Whose father then, as men report
> Thou orphans' father art,
> Thou shouldst have been, and shielded him
> From this earth-vexing smart.

The mother describes Posthumous the infant, a 'thing of pity'; Sicilius and a brother praise his incomparable greatness. Then, having thus indicated two of Shakespeare's primary symbols, they return again to the question: why has not Jupiter shielded him from suffering and sorrow? And they appeal to him to

> Peep through thy marble mansion; help;
> Or we poor ghosts will cry
> To the shining synod of the rest
> Against thy deity.

Jupiter then appears and asserts the justice of his ways:

> Be not with mortal accidents opprest;
> No care of yours it is; you know 'tis ours.
> Whom best I love I cross; to make my gift,
> The more delay'd, delighted. Be content;
> Your low-laid son our Godhead will uplift:
> His comforts thrive, his trials well are spent.

At the close of the play a soothsayer is present to interpret the will of the gods, and Cymbeline, in the last speech of the play, promises a visit to the temple of Jupiter. In *The Winter's Tale* it is the oracle of Apollo which condemns Leontes; and Hermione comes to 'life' in a chapel in the house of Pauline. In *The Tempest* there is Prospero who seems invested with the powers of Deity.

Of these manifestations of Deity, it is that in *Cymbeline* which is the most striking. It is possible that Shakespeare did not write it; it is more likely, as Mr. Wilson Knight insists,[1] that he did. And I should say that its crudeness, so far from being evidence that he did not write it, is evidence that he did. It illustrates again the warfare of Shakespeare's dramatic art and his purpose which as such is not dramatic at all. In this episode he comes to a franker expression of his religion than perhaps anywhere; yet in so doing he writes with a clumsiness which would be amazing if we did not realize the two stools between which, in all these plays, he is constantly falling. Though his purpose be to justify the ways of God to man, he struggles to maintain the limits imposed by secular drama; and the result is that he writes neither religious nor secular drama, but, in some scenes, a crude parody of high religious significances. And as he never again after *Pericles* repeated a situation of literal resurrection, so after *Cymbeline* he never reintroduced on to the stage an appearance of Deity.

It is of interest to observe the differences between *Pericles* and *Cymbeline* on the one hand, and *The Winter's Tale* and *The Tempest* on the other. As we have said, in the two latter plays, Shakespeare avoided such frank religious symbolism as we have in the two earlier. Thaisa and Jupiter are rigorously banished. There is indeed in *The Tempest* the masque of Iris and Ceres; but their introduction is conventional, and they are called up as spirits by Prospero. They are clearly not intended as a part of a serious symbolism. It is true also that in *The Winter's Tale* Apollo speaks, through his oracle, to the state of affairs in Sicilia, and that Prospero in *The Tempest* is a kind of deity. But Apollo confines himself to the statement of bare

[1] *Myth and Miracle*, p. 20.

facts; and Prospero, if he is a deity, is also a very irritable old gentleman. And with this avoidance of fairly explicit religious symbol goes another difference also, which may be closely bound up with it. In neither *The Winter's Tale* nor *The Tempest* does such terrible suffering assail the heroes and heroines as in the two former plays. Marina, Posthumous, and Imogen, as grown-up persons, undergo suffering in a degree very much greater than falls to the lot of Perdita, Miranda, and Ferdinand, when grown up. And it is probably not an accident that avoidance of fairly explicit religious language and symbolism in the last two plays is accompanied by a diminution of the amount of suffering undergone by the heroes and heroines. It is likely that Shakespeare found such a diminution of suffering a condition of easier avoidance of obvious religious symbol. It is Thaisa who dies in the midst of tempest, and Marina who is sold to a brothel, and Posthumous, whose sufferings reduce him to something like Troilus and Hamlet rolled into one, who are most directly associated with the plainest religious symbolism in all the plays—the resurrection of Thaisa; the unusually clear symbolic character of Marina's lost royalty; the appearance of Jupiter to Posthumous when he thinks Imogen dead. Hence if in the later plays there is avoidance of such suffering, we may not unreasonably think that it is connected with avoidance by Shakespeare of too plain a symbolism. Perdita is indeed threatened with life-long poverty when Polixenes reveals himself at the feast; Caliban is a threat to Miranda, and Ferdinand suffers shipwreck. But the tone of *The Winter's Tale*, wherever Perdita appears, is incorrigibly delightful, however much Polixenes may thunder; and we know that in all that happens in *The Tempest* the benevolent magic of Prospero is present. Where, in the earlier plays, such an extent of suffering occurs, Shakespeare was under compulsion, too clearly, for his secular art, to justify the ways of God to men; hence by lightening the tone of the later plays he released himself, at least to some extent, from that compulsion. It is certainly true that the later plays at once contain less obvious symbolism and are gayer in their tone. Certainly there is no character in the last two plays who display the utter depravity of the brothel keepers, or the vileness of Cloten and the Queen; for Leontes' jealousy is, we know, an aberration in an essentially good man; Autolycus is a desirable member of any right-minded community; and Caliban is surrounded by the power of Prospero.

Yet, in thus reducing the amount of suffering in the last two plays, Shakespeare, in a measure, weakens his most desired effect, namely that of a sense of deliverance from the tragic character of all human life. The myths of the finding of what is lost and of the recovery of a lost royalty remain; but they remain without the reinforcement which, in the earlier plays, it derived from the spectacle of hideous evil overcome or destroyed, and of demoralization and despair, such as that of Posthumous, dissipated. But this weakening of effect was inevitable if he was to avoid too obvious religious symbol.

8

In *The Tempest* Shakespeare made a last and desperate effort to cope with his impossible task, and to aid himself confined himself within the limits of the unities. To do this, the story of the originating evil has to be told in retrospect and gave Shakespeare an opportunity to show his amazing powers of plain verse narrative. But also, by so doing, the effect which Shakespeare sought to convey is heightened; for from the start we have the impression of a long and disastrous story being brought to a conclusion, a sense of imminent finality. Moreover, from the outset there is a presiding and omnipotent genius; nothing, we know, can resist the power of Prospero. He is a necessity which all must choose. Hence, if there is to be finality it is at once an inevitable, agreeable, and benevolent one. The tone of the play is thus set in its early phases. This is indeed a new situation, one which does not appear elsewhere.

Now the framework of the plot, despite this novelty of situation, is yet strikingly like the older plays—there is shipwreck and storm, the loss of an heir, the belief that he is dead, his recovery, and with his recovery repentance and joy in the workers of the original evil. Yet the plot of *The Tempest* is entirely presided over, and is indeed, with the exception of the original evil of Alonso and Antonio, planned by Prospero. It is no longer a story which, as in the earlier plays, winds its uncertain and precarious way to a happy ending; it is a story issuing from the commanding magic of Prospero. This is the supreme difference between *The Tempest* and the earlier plays. And it is to be noted that in the course of the play there occurs a conspiracy directly analogous to that which dispossessed Prospero and Miranda of their crown—that in which Antonio plots to dispossess Alonso and his heir, Claribel. The analogy is too obvious to be missed. But this conspiracy, unlike the earlier one which sent Prospero and Miranda on their travels, is stopped—it is subject to the omniscience and omnipotence of Prospero. Thus cunningly does Shakespeare make all evil, as well as love, subject to the power of Prospero. Over the entire course of human destiny, therefore, there presides Prospero who is in this respect the Jupiter, however heavily disguised, of *Cymbeline*. For by being master even of such an evil as drove Prospero himself from Milan, Prospero is no longer the injured man of earlier years doomed to suffer evil, but the god who commands evil for his purposes. Yet, though Prospero be the Jupiter of *Cymbeline*, he is indeed Jupiter in a heavy disguise of mortality. Here is no crude descent of a god. God Prospero may be; but he is also a very human, impatient old gentleman. His humanity is as perfectly set out as his divinity. Here is no stiff and pompous Jupiter. Shakespeare no doubt was on his guard against another such Jupiter as he made in *Cymbeline*. But to do so he had to resort to making an all too human character of his divinity in *The Tempest*.

But it is not only that Prospero is the controller of human destinies as they are symbolized in the story of the play, the essential plot which *The Tempest* has in common with the three other plays. He is here also lord of Ariel and Caliban. As we have said, Caliban, even if he be the evil of the world, our 'worser genius', is not merely that—that could not be. He has imagination and dreams of an almost intolerable beauty—

> Sometimes a thousand twangling instruments
> Will hum about mine ears; and sometimes voices,
> That, if I then had waked after long sleep,
> Will make me sleep again; and then, in dreaming,
> The clouds methought would open and show riches
> Ready to drop upon me; that, when I waked,
> I cried to dream again.

That being so, the harshest judgment we can pass on him is that he is very foolish. For this was his judgment on himself:

> What a thrice double-ass
> Was I, to take this drunkard for a god,
> And worship this dull fool!

And if Ariel is the imagination, singing an unearthly music, seeking liberation into worlds unrealized and destined to achieve it, Caliban too has his divinity. His is the labour of humanity which, though it cannot fail of a sense of beauty greater than the world can show, yet follows foolish gods; must suffer disillusion and exclaim, with Caliban—

> and I'll be wise hereafter,
> And seek for grace.

Caliban and Ariel, after all, are one. To show this identification Shakespeare lavished, in Caliban, his most consummate art, for it was the goal and consummation of all his work.

Yet, as has often been said, Prospero is not only divinity, the Eternal Being; he is also the genius of poetry, whether of Shakespeare, Wordsworth or Keats, or any other of the great poets, which raises the tempest of tragedy, the "agonies, the strife of human hearts", and allays it with "heavenly music"; and which sees that Caliban and Ariel are one, though Caliban be kept in bondage and Ariel be set free. For Caliban is the tempest which passes into the music which is Ariel. Yet, if Prospero be at once divinity and poet, there is here perhaps no inner contradiction in the symbol. For if we may borrow Coleridge's thought for a moment when he said that the imagination is 'the repetition, in the finite mind, of the infinite I AM', the universal inclusive imagination of the great poet may perhaps be the completest repetition which we can know in the finite mind of the 'infinite I AM'. For the great poet is creative to the greatest possible degree; he creates in his art a world of humanity. And then seeks the dissolution of it, an 'insubstantial pageant faded', in the face of a transcendent and incomparably greater reality. "It dissolves, diffuses, dissipates . . ."

> The cloud-capp'd towers, the gorgeous palaces,
> The solemn temples, the great globe itself,
> Yea, all which it inherit, shall dissolve,
> And, like this insubstantial pageant faded,
> Leave not a rack behind.

The Tempest is the record of the final dissolution, the ultimate destruction, of the world by the imagination. Shakespeare dissolved the world he had created; his interest was no longer in it; it was beyond it, and beyond the human. And he dissolved it, never to recreate it. In *The Tempest* humanity is destroyed, and with it poetry—

> —I'll break my staff,
> Bury it certain fadoms in the earth,
> And deeper than did ever plummet sound
> I'll drown my book.

For human life is a "little" thing and is 'rounded with a sleep'.[1]

[1] To many readers it is likely that this statement will seem enough to disprove my argument in this chapter. I will only say that there is no need to assume that 'rounded' means 'finished off'; it may equally well be taken to mean 'encompassed by' and therefore 'occurring within' a 'sleep'—'we are such stuff as dreams are made on'. Taken in this way, the identity of Shakespeare's thought with that of Keats is clear.

CHAPTER VIII

POETRY, DOGMA, AND THE MYSTICAL

I saw a chapel all of gold
That none did dare to enter in,
And many weeping stood without,
Weeping, mourning, worshipping.

I saw a serpent rise between
The white pillars of the door,
And he forc'd and forc'd and forc'd,
Down the golden hinges tore.

And along the pavement sweet,
Set with pearls and rubies bright,
All his slimy length he drew,
Till upon the altar white

Vomiting his poison out
On the bread and on the wine.
So I turn'd into a sty
And laid me down among the swine.

BLAKE

I

THE work of literary criticism is not one which can hope to be carried out successfully without a synoptic view of human nature in all activities and experiences; it draws its vitality, such as it may be, from sympathetic contact with the whole range of human apprehension of the world. Clearly the work of criticism is not a specialized department of knowledge and judgment which can operate in disregard of any part of experience; on the contrary it demands for itself the best and most inclusive reflections on human experience in its entirety as a condition for assessment of the place and significance of creative imaginative work. Whatever value we may attach to that aspect of literary criticism which is virtually a part of history, the tracing of facts relating to the

creation of literature and of literary form, there remains, as
the final labour of criticism, the judgment of literary work,
not as a historical occurrence, but as an imaginative apprehension which is complete in itself, and which the historical
judgment does not affect. Such a process of judgment demands
a previous labour of reflection and construction which, resulting
in a unified view of human activity, is capable at once of imaginative sympathy with the work in question, and of emphatic
judgment of its significance. The great need of our civilization
is such a unification in our view of human experience, a unity
in which no major activity of the human mind is sacrificed to
others, but is related to others in a way which detracts from
the importance of none of them for the well-being of life.

Such a unity of self-knowledge is what the human mind
in our own day notoriously lacks. It is a commonplace of reflection that the modern world, issuing from the unity of Catho-
licism in the Middle Ages, became a scene in which the different
modes of experiencing reality were set in conflict. Where
previously philosophy, art and the entire conduct of life were
unified in the Catholic view of the universe, and of the place
of man in it, the modern world is one in which there is no
stabilized centre around which our varied activities may move,
and to which they may constantly be related. The addition,
to this disruption, of the scientific attitude added enormously
to the difficulties; to-day we seem to be little nearer to
effecting a unity of experience than were the men and women
of the seventeenth century. The fundamental trouble of our
civilization is precisely this disruption of the inner unity of
human experience which began with what we call the modern
world. This inner conflict is necessarily a devitalization, a
weakening of the mind which increasingly renders us more
helpless to deal successfully with the outer chaos into which our
inner division issues. A house so divided within itself must fall
sooner or later; and our only hope lies in the discovery of a
degree of self-knowledge which can harmoniously relate to
each other all our activities to the detriment of none.

It has sometimes been said that the Romantic poets were those who, in the history of English literature, came nearest to achieving such a unified view of experience. Wordsworth, Coleridge, Keats, and Shelley were all of them men of wide and deep reflection as well as of powerful imagination. Yet, if we consider Wordsworth in the days of his maturity, it is impossible, as we have said, not to see in his attitude to science evidence of an underlying disquiet. Although on the surface he endeavours to give the appearance of an absence of the least antagonism between science on the one hand and religion and poetry on the other, the alliance between them which he describes is a strikingly uneasy one. I have tried in a former chapter to describe how intolerable Wordsworth's attitude towards science really is; and it is difficult not to conclude that scientific inquiry so far from being in Wordsworth's view a support to the poet's religious attitude to life, was, for him, a source of the greatest fear. Wordsworth's error, as we saw, lay in thinking that scientific inquiry is a means whereby the ultimate nature of reality may be disclosed; his attitude towards it was therefore that of a man who placed in a cage with a tiger tries desperately to conciliate the tiger as the only possible hope of not being eaten up. The result was that Wordsworth at once thought too much and too little of science. On the one hand he seems to attribute to it the power of ultimate metaphysical disclosure; on the other he fails to recognize the enormous value and importance of science. He at once minimizes the true dignity of science, and attributes to it powers which in fact it does not possess.

In respect of religion, Wordsworth, in contrast to Keats, finally accepted Christianity; he came increasingly to see in the Christian representation of the world an expression of all that was best in his own imaginative life. Shakespeare and Keats struggled to create a mythology adequate to their apprehension; Wordsworth rested from any such labour in the possession of Christian dogma. The poetic lives of Shakespeare and Keats ended with their efforts to create adequate mythology; Wordsworth's poetry declined with his acceptance of Christianity. If Shakespeare and Keats failed to create adequate mythologies, Wordsworth was content with what Christianity gave him. Yet, dogma is not poetry, nor a mere mythology. Mythology is the use of symbols which is not bound up with belief in its symbols; but dogma is bound to the denial that it is using mere symbols and to the assertion of the historical truth of its "symbols". In dogma belief is vital; and with it goes acceptance of authority. And in accepting Christianity Wordsworth was not accepting, nor could he possibly imagine that he was accepting, a mythology which may be highly expressive. Christianity could not be for Wordsworth, any more than for anyone else, a mere poetry, however adequate, and it necessarily laid compulsion upon his poetry. Keats on the other hand was curiously unsympathetic towards Christianity, and described the structure of Christian dogma as 'pious fraud', although the man whom more than any other of his day he admired had shown in *The Excursion* the submission of his imagination to Christianity. As for Keats we certainly can say that he showed in this respect a striking insensitiveness to the expressiveness of Christian dogma. It is of the greatest interest to observe two such strikingly different attitudes on the part of the two great poets towards dogmatic religion, and to consider how two powerful imaginations in certain important respects so fundamentally alike, should entertain such extremely differing views of Christianity.

2

What is of the greatest importance is to try to realize the place of dogma in religion and its necessity for a religion. To many people to-day, we may be sure, religious dogma is an inexplicable mystery which they feel it necessary to condemn wholesale. What makes dogma an impossible stumbling-block to many such is of course its assertion of the miraculous[1];

---

[1] I use the word 'miraculous' to include the claim of a final revelation made at a definite period of time through Christ.

but what alone can dispel, to any degree, its impossibility in this respect is the realization of the inevitability of miracle for religion, and the understanding that a great religion demands, as a condition of its vitality, a structure of belief in what is shot through with the miraculous. Unless we can realize that this is so, we shall either stand outside Christianity and condemn it, as Keats did, or we shall, if our attitude be religious, be one of the many modernist apologists for Christianity who, we may believe, do harm to their religion by seeking carefully to extract from it all element of miracle. Such teachers may, indeed they often do, reduce dogma to the status of a symbol, beautiful and expressive perhaps, but yet only a symbol; and they thereby weaken its vitality and value. The historical basis which Christianity claims is fundamental to its existence, and to deny it is to rob Christianity of its potency in the world.

It is of course the case that the Christian creed is not wholly a statement of what is stated to be historical fact; and it may be said that we can accept the idea of revelation without committing ourselves to belief in the historical truth of many Christian dogmas. But nevertheless, if we are to be Christians, we cannot thus separate out its various elements, rejecting some and accepting others; and to reject the historical basis of Christianity with its great miracles in whole or part is an act which must finally, if it is to be consistent, be content to recognize that the Christ-myth doctrine, if it attained to general credence, would not affect the life of Christianity in the world. If we are willing to view any part of the life of Christ as symbolic merely, there is no overwhelming reason why we should not be prepared to view Christ himself as a symbol, one of unusual power and expressiveness, but only a fictitious creation. As is well known, there have been attempts from the early days of Christianity to effect this reduction; but the Church has consistently recognized that its continued existence depended upon the destruction of any such tendency. The revelation which Christianity claims to convey is irrevocably bound up with the assertion of historical fact; and to refuse to see that this is so is to aim at the foundation of Christianity.

The reason for the importance of the historical element in religion is not far to seek. A great religion is the answer to humanity's imperative demand for an absolute and final revelation. And that being so, as Professor A. E. Taylor has pointed out, it is clear that what is claimed as a final revelation of God is strengthened, and not weakened, if it be asserted that that revelation was effected through a particular life which was lived under certain historical conditions and in intimacy with other men and women; if, that is to say, the revelation occurred in the midst of the ordinary goings-on of the world. Such a claim must necessarily give to a religion a power, and a command of men's imagination, which no abstract philosophy or collection of abstract truths about the nature of God and his relations to man could possibly have. "The completest revelation conceivable", says Professor Taylor, "would be an actual temporal life, subject as such to the contingency characteristic of the temporal, which should be also, in all its detail, the complete and adequate vehicle of the eternal."[1] And again,

So long as we have the strictly eternal on one side, and the merely creaturely, however faultless, on the other, the actual interpenetration and enfolding of the temporal by the eternal remains incomplete. If the full resolution of the ultimate dissonance is to be achieved, what is necessary is a life which is at once everywhere creaturely and yet also everywhere more than creaturely, because its limitations, circumscriptions and infirmities, whatever they may be, interpose no obstacle to the divine and eternal purpose which controls and shines through it, but are themselves vehicles of that purpose.

As Professor Taylor goes on to point out, the Christian conviction that such a life has been lived is not established from empirical evidence; it is, he says, "an act of walking by 'faith' and not by 'sight'. That the Word has been 'made flesh', and

[1] *The Faith of a Moralist*, Vol. II, p. xii.

made flesh in just the specific person whom a Christian calls Lord, is a proposition which admits of no establishment by the empirical appeal to certified fact."[1]

The assertion of this supreme historical fact is further added to by assertions of miraculous occurrences in the life of Christ. With the philosophical arguments which may be advanced to show the possibility of miraculous occurrences we are not concerned; it may be argued that there is nothing intrinsically absurd in believing in miracle, if we once grant the point from which religion starts. The general fact with which we are concerned is that it would be impossible to remove from Christianity its belief in miracles without profoundly changing it. And a religion which is to hold itself as a final revelation of God cannot, what it would not wish to do, rid itself of such a belief. For miracle is for religion, believing in the reality of God disclosing himself to man, the intrusion of the supernatural into the natural and the assertion of the supremacy of the supernatural. That the extraordinary and miraculous will accompany any direct revelation of God through any chosen person is a belief to which mankind has ever been prone; and it would naturally be inconceivable that a religion, which holds that God has in a certain life made a final revelation of himself, should not hold fast to miraculous occurrences which were claimed to have occurred during that life. And there is no reason to believe that, in the belief in miracles, there is anything intrinsically unreasonable; there is nothing in miracle which conflicts with a view of the world as a rational order; and indeed miracle, so far from being in the eyes of religion an inexplicable marvel, is rather a higher manifestation of a supreme purpose showing itself to its creatures. It is true that in a sense miracle is, for the religious consciousness, something inexplicable, if we view it from the standpoint of physical science; yet also, for religion, its inexplicability from that point of view is necessary in order to make it explicable as a revelation of transcendent purpose. Any attempt by a

[1] *Faith of a Moralist*, Vol. II, pp. 125–6.

modernist Christianity to explain away the miracles, that is to say, to find for them a natural explanation, must necessarily be unwelcome to many Christians. For such an attempt arises from viewing miracle as something formerly unexplained yet now explicable. But to do that is to fail to understand the unique importance of miracle for the spiritual life, for, in the spiritual life of Christianity, belief in miracle is an act of faith which sees in a given event a direct sign of the purpose of God; and in order that the event may be so regarded, and that belief in the event may be an act of faith, miracle must be placed beyond the scope of natural explanation; its immediate cause must be the free activity of God. It is by belief in miracle that religion makes powerful testimony, in faith, to the reality of God and his dealings with men.

Moreover, it is not the case that in the days in which the belief in miracle grew up the human mind was not acquainted with the notion of the world as a regular and uniform order. It is sometimes thought that the belief in miracle was possible only in pre-scientific days before our modern scientific attitude grew up, and that therefore beliefs which were possible in earlier days can no longer be maintained. But this view has no real foundation. Miracle indeed would never have come to occupy the place in religion which it has always had unless the idea of nature as a regular order had grown up; its significance depends upon its occurrence within a world which is regular and uniform in its occurrences. And indeed so far from the growth of belief in miracle being evidence of the failure of earlier generations of men to grasp the notion of the world as regularly and lawfully connected part with part, it is instead evidence that that notion was strongly present in their minds. It is only because it was so that belief in miracle, as an act of faith in the transcendent purpose of God, could possibly arise. In a similar manner it is sometimes said that only a philosophy such as that of Hume, which makes the world order irrational through and through, can make belief in miracle at all intelligible. But this is an extreme misstatement; it is only in a world which is rational that miracle can have, as issuing from the Mind which is the source of the world's rational structure, its enormous significance for faith and become itself a part of a rational universe.

It is the same with religious convention. Christianity is associated as we know with a large number of institutional observances which are dogmatic in the sense that they are, in their observance, means of grace which grew up in the course of time, and became sanctioned by authority. The social character of religion necessarily led to this result, as uniformity between individuals in the means whereby grace is sought. The value of such conventions, religious observances regularly carried out by all members of the Church, is obviously very great; a great religion could not conceivably grow up without them, and they naturally become enjoined upon the individual as necessary to his spiritual well-being. For the individual to seek to depart from them must necessarily be viewed with grave disfavour by the Church. They become inwoven into the structure of dogma, and constituent parts of the dogmatic framework, means sanctioned and instituted by divine authority for the reception of grace. This does not, of course, involve denial of response to divine reality through private channels; but the Church inevitably insists at least upon these authoritative channels. This is right and inevitable; and the ritual of Christianity becomes therefore of a piece with its entire tissue of dogma, and inseparable from it. The individual in Christianity therefore is committed not only to belief in a final revelation of God in history; that act of faith becomes one with the series of conventional observances which the Church demands. The act of belief is inextricably associated with the practice of religious observance, which regularly carried out invests the whole of life with a sacramental character. The acceptance of dogma without traditional observances is not a Christianity; the belief in a final historical revelation shows itself in acceptance of religious convention.

It is, of course, the case that this involves acceptance of

authority, of a means through which the ultimate divine authority speaks. The social character of religion makes this inevitable. The dangers of ritualism and convention in religion may be great; so may submission before authority. Yet authority in the Church, like ritual, is clearly indispensable. The Church must necessarily remain critical of itself; it must also avoid the destruction of freedom and initiative in the individual. But however much this is so, ritual and authority must remain. If a final revelation of God has been made, there must be authority through which that revelation is maintained and by which it is asserted, and before which the individual, in association with others, must submit. To attempt to dispense with authority is necessarily to initiate anarchy and decay; for if a Church which claims to be a vehicle for a final revelation is to be universal, it can be so only on the basis of an authority which is absolute. This must mean in the last resort the acceptance of authority not because it appeals, by its judgments, to personal reflection, but for no other reason than that it is a final authority. Authority again therefore is part and parcel of the dogmatic structure of religion; it is indeed foundational to it. The official representative of religion is, so to speak, himself dogma, in so far as he is part of the chosen means whereby the final revelation of himself made by God is proclaimed. He is therefore not one man among others; his position is recognized, through an act of faith, as authoritive, enjoining religious creed and practice alike. And in general, we cannot hope to enter into the spirit of Christianity unless we realize that its life is a walking by 'faith' and an acceptance of that which cannot be established by appeal to empirical evidence. The craving of the spirit is for an absolute disclosure of reality. That such a disclosure has once and for all been made, and that there exists an authority sanctioned to convey it, cannot be established by argumentation; Christianity is an act of faith. Until we grasp this essentially simple situation the entire structure of Christianity is for us, as it was for Keats, simply 'pious fraud'.

But if, on the other hand, we see belief in Christian dogma as fundamentally an act of faith in an ultimate revelation, made through a historical person and continuing to be proclaimed authoritatively by the Church, we also see the entirely impregnable position which it enjoys. Its invulnerability is complete. For there is no argumentation either of a philosophical or scientific kind which can overthrow it. Belief in God and in a revelation of himself in the life of Christ, even if it cannot be established by philosophical argument, can neither be overthrown by it; and the evidence of a historical kind which has come down to us, while it may not establish the historical dogmas of Christianity, is not incompatible with them. So much no doubt can be said; but the positive acceptance of dogma is far from depending on this for its occurrence. For such acceptance, issuing from an act of faith, does not appeal to empirical evidence. For this reason, it is unassailable. And the increase of the strength of the scientific consciousness in our time, so far from making acceptance of dogma impossible simply has not relevance to that acceptance as expression of Christian faith.

3

No doubt there will always be two types of religious minds, those who fail to respond to Christian dogma and those who find in dogma and Christian practice the only possible means to spiritual health. And Keats, who seems to have been incorrigibly of the first type, was yet so near to Wordsworth, who became one of the latter type, as to find *The Excursion* one of the three finest things of his time. Whether Keats, had he lived, might have come, like Wordsworth, to a perception of the power and depth of Christian dogma, it is useless to speculate. Probably he would not have so changed, though we have to remember that for many years of poetic vitality Wordsworth failed to realize the significance of Christianity. But our present purpose is to observe that the most acute spiritual and cultural crisis of our time consists in the increasing inability of many religious people to accept dogmatic religion, in contrast to those who find in revealed religion a necessity for their spiritual life. The poetry of Wordsworth and of Keats and their respective attitudes towards Christianity present the issue; and it is a question of the greatest importance for the whole of modern life and the future of civilization.

Now dogma may be regarded as a concrete mode of apprehending what, if it were stated abstractly in propositional form, would become a philosophy and as such cease to command the minds of men. Religion is not philosophy, and dogma is not mere proposition. A dogma may be regarded as a mode of apprehending what evades expression in abstract form, and which, by its appeal to the imagination, remains the form in which what is claimed as religious truth may be most effectively and compulsively conveyed. A condition of the power of religion which is to be universal is that it be available and effective for all minds, educated and uneducated alike; and the concrete historical form of conveying the religious imagination of the world is for that reason the only possible one. That is not to say that Christian dogma was deliberately adopted, in the growth of the Church, as the most signal way in which what was originally grasped as a philosophical whole might have expression and find its way to men's minds. For Christian dogma has never been resolved by Christian thinkers into a philosophical scheme having universal acceptance; nor did dogma take its rise from such a scheme. Dogma was the natural way in which the religious apprehension of the world occurred; it was not, that is to say, a piece of 'pious fraud' deliberately and deceptively imposed on a too credulous world. It was only as dogma that Christianity first fired the imagination and lives of men; and only as dogma will it in the future continue to do so. It is the only way in which the craving for an absolute and final knowledge could and will find satisfaction, a final revelation embodied in a life lived under conditions of space and time. Only thus could the wealth of thought and feeling which is in religion find a clear and emphatic crystallization of itself, and thereby make itself available for the simplest mind. Dogma is a necessity for religion if only in the sense that in that way alone can religion convey its tremendous burden. The expressiveness of dogma lies in its concreteness, in its avoidance of theory, and its assertion of certain definite historical occurrences.

Thus, to express the sense of the overwhelming reality of the supernatural order, there is no means conceivably more effective than revelation and miracle, the disruption of the natural; to show the reality of God, there is no means comparable with the story of Christ who was both God and man; to show the relation of the human to the divine, the story of Christ's despair, sacrifice, dereliction, and resurrection exceeds anything which has ever been thought or imagined. We may endeavour to extract from these dogmas volumes of theology, but they will be, from the point of view of religion, pitiable in comparison with the simple story from which they take their origin. Theology is, in a sense, a desecration of the superb poetry of religion; it destroys its magical power and gives us the dry dust of abstraction. That is not to say that theology can or ought to be done away with, any more than criticism and interpretation of great poetry ought to be prohibited because it is not itself poetry. Theology no doubt is a necessity doomed to end in failure, which we cannot avoid. Yet whatever value the effort to explicate dogma into theology may be, it is the contemplation of the dogma itself which is central to the Christian life. Theology may very well enrich that contemplation, and therein lies its sole justification: as the study of criticism of poetry is justified only in so far as it enriches the later contemplation of the poetry itself. But considered in itself, theology is for religion a pernicious substitute, as reading about a poet is a pernicious substitute for reading the poet.

That is not, of course, to say that, to religion, dogma is but a poetry. That indeed is precisely what it can never be. And to talk about dogma as a kind of poetry is already to have put oneself outside religion, to have excommunicated oneself from its inner simplicity and wholeness. As we have said, religion insists on its historical basis; indeed thereby it defies the destructive heresy that religion and dogma are but a poetry and a symbolism. The story of Christianity suggests that religion is always and for ever menaced by just this danger, a menace which, could it gain general assent, would be the end of Christianity. For Christianity is built upon beliefs in historical occurrences which for faith are beyond dispute and attack; for these are occurrences directly manifesting God in the world, and thus, as we have said, showing forth the rationality of the universe. The greatest danger to religion is not from critics outside the Church, but from those within organized Christianity who are constantly urging the recognition of all miracle as either explicable or as a poetry.

4

Yet, to many minds, dogma is a poetry and a symbolism, however perfect and final, a mode of expression, not assertion of actual historical occurrence.[1] Such people, to whom Keats' view that religious dogma is an accretion issuing from pious fraud is abhorrent, yet cannot reach orthodoxy; or if they remain nominally Christian are kept in a constant inner disquiet by what they know to be the falseness of their position. We may say that it is the very invulnerability of religion from attack, and the perfect security of its position, which makes dogma difficult of acceptance for many minds. Religion is impregnable against attack from any scientific point of view because the historical events on

[1] I wish to add here that my concern is not to advocate the view of dogma which is expounded in this section. My desire is merely to set out the nature of what seems to me the primary spiritual crisis of our time.

which it bases itself are accepted, by faith, as the manifestation of God; to such minds as those of whom now we speak, religion is immune from such attack because the power of dogma is of the same order as the power of a great play, a perfect manifestation of the world, as it is present to the imagination, which is not bound to limit itself for its purposes by any calculation of probability. From such a point of view, it is as absurd to impugn the historical basis of Christianity as to impugn the reality of the characters and events in a Shakespearean play; for questions of fact in such an apprehension of the world, through the particular and the concrete, do not present themselves for consideration. It is enough that the world as it is present to the religious imagination is vividly apprehended. In such an attitude to dogma, the question of fact and fiction simply does not occur, as it does not occur in the beholdment of a tragedy. Statement in dogma is not commensurate with ordinary statement of fact, as the statements in a great work of art are not so commensurate. The question of truth and falsity does not occur in either case in relevance to such statements; all that is important is that an imaginative apprehension of the world is conveyed through them. Nevertheless, as we have said, to view Christianity as a poetry, however perfectly expressive, is to have put oneself outside the Christian community; to sever the identity of symbol and reality in religion is to destroy the necessary foundations of that religion. Hence, as we have suggested, the menace to religion does not arise from so-called scientific attack; but from the angle of perception in which the impregnability of religion against such attack is seen as arising from the essentially artistic mode of religious apprehension. Religion is seen as an artistic mode of apprehension which is compelled to assert the reality of its mythus. It is therefore, when thus viewed, seen as containing an inner contradiction, yet a contradiction which, for the continuance of religion, must be preserved at all costs.

But such a state of affairs is, it is held, necessarily unsatisfactory, and if we view religion in this light, orthodoxy is seen to be a factor in experience which necessarily occasions inner conflict and disquiet, a factor which will be eliminated in the course of the growth of man's mind and of increase in self-knowledge. For from this point of view religion is a poetry which must refuse to know itself for a poetry. But such a refusal, it is argued, must be overcome; and as civilization advances dogmatic religion must increasingly be seen as primitive, and a stage beyond which man must pass. This transition, it is held, is what is most painful in the present stage of our civilization. It is not true, as is often thought, that the cultural crisis of our time issues from the so-called conflict of religion and science. Such a conflict does not exist. The significant conflict of our time is that which occurs in the minds of those who, seeing in dogmatic religion the only possible form of a religion which is to be universal, saving, and missionary, yet are compelled to view dogma as a form of religion from which they must, in honesty, deliver themselves.[1] It may be put in another way by saying that for such minds the difficulty is not in accepting dogmatic religion; to seek membership of the community of a Christianity can be only too easy. The difficulty is rather in rejecting a religion which is thought to be, as a religion, final and absolute.

When we consider the tradition of English poetry since the Reformation, it is obvious that it is not a Christian poetic tradition. None of the major poets, with the exception of Milton, have written as Christians. The case of Wordsworth therefore is of enormous interest and importance to us. During the years of his greatest poetic output he wrote as a man of passionately religious imagination, but not as a Christian. After his acceptance of Christianity he wrote indeed much fine poetry; but the fact of a decline of his poetic power is undeniable.

[1] This crisis has not arisen, it must be repeated, as a result of the growth of natural science; it has arisen pre-eminently from growing knowledge of anthropology and of primitive religion. I need hardly add, however, that it would be erroneous to think that the latter studies have made Christian belief irrational.

Keats and Shakespeare sought to evolve their own mythologies;
Wordsworth satisfied his imagination in the contemplation of
Christian dogma, which considered as a mythology is absolute,
where those of Shakespeare and Keats are halting and inexpres-
sive. But a dogma is not merely poetry, as we have said. It is
a great deal more. In Wordsworth the non-Christian tradition
in English poetry once more adopted Christianity; but to its
detriment. Wordsworth's later poetry is therefore the most
perfect comment we have upon the present state of the mind of
our civilization; for Wordsworth, who, when all is said and
done, possessed one of the most powerful imaginations of
our time, sought out Christianity and made it his own, only
to impair, though by no means to destroy, the sources of his
poetry. And we choose before the dogmatic poetry of the later
Wordsworth the poetic failures of Keats and of Shakespeare.

5

There is, before we proceed briefly to summarize
the argument of this essay, another aspect of the relationship
between poetry and religion which calls for comment. And it
is an aspect which we can discuss through the help of M.
Brémond's remarkable book *Prayer and Poetry*. The argument
of M. Brémond's book is sufficiently familiar to excuse me from
attempting to summarize it at any length. It is, in effect, that
all poetic apprehension is essentially mystical, that the movement of the poetic mind is necessarily towards a state of prayer,
a goal and consummation from which the poet turns away
in order to carry through the task of expressing himself in
his verse. The thrill which great poetry affords is the thrill
of a mystical experience which does not know itself for what
it is, and which therefore does not proceed to the finality of the
actual mystical contemplation of, or penetration to, the transcendent. Such 'secondary' mystical experiences as we are given
in poetry are, in their essential character, moments in which
we enjoy an awareness which is not intellectual but intuitive;

and because, it is held, this is so, poetic experience is fundamentally akin to the mystical, and would, if given scope to develop itself, become mystical experience proper. In M. Brémond's theory there are many elements, and the relation between them is often far from clear. But in general there is good reason to believe that his theory is too drastic, and an excessive reduction, into the limits of a sweeping theory, of the enormous varieties of expression which mark the past and present of poetry. And in particular, it may be asked whether to use the word mystical in so wide a sense is not at once to divest it of its essential significance, and to build the argumentation on shifting sands. So strongly did M. Brémond hold that in poetic apprehension the intellectual element is unimportant that he held, indeed, that what is strictly poetic is that which is other than the intellectual in it, and that in poetry the intellectual content is irrelevant to the experience we enjoy. Now it may very well be the case that in what we have called the imaginative act, the conceptual element is secondary to that power whereby the object is grasped as an individual whole. Nevertheless, the imagination and the intelligence cannot be conveniently sundered apart, but at every point involve each other. And in poetry we see the union of the two, expression in words, necessarily expressive of intellectual content, and also conveyance of a sense of the individual wholeness of the object. And however true it may be that poetic apprehension is not merely an affair of concepts and categories, poetry is yet an affair of words, and depends for its expressiveness on what are necessarily, in one aspect of their usage, vehicles of abstraction. However true it may be that in poetry the poet uses words with an art which compels them to be much more than such vehicles of abstraction, yet he cannot destroy, in the use of them, the intellectual content which is necessarily present in the use of words. M. Brémond indeed does not deny the presence of such an intellectual content; yet he does frequently appear to speak as if in poetic apprehension such content completely fades out; or if it remains present, is entirely irrelevant to what is strictly poetic in our experience. It is true, obviously, that poetry is not merely an affair of concepts. But that does not drive us to deny a conceptual element which is present and relevant to the other elements active in our experience. It may no doubt be the case that 'a thing of beauty is a constant joy' is not poetry, while 'a thing of beauty is a joy for ever' is, although the intellectual content is the same in each case. But it is clear that all that this shows is, not that intellectual content is irrelevant to poetry, but that poetry depends on something more than expression of intellectual content. And it may be added that even if formal sentences be not used in poetry, the mere use of words implies conceptual expression; and in the creation or reading of poetry, that expression cannot fail to be a constituent part, upon which the entire effect of the poetry must to some extent depend. So long as words are used they cannot fail to be indicators of classes of objects.

We are compelled therefore to ask whether, when M. Brémond said that all poetic apprehension is mystical, he meant anything more than that poetic apprehension involves something more than awareness of a meaning? In other words, is anything more implied than is present in saying that poetry is the effort after vivid conveyance of an object present in its unity to the imagination, an effort which is not active in scientific inquiry or prose statement? It may be the case that, as M. Brémond, quoting Arnold, says, it is Shakespeare who has given us the life of the flower 'taking the winds of March with beauty', and not the botanist; or Wordsworth the bird 'breaking the silence of the seas' and not the zoologist. But this is hardly saying more than that the flower and the bird were present to the poets' minds in a fashion unusual to people whose main concern is conceptual explication. The mysticism which M. Brémond detected in poetic apprehension is surely nothing more than the enjoyment of acute imaginative apprehension of the being of an object, an experience enjoyed by the poet himself in the first place, and then conveyed by his subtle use of words through his poetry to the reader. The enjoyment of such pure imaginative experience, in which release is found from the ordinary immersion of the mind in the life of practice and of the will, is itself the thrill, the 'passing of the current' of which M. Brémond spoke. The sense of being uplifted above the world, allied with unusually penetrative perception of the world, is what M. Brémond chose to call a mystical experience, but which it is surely better to describe simply as the essence of all imaginative experience whatsoever; and it must surely only make for confusion thus to render the terms interchangeable.

6

Yet it is true that poetry is often mystical, in the strict sense of the term, embodying the movement of the imagination to penetrate to what is beyond our world. In what has gone before we have tried to illustrate this in writing of Wordsworth, Keats, and Shakespeare. It is not indeed true to say, as we have suggested, that the life of poetry is one of mere disinterestedness in the sense that the whole life of the poet does not seek in poetic experience an inner satisfaction and fulfilment. To view poetry as merely and wholly disinterested would be to view it as something which could occur at the will of the poet; in other words, to divorce it from life in its pursuit of an absolute fulfilment. And as in science the formulation of a theorem must lead to further inquiry and research, so in poetry the enjoyment of poetic experience of any part of the world is fraught with the necessity of discovering a wider and more inclusive imaginative apprehension, in which more and more elements in experience are caught up and incorporated. The imagination of the great poet at least never rests from this momentous labour which endeavours to encompass the whole of life, and to achieve a comprehensive unity of imaginative pattern. In many minds, though by no means in all, such a labour, issuing in a failure to achieve such a unity and to perceive in experience such a harmony, leads on to an imaginative apprehension of life in which the world or our experience is seen as only fragmentary, and as a part of a wider reality which in its totality is susceptible only of the dimmest apprehension. Only in the light of that wider reality is this world seen as bodying forth a unity, a unity which in itself it does not possess. For some minds such an imagination of life comes to have a compulsive and controlling reality; an 'unknown and no more' takes on an overwhelming significance for the whole of life. The imagination in its passion for unity and harmony is driven to the indulgence of this 'dream', which, whether in reality it be 'dream' or not, is 'a presence which is not to be put by', and which conditions the whole of life. In other words, it is precisely the encompassment of the world by the imagination which is seen to be impossible; the essential labour of the imagination, its passion for unity and order is defeated by experience; and whatsoever of unity and order life is seen to possess hangs on the sense of that which baffles the imagination.

Such a state of affairs, while alone it affords to the imagination release from a sense of total failure, is one in which poetry must struggle for its very life; for it imposes upon poetry the task of conveying the ineffable and what lies beyond human life. Only when it endeavours to do so is poetry strictly mystical; but if this is so, mysticism occurs as the consummation of the poetical life not, as M. Brémond would, it seems, have us believe, as its original and necessary condition. Yet there is at least this truth in M. Brémond's view; that in some poets, and in some of the very greatest poets, their poetry moves to an end which is indeed that which Christianity calls prayer, the aspiration towards transcendent perception. It is of course the case that some poets begin their poetic life haunted by 'Adam's dream'—Keats is a notable instance, and his poetry has from the outset a mythical character. But there are many poets whose work is of the greatest worth but which does not at all try to convey such a response to life; and there

are others of whom Shakespeare is the greatest example,
in whom we can see the 'human and dramatic' imagination
suddenly transformed into the 'enthusiastic and meditative'
under the compulsion of suffering. M. Brémond's generalization
was therefore based on too vague and inexact a use of the word
'mysticism'; the most that we can say is that in some cases
the imaginative life finds its consummation in the mystical,
that in others the imagination is naturally and consistently
mystical; but that there are notable instances of poetic work,
the worth of which is generally beyond doubt, of which it
would be wholly misleading to say that it is mystical. Yet,
when this has been said, M. Brémond may well be right in
what is most fundamental in his doctrine. For though it is
the case that there is much poetry, such as that of Hardy,
which it seems mistaken to describe as in any way mystical,
we have to take account of the following situation. As Mr.
Eliot has said, religion is never wholly freed of scepticism;
but it needs to be added, what is equally true, that scepticism
can never wholly liberate itself from faith. Faith is 'somehow
integrated' into scepticism, just as scepticism is 'somehow integrated' into faith. In these matters it is not given to us to *know*.
The 'denial' into which some scepticism issues cannot be
absolute. As Kant said, religion is an affair of the *practical*
reason; and for this reason explicit assertion or denial is superficial in its implications. Thus, it is in effect impossible to draw
a line of division between what we call faith and what we call
scepticism, for each is, whether it realizes it or not, 'integrated'
into the other. If this is so, the poetry of mysticism exhibits
something latent in all imaginative apprehension of the world
which seeks to be comprehensive.

7

There is another matter arising out of M. Brémond's
discussion, in particular from that part of it in which he speaks
of the poet as if he were one who turned from mystical contem-

plation, or from the movement of his mind towards mystical
contemplation, in order to carry through the task of composition. The implication appears to be that the poet, in order to
be a poet, must deny the mystical in himself; must stifle
the incipient mysticism of his experience in order that poetry
may be made. But it is difficult to see the grounds of this
alleged conflict between the creation of poetry and the culti-
vation of the religious life. Such a conflict is thought to exist
only on the assumption that all poetry whatsoever is in some
sense mystical, an assumption which induced M. Brémond
to think that when the imagination is 'human and dramatic'
the poet is constantly forcing his imagination away from the
transcendent to the human and the finite. But in fact, as we
have noted, there is no good reason to believe that this assumption is true. When the imagination is 'human and dramatic'
we have to believe that the poet is content with his imaginative
life, and is not denying any supposed tendencies towards the
mystical. On the other hand, in the case of unmistakably
mystical poetry, the fact that the poet undertakes expression
of his response to a transcendent object is no indication that
he is denying that response. All the great mystics have attempted
expression; but we do not for that reason allege against them
a failure in their mystical life. They may indeed fail in their
attempt at expression; it is likely that they must do. But a
failure of expression is in itself no sign of redirection and ill-
direction of their inner life. All poetry is not mystical. There
is much that is; and it is natural that the failure of the secular
imagination to find fulfilment for itself in the contemplation
of human life should be succeeded, in those cases where the
previous labour of the imagination has been long and strenuous,
by the mystical imagination. But instead of saying that poetry
cannot occur without mysticism, it would be truer to say that,
when mysticism does enter into the poetic experience of life,
poetry is reaching a stage of impotence and of failure. Therefore,
however strongly we may believe that the true consummation
of poetry is in mysticism, we are compelled to recognize that

poetry is primarily an affair which is 'human and dramatic', and that the perfection of its life and its greatest attainments, judged as poetry, and not from any religious interest, occur in that pre-mystical stage in which it is seeking to convey its apprehension of the finite. In mystical poetry it is pre-eminently only the brief lyrical poem which stands to be successful. It is the *Ode to the Nightingale*, not the *Hyperion*, which accomplishes its end; where the eternal is vaguely symbolized and suggested, and not where the poet labours with a detail of mythology to figure forth that before which his imagination struggles hopelessly for life and expression. Yet the true mystic who is also a poet is driven on to attempt to overcome these impossible difficulties, and must therefore meet with a final frustration. The ship of poetry must, to use a famous phrase, suffer shipwreck at the entrance to harbour. We may believe that the greatest shipwreck which fine poetry has ever suffered is to be witnessed in the symbolical and prophetic works of Blake. Hence, as against M. Brémond, it seems more satisfactory to say that the poet may seek mystical apprehension and no less endeavour to effect communication in poetry; but that therein he must experience failure.

8

The task of the critic, as we have said, demands a catholicity of imaginative enjoyment which is possible to the greatest degree only when the critic is able to grasp the forms of human experience both in their singleness and in their relation to each other. Without this he will quickly become the victim of prejudice and fashion, able perhaps to catch the ear of the devotees of a passing emphasis or cult, but unable to contribute to the creation of an inclusive and universal culture. We have pointed, in speaking of Wordsworth, a man of mature and wise judgment, to his failure to co-ordinate scientific inquiry into his total view of human experience. This failure arose from the belief in a conflict between the intellectual and imaginative life, a conflict for the existence of which there is no evidence. Now what is called the romantic attitude in literature is notoriously apt to decry and minimize the place of intellectual inquiry in life, a tendency which must, inevitably and rightly, have weakened its influence. In our own time the cry is frequently heard that our life has become excessively and woefully dominated by our intellectual faculties, and that our imaginative powers are undergoing serious decline. In this there may be an element of truth; but the view is surely false if it implies that the pursuit of the intellectual life, whether in science or philosophy, is of a kind which necessarily results in a diminution of the imaginative life. Many writers who spend their time in decrying the intelligence show the essential feebleness of their plea by the semi-hysterical, unrestrained, and ultimately obscurantist character of their writings. There has been altogether too much of this kind of thing in our own day, the suggestion that in the exercise of the intelligence we are betraying the best that is within us. The intelligence cannot be denied, nor its necessity ignored; and the exercise of it is a moral as well as a biological necessity. However much we may admire the great romantic poets of a century ago, the duty of those who sympathize with what they were attempting to do is to set right the tendency which we have noted in Wordsworth, the tendency either to decry or patronize intellectual inquiry. Such an attitude must, in the long run, seriously undermine what stability of culture we possess, and make impossible the increase of that stability. It may be that the issue of philosophical investigation will be anti-intellectualist, in the sense that it will show the inability of the intelligence to deal with matters with which formerly it was thought competent to deal. But the cause of culture will be advanced only if such a conclusion is reached after the most strenuous and stringent efforts of the intelligence. The hysterical preaching of an anti-intellectualism can have only the most degenerating effects upon personality and literature alike. It is nonsense to think that a flight from reason is necessarily an advance towards a more powerful imaginative life. The discipline of the intellectual life is an altogether saving factor in any culture worthy of its name. If therefore the issue between the romantic and the classical attitudes were a difference in their respective views of the intelligence, the one decrying or patronizing it, the other upholding it, there would be no question as to where our choice should lie.

The issue between the romantic and classical attitudes is of course not so simple as this. Perhaps the most important factor in the dispute has to do with the view to be taken of the relation of the individual to society and tradition, the one tending to assertion of the individual as opposed to society and tradition, the other asserting the supremacy of the latter. But the issue is, when all is said and done, primarily a matter of emphasis, which by no means excludes recognition of the great importance of what each side in the dispute is concerned to uphold. It is true that according as weight is given to the emphasis two different kinds of sensibility tend to occur, two attitudes which we may understand and into which we can and must sympathetically enter. Unless we can effect such imaginative enjoyment of both attitudes, we disqualify ourselves from the first necessity of criticism. It is fatal for the critic to encase himself in a steel frame which disables him from appreciation of a different mode of sensibility from his own. If the critic enters either opposed camp, we can be sure that his appreciation and judgment will suffer; he will become the mouthpiece of a militant sect and his deliverances warped. But if the critic must, in an important degree, disqualify himself by such action, it by no means follows that he has nothing to say by way of judgment and assessment of significance in regard to such a clash of sensibilities. In so long standing an issue it is unlikely that neither side in the dispute has anything of vital importance to contribute towards a permanent culture; and it is obviously the case that the situation in which at any time in history we find ourselves is one of necessary tension between individual and society, a tension which is ultimate and unavoidable, and in which neither the individual nor social tradition can be sacrificed. In that tension, whether in social, literary, or religious matters, humility and adventurousness must live together; the loss of either is fatal, and the danger which attaches to the two attitudes respectively is that resulting from an over-emphasis of one at the expense of the other. There are some profound words of F. H. Bradley, which have, in this connection, a universal application, in which, speaking of the moral life in relation to society, he refers to the intuition 'which tells you that, if you could be as good as your world, you would be better than you most likely are, and that to wish to be better than the world is to be already on the threshold of immorality'. This, he goes on,

perhaps 'is a hard saying', but it is least hard to those who know life best; it is intolerable to those mainly who, from inexperience or preconceived theories, cannot see the world as it is. Explained it may be by saying that enthusiasm for good dies away—the ideal fades—but better perhaps if we say that those who have seen most of the world (not one side of it)—know most also how much good there is in it. They are tolerant of new theories and youthful opinions that everything would be better upside down, because they know that this also is as it should be and that the world gets good even from these. They are intolerant only of those who are old enough, and should be wise enough, to know better than that they know better than the world; for in such people they cannot help seeing the self-conceit which is pardonable only in youth. . . . It is not wrong, it is a duty, standing on the basis of the existing, and in harmony with its general spirit, to try and make not only oneself but also the world better, or rather, and in preference, one's own world better. But it is another thing, starting from oneself, from ideals in one's head, to set oneself and them against the moral world.[1]

Though Bradley is here writing of morals, his words have an application throughout life; and they are instinct with a wisdom which sees beyond the antagonisms and party catch-words with which all departments of life—social, political, literary,

[1] *Ethical Studies*, pp. 199–200.

and religious—are compact, and it is with such a wisdom that the critic, if he is to do his work, must be armed. In the last resort the long-drawn debate between romanticism and classicism issues from a failure to possess such a wisdom, and from a narrowness of vision which cannot command a full conspectus of the fundamental situation. The critic must therefore see the necessity of both these attitudes; but he must also be possessed of that in virtue of which both are resolvable into a unity of attitude which includes, by transcending, both. If to decry the intelligence were necessary to romanticism; or if to decry adventurousness were necessary to classicism, the position would be different. But it is not so; and one of the chief labours of criticism, in addition to pointing to the flaws and inadequacy which arise in literary creation through an ignoring of the essential situation, is to show that it is not so, and by so doing to achieve a unity and consensus of literary ideals. Most often, we think of the romantic poet as one who, in a general disregard for tradition, ignores the great religious tradition of his country or civilization; on the other hand the classicist, in his general reverence for tradition, aligns himself with orthodoxy in religion. And there can be no doubt that here is the most important point in respect of which they are divided, the respect in which it is most difficult to unite them. The issue here is not one between two views, the one secularist, the other religious; it is between two different modes of expressing one fundamental religious apprehension of the world. I have tried, by writing of Keats and Wordsworth, to show that this is so. It is sometimes said that the acceptance, by men whose outlook is classicist, of the dogma of original sin must wholly divide them from any identity with romanticism. But this mode of stating the distinction is superficial, and not profound. For if we interpret the Fall to indicate the essential and necessary character of human life as self-assertion, a state which necessarily divides us from God, and only to be overcome by dying to self, a process which clearly the finite cannot effect, there is in this nothing with which the romantic poets

of a century ago, with the exception of Shelley in one aspect
of his teaching, are at variance. In Keats there is nothing, so
far as I know, which constitutes a denial that our 'mortal
state' is one from which, as Keats said, we are 'spiritualized'
by the divine; and Wordsworth delivered himself from a
flabby pantheism. None of the great romantic poets rested
in any shallow naturalism (and this is true, I should say,
of Shelley as of the rest, though it is undeniable that there
is a strong vein of naturalism in some of his work. But Shelley
never long forgot his Platonism). There are no grounds for
thinking there is a necessary connection between romanticism
and any form of naturalism. What marks the romantic writer
is his difficulty in accepting Christian forms of expression,
and we noted Keats' attitude to Christian dogma when he
styled it 'pious fraud'. Keats was a more mature and balanced
personality than Shelley; and we cannot refuse to see in his
remark a grave weakness in the romantic mentality. But here
again, as in the case of Wordsworth's deprecation of science,
is an element which, while we must deplore it, is not essential
to the burden of Keats' work. Religion, as we have pointed
out, is always threatened from within by a tendency to reduce
its historical basis to the status of mythology. And we must
not therefore be surprised if some minds, undeniably of great
power and insight in many ways, fail to see in Christian dogma
anything but a deception, however well-intentioned. This is
not to justify Keats' remark. What Keats lacked was a historical
and traditional sense which would have compelled him to
see in the structure of Christian dogma something more than
fraud. Wordsworth, who was the only one of the great romantic
poets to grow to maturity in health of mind, came strongly
to acquire this sense; but certainly he was comparatively
late in acquiring it. But if we take the case of Keats as crucial
we have to ask whether, in so summary a rejection of Christianity,
we have not that mark of the romantic mind which must for
ever differentiate it from that type of sensibility which demands
Christian forms of expression and worship for its greater

fulfilment. It does indeed appear that in this case a reconciliation is not possible. For here it is not primarily an affair of emphasis; the difference between the acceptance and rejection of Christianity is in one sense absolute and cannot be mitigated. For either one is a Christian or one is not. That is to say, the claim of Christianity to be, in the form in which it is set out, with its historical basis, a final revelation of the nature of the universe, is in the last resort one which one must either accept or reject. There is no possible compromise.

And yet, even if with Keats Christianity be rejected, such a rejection need not, and certainly should not, occur in the spirit of almost contemptuous dismissal which marks Keats' words. As I have said, many may find it impossible to be Christians, and yet, wholly indeed without any smugness and complacent condescension, see in it a final expression of the religious apprehension of the world, and maintain towards it an attitude of the greatest humility. Here too, it may be said, Bradley's words have an application. Certainly it will be said by many to-day: "if I could be as good as Christianity has made countless men, I should be better than I am. But if I find myself unable, after careful self-examination, to see in my inability to be a Christian mere 'self-conceit', what am I to do? Hence it is necessary for me, if I feel it impossible conscientiously to call myself a Christian, to strive to maintain the isolation which is thus compelled upon me; but to maintain it in the company of respect and reverence for the religious tradition which has given me what grasp of religious truth I have." That it was a flaw in Keats to fail to see the necessity and expressiveness of Christianity is undeniable. But that there was such a failure in Keats' life does not mean that to be unable to be a Christian need imply anything but humility before and respect for the Christian tradition. We may hold Wordsworth and Keats in the greatest respect, yet deplore their attitudes to science and Christianity respectively. Certainly if romanticism were necessarily bound up with deprecation of intellectual inquiry and Christianity, it should be rejected summarily. This is not to say that it is one of the requirements of good criticism that it should adopt an attitude which is one of improved and more catholic romanticism. The so-called opposition of romantic and classicist is one which should and can, in the interests of poetry, be overcome. Certainly the greatest difficulty in a resolution of this opposition, which is also the spiritual crisis of our time, is in regard to Christianity. But it is certain that to attempt the task of criticism without the deepest reverence for, and understanding of, the Christian tradition is to disqualify oneself from the outset for the work in hand. And in this sense at least this aspect of the opposition between these two different sensibilities may be resolved.

9

But if the work of criticism demands the greatest power of appreciation of entry into the religious apprehension of the world, whether Christian or not, it is equally true that the secular mind, if we use the phrase to indicate response to experience which is entirely free from any sense of the supernatural, calls for 'enjoyment' by the critic. There must be no form of response to experience, if it be serious, which lies outside the domain of critical appreciation. The ability of the critical mind to effect this range of 'enjoyment' has, as we have noted, been discussed in recent years. Difference of belief, it has been suggested, may be a serious difficulty in the way of such enjoyment. But as we have argued, belief in such matters is but the active response of personality to the world as imaginatively apprehended, the control wrought over the poet's life by the world as it is present to his imagination. And because this is so, the formal beliefs which may be expressed by the poet are but indications of, and aids to, the creation, in the mind of the reader, of the imaginative pattern which has formed in the mind of the poet, and which the poet is endeavouring to communicate. The world which the imagination of the poet has created is that which is real for him and which must, in the process of criticism, become real for the critic. Unless this happens, any judgment passed by the critic is necessarily poorly founded, and involves injustice to the work in question.

Finally, we need hardly repeat the need that the critic should constantly be on his guard against any tendency towards being what is called, by a gross abuse of the word, 'scientific'. The assumption that science is a form of apprehending the world which can issue in final and conclusive deliverances as to the nature of reality and human life, arises from simple failure to see what is involved in scientific inquiry. It is the inability of science to do this, and its irrelevance to the issues with which human life is confronted, which the critic must keep severely in view. To do so is not in the least, as is sometimes thought, to discredit science and scientific inquiry. The notion that one is giving affront to science by pointing to its limitations is merely sentimental; just as the view of science which upholds it as the final arbiter on all issues of life and death is 'emotive'. A healthy criticism can be built only on a respect for scientific inquiry; a respect which has incomparably greater value arising from a scrutiny of what science is and can do than an adulation of science which arises from prejudice and sentimentality.

But if science is unable to solve for us the problem of life, we have also to remember that the poetic imagination cannot hope to shake itself free of scepticism. I have argued that it is impossible to claim that the imagination can give us what can be known for truth, or what may, in all strictness, be called knowledge. Keats, whose reflection on the imagination is perhaps the profoundest in our literature, was careful, as I have tried to show, not to make this claim for it. In a recent article in the *Times Literary Supplement* the writer quotes A. C. Bradley as saying: "Wherever the imagination is satisfied, there, *if we had a knowledge we have not*, we should discover no idle fancy but the image of a truth." And the writer goes on to make the following admirable statement:

The qualification is important. Bradley did not believe that even imagination could pluck out the heart of the mystery; he did not believe that mankind would ever come to possess the knowledge that would enable it to make the fateful transmutation of beauty into truth. In a sense, it was inherent in mortality that even those most highly gifted with the true imaginative power should feel themselves to be the incessant prey of

> Blank misgivings of a creature
> Moving about in worlds not realized.

. . . Not even by imagination can we make the universe our home— indeed, it is the imagination that tells us that it cannot be; nevertheless, it is through imagination that we learn to take into our souls and accept the ultimate mystery. By imagination its nature, though not its secret, can be revealed to us.[1]

[1] Leading article on A. C. Bradley, *Times Literary Supplement*, May 23, 1936.

INDEX